P9-CKN-768

EXPERIENCING THE ROLLING STONES

The Listener's Companion
Gregg Akkerman, Series Editor

Titles in **The Listener's Companion** provide readers with a deeper understanding of key musical genres and the work of major artists and composers. Aimed at nonspecialists, each volume explains in clear and accessible language how to *listen* to works from particular artists, composers, and genres. Looking at both the context in which the music first appeared and has since been heard, authors explore with readers the environments in which key musical works were written and performed.

Experiencing David Bowie: A Listener's Companion, by Ian Chapman
Experiencing Jazz: A Listener's Companion, by Michael Stephans
Experiencing Led Zeppelin: A Listener's Companion, by Gregg Akkerman
Experiencing Leonard Bernstein: A Listener's Companion, by Kenneth LaFave
Experiencing Mozart: A Listener's Companion, by David Schroeder
Experiencing the Rolling Stones: A Listener's Companion, by David Malvinni
Experiencing Rush: A Listener's Companion, by Durrell Bowman
Experiencing Stravinsky: A Listener's Companion, by Robin Maconie
Experiencing Tchaikovsky: A Listener's Companion, by David Schroeder
Experiencing Verdi: A Listener's Companion, by Donald Sanders

EXPERIENCING THE ROLLING STONES

A Listener's Companion

David Malvinni

ROWMAN & LITTLEFIELD
Lanham • Boulder • New York • London

Published by Rowman & Littlefield
A wholly owned subsidiary of The Rowman & Littlefield Publishing Group, Inc.
4501 Forbes Boulevard, Suite 200, Lanham, Maryland 20706
www.rowman.com

Unit A, Whitacre Mews, 26-34 Stannary Street, London SE11 4AB

British Library Cataloguing in Publication Information Available

Library of Congress Cataloging-in-Publication Data

Names: Malvinni, David.
Title: Experiencing the Rolling Stones : a listener's companion / David Malvinni.
Description: Lanham, Maryland : Rowman & Littlefield, [2016] | Series: Listener's companion
Includes bibliographical references and index.
Identifiers: LCCN 2015035072 | ISBN 9780810889194 (cloth : alk. paper) | ISBN 9780810889200 (ebook)
Subjects: LCSH: Rolling Stones. | Rock music–1961–1970–History and criticism. | Rock music–1971–1980–History and criticism.
Classification: LCC ML421.R64 M34 2016 | DDC 782.42166092/2–dc23 LC record available at http://lccn.loc.gov/2015035072

∞ ™ The paper used in this publication meets the minimum requirements of American National Standard for Information Sciences Permanence of Paper for Printed Library Materials, ANSI/NISO Z39.48-1992.

Printed in the United States of America

To my family, Valerie, Sofia, and Joe, for all their love and support.

Know what rhythm holds men.—Archilochus, fragment 128, as quoted by Maurice Blanchot, *Writing of the Disaster*, 5

CONTENTS

LIST OF TABLES

FOREWORD

Experiencing the Rolling Stones for the First Time Again

The Rolling Stones were the first band I ever loved. Long before I was ever passionate about any other band, it was the Stones that kindled my love for popular music in all its forms. My parents had given me an 8-track tape of *Metamorphosis* (1975) when I was, like, six years old. I played that until it didn't play anymore. Then during the summer of 1978 my father got a seasonal job in Tucson, Arizona, and at age eleven I started hanging around the Record Bar store. The staffers loved the Stones and turned me onto more of their work. One of the staffers showed me a photo of the band from the 1975–1976 tour with Billy Preston and Ollie Brown, where a shirtless Mick is laying his head on Bill Wyman, and Keith and Woody are smoking cigarettes. I stared at this photo for what seemed like hours. Wow! For fifty cents an album, I bought used copies of *Rolling Stones: England's Newest Hit Makers*, *12 X 5*, *Flowers*, *'Get Yer Ya-Ya's Out!'*, and *Out of Our Heads*, in addition to albums by other artists—a few that come to mind from this era are Cheap Trick's *In Color*, Eddie and the Hot Rods' *Life on the Line*, the Dickies' *Paranoid*, the Sex Pistols' *Never Mind the Bollocks* (of course), Television's *Marquee Moon*, the Modern Lovers' *Live*, Led Zeppelin's *In Through the Out Door*, Emerson Lake & Palmer's *Works*, Jethro Tull's *Heavy Horses*, Pink Floyd's *Animals*, Black Sabbath's *Sabotage*, Yes's *Tormato*, Iggy Pop's *Lust for Life*—but it was the Rolling Stones that I listened to the most. The first "fan" magazine I ever got was about the band. For my birthday my parents bought me the newly released *Some Girls*. I played it over and over again until the grooves no longer existed. Then for Christmas 1978 my parents gave me a beautiful silver poster of the Stones (wish I still had it and that "fan" mag). I loved that poster, and its shininess fascinated me. Of course I tried to get whatever albums I was missing, like *Aftermath*, *Sticky Fingers*, *Goats Head Soup*, *Got Live If You Want It!*, *Exile on Main Street*, *It's Only Rock 'n' Roll*, and oddly, *More Hot Rocks*. (For some reason I didn't get *Black and Blue*; *Between the Buttons*; *The Rolling Stones, Now!*; *Tattoo You*; or *December's Children* until many years later as an adult.)

When the Stones played on *Saturday Night Live* in 1978, it was like seeing the Greek Gods come to life. Simply amazing! I even obtained copies of solo projects like *Jamming with Edward!*, Bill Wyman's *Monkey Grip* and *Stone Alone*, and Ron Wood's *Gimme Some Neck*. The first bootleg album I ever purchased was from the 1978 *Some Girls* tour. My parents were strangely concerned when the record seller told them that the F-bomb was strewn throughout the bootleg, though the word escaped their notice on the *Some Girls* LP itself. They let me buy the bootleg anyway (I was pretty ticked off at the record store owner for warning them; no wonder the store went out of business). When *Emotional Rescue* came out in 1980, I also played the album till the grooves bled, and loved the album's poster.

The band often gets tagged as the "world's greatest rock and roll group" and of course this is true, and ALWAYS will be. But why not tag the band as one of the "supreme blues ensembles" in the history of popular culture? Honestly, that is not said enough. I suppose there are those critics who would say that the Stones are pretenders to the blues throne, having little in common musically with Robert Johnson, Lead Belly, Charlie Patton, Muddy Waters, Mance Lipscomb, Reverend Gary Davis, Howlin' Wolf, Freddie King, or any of the historical blues greats one could name. Well, the truth is the Rolling Stones are NO pretenders to the throne when it comes to the blues. They never were and never will be (as David Malvinni amply demonstrates in this volume) pretenders playing the blues. One only needs to listen to the Stones' covers of blues classics like "Little Red Rooster," "I'm a King Bee," "Love in Vain," "You Gotta Move," or original songs like "Fancy Man Blues," "Down in the Hole," "Sister Morphine," "No Expectations," and "Cook Cook Blues." The Rolling Stones understand the blues perhaps as well as, if not better than, any rock band ever has.

However, it does not stop with the blues. Some fifty-plus years after Charlie Watts first sat down to play with the band, it becomes apparent that the Rolling Stones can and do adapt to any kind of music: from basic rock and roll to R & B, funk, new wave, folk, soul, dance-techno, country, gospel, jazz, punk, reggae, world, pop, and disco—all are there in their massive musical catalog. From "Tell Me" to "Doom and Gloom," the Rolling Stones' catalog continues to sound fresh and is a testament to the band's ability to transcend musical trends.

It's often been said that the Rolling Stones have defied all odds by existing in the popular music world for fifty-three years and counting at the time of this writing. The Stones, like the Grateful Dead, Yes, Chicago, ELP, the Who, the Beach Boys, and the enduring popularity of bands and artists like Led Zeppelin, Jimi Hendrix, and Pink Floyd, show that these artists certainly have made some timeless music and have a great deal of lasting value to today's musical scene. Yet it is more in the way the Stones defied the odds and critics that make them so unique. When Brian Jones left, and subsequently died, most critics thought the band was washed up. As they entered the 1970s the band was thought of as a spent force creatively, but as Dr. Malvinni so eloquently details here, they entered their most creative musical period with albums considered rock classics (*Sticky Fingers* and *Exile on Main Street*). Then Mick Taylor left, and Ron Wood joined. In the late 1970s the punks considered "the Rolling Stones" to be dirty words and boring old farts, but with *Some Girls* the band out-punked (whether intentionally or not) much of the punk rock at the time. The band entered the 1980s with the biggest tour up to that time and a hit album, but critics again said the band could never compete in the MTV rock video age with the newer video bands. In 1983, the Stones released videos for "Undercover," "Too Much Blood," and "She Was Hot," all of which garnered heavy rotation on the fledging MTV. When the band almost broke up during the Jagger–Richards feud of the mid-1980s amid the releases of Jagger's solo work *She's the Boss* and the Stones' *Dirty Work*, critics thought the band was through. They reckoned, yet again, that the band was finally over and now the haters could gloat. The Stones weathered that storm too, and in 1989 launched the successful *Steel Wheels* album and tour. This too proved to be a milestone. Original band member Bill Wyman would leave, and once again it was thought the band couldn't endure such a drastic change. Yet the first post-Wyman release, *Voodoo Lounge*, was a solid album and the Stones toured the world once again. Even in 1994, I remember attacks on message boards and in the press referring to the band as the "Strollin' Bones." By the time of the band's fortieth anniversary tour, dubbed "Forty Licks," in 2002, critics were really flummoxed. When fifty years rolled around in 2012 it was hailed as a celebration, but what was surprising was just how good the band still was live. The Rolling Stones came out as one of the top live bands of the year in polls, proving you are NEVER too OLD to rock and roll.

What all the above shows is that the Rolling Stones continue to remain relevant because they are relevant. Sure, they may never top the charts in the same way, but what does that matter when you can play to 80,000 people on a given night? Still, the band proves it can be relevant musically; "Doom and Gloom," the 2012 fiftieth anniversary single, rocks with a ferocity that puts many younger bands to shame. I would argue that rather than aping popular culture, the Rolling Stones (and particularly Mick Jagger) have always had their pulse on it. Jagger is able to adapt the Stones' music and lyrics to reflect the times so it always remains contemporary, but the band is also always the Rolling Stones (with input from Richards, Wood, and Watts, Wyman, Taylor, and Brian Jones of course, and others at times). However, the band never loses sight of its blues and rock roots either. It's a balancing game!

One could ask, why don't Mick Jagger and the rest of the band grow old gracefully? Where is the fun in that? I remember hearing critics say years ago that no one will accept a fifty-year-old Mick Jagger singing "Satisfaction." Well, now we have a seventy-plus Jagger singing it, and it's great. So what? The fact that Mick Jagger can run around the stage better in his seventies than most can in their twenties is a testament to the power of music. This is a cause for celebration, not for criticism! I tend to view this as showing there is hope for the rest of us. Sir Mick rocks, and let's hope he keeps doing so for a long time. He killed it on the 2011 Grammy Awards and when he hosted *Saturday Night Live* in 2012.

And what about the other members of the band? Keith Richards is definitively the coolest guy in rock and roll and the most durable! He has a "chugging" guitar style that is instantly recognizable. Brian Jones was the most versatile guitarist the band ever had. As this volume shows, Jones could pick up nearly any instrument and learn to play it. Mick Taylor was probably the best guitarist the band ever played with, and he had a virtuoso's understanding of the instrument. Wyman kept the rhythm during his tenure and although he looked stoic while playing, he was vital to the band's development and sound. It's too bad that Jagger and Richards wouldn't let Wyman have a song or two per album (or even Mick Taylor, as his timeless "Leather Jacket" shows from his first solo album), the way Pete Townshend did for John Entwistle on the Who's recorded output. The few official songs that Wyman did write for the Stones are very good indeed: "Goodbye Girl," "In Another Land," and "Downtown Suzie," while the unofficial ones ("Jumpin' Jack Flash" springs to mind) are musical classics. Wyman's first couple of solo albums have some pretty good songs too. Charlie Watts kept the backbeat and it was his joining the band that is regarded as the true birth of the Rolling Stones in 1962. Watts is the glue that kept and keeps the Stones chugging along. Ron Wood is just about the perfect member of the Stones. He fits in with Jagger and Richards both personally and musically in a way that Jones and Taylor never did. He's a darn good player as well. He's a Rolling Stone through and through!

Which brings me to the subject of David Malvinni's book, *Experiencing the Rolling Stones*. Sure, there are lots of books on the Rolling Stones and even more written material in magazines, online articles, and book chapters, so one might wonder what else could be said about the band. Fortunately, plenty, and Dr. Malvinni penetrates to the heart of the Stones' music in a way I've not seen before. This is a volume that will please the casual fan AND the musicologist. There is plenty here for both parties to enjoy. The author does not simply dissect the music in a sterile way that sucks the life out of it. On the contrary, he digs deep into the songs and forces the reader to think about them in a unique way. He understands the Stones' music and history in a way that few academics or fans really grasp. It is a testament to Dr. Malvinni's musical understanding to be able to analyze the music as seriously as he does. His analysis of Keith Richards gives the guitarist and songwriter the musical credit he deserves. Each of the albums and songs discussed in this volume takes the reader beyond thinking about the Rolling Stones as just some no-good bar band that became famous on the Beatles' coattails. Peppered throughout the chapters is a "Listening Vignette" feature where Dr. Malvinni writes about experiencing the Rolling Stones in a new and unique way. With a "you are there" approach, the author conveys what it was like to get the new Stones album or see the band live during their first ten years. This innovative writing gives the reader an inside look into how exciting it was to get the new Stones album and just how important it was for many a young person. In fact, I found myself not wanting these chapters or this book to end, which is the greatest praise one can give a writer.

—Robert G. Weiner

Robert G. Weiner hails from West Texas and Lubbock, the home of the Rolling Stones saxophone player, Bobby Keys. He is the popular culture librarian at Texas Tech University and sometimes teaches honors classes. He has written, co-written, edited, or co-edited articles and books on the Grateful Dead, grindhouse cinema, Lubbock music, sequential art, and other popular culture topics. His works include The Grateful Dead and the Deadheads*;* The Storyteller Speaks: Rare and Different Fictions of the Grateful Dead*;* James Bond in World and Popular Culture: The Films Are Not Enough*;* Web-Spinning Heroics*;* Graphic Novels and Comics in the Classroom*;* Graphic Novels and Comics in Libraries and Archives; *and* From the Arthouse to the Grindhouse. *His most recent book is the co-edited volume* The Joker: A Serious Study on the Clown Prince of Crime. *He can be seen in the music documentaries* Lubbock Lights *and* Tommy Hancock: West Texas Muse. *Weiner wrote the Rolling Stones entry for* The Guide to United States Popular Culture.

TIMELINE UP TO *EXILE* (1972)

1962

April 7	Mick and Keith see Blues Incorporated at the Ealing Club and meet Brian Jones and Charlie Watts.
May	Ian Stewart answers an ad placed by Brian Jones, and they start rehearsing together.
June	Mick Jagger, Keith Richards, and Dick Taylor take up with Jones and Stewart for weekly rehearsals at the Bricklayers Arms Pub in Soho.
July 12	The Rollin' Stones substitute for Blues Incorporated at the Marquee Jazz Club on Oxford Street for their first gig, with Mick Jagger, Keith Richards, Brian Jones, Dick Taylor, Ian Stewart, and possibly Mick Avory on drums. Ian Stewart wrote down the set list of American R & B covers.[1]
August	Drummer Tony Chapman of the Cliftons, Bill Wyman's group, answers an ad and joins the group.
October 27	At the instigation of Jones, the Rolling Stones record three cover demos at Curly Clayton Sound Studios, London, including Dixon's "You Can't Judge a Book by Its Cover."
December 14	Bill Wyman debuts with the Rolling Stones at the Ricky Tick Club.

1963

January 12	After going through multiple drummers and bass players, Charlie Watts plays his first concert with the Rolling Stones at the Ealing Club; with Bill Wyman present, this marks the first concert with all of the band members.
March 11	First demos by the full band at IBC Studios in London. This was finally officially released as a bonus disc on 2012's four-disc *GRRR!* "best of" package.
April	The Stones are well established in London club scene, with a now-legendary residency at Giorgio Gomelsky's Crawdaddy Club, in Richmond; the popularity of the Stones effectively ends the London "Trad" jazz scene; they meet Andrew Oldham and Eric Easton who become the band's managers.
May 1	On Oldham's recommendation, Ian Stewart steps down from the official lineup and becomes road manager; he would continue to play with the band until his premature death in 1985.
May	Brian Jones signs the Stones to a three-year recording contract with Decca; the band records their first single, "Come On" by Chuck Berry.
Summer	Touring schedule takes them beyond London to bigger venues.
September	Brian Jones leaves the band's flat in Edith Grove to live with girlfriend Linda Lawrence's parents.
September 15	The Stones perform at the Great Pop Prom at the Royal Albert Hall, first time with the Beatles, who close the show.
October 7	The band records their next single, Lennon/McCartney's "I Wanna Be Your Man"; band finds out Brian Jones is taking more pay, which is met with anger and will eventually lead to his isolation in the band.

November 5	The Rolling Stones perform at the Cavern Club in Liverpool.
November	Jagger/Richards compositions are shopped around by Oldham, solidifying the power shift in the band away from Jones.

1964

January	The Stones start recording for their first album; *The Rolling Stones* EP is released.
February 14	The band performs "Not Fade Away" on British TV's *Ready, Steady, Go!*; the song is then released as the third single.
April 17	Release of first album, *The Rolling Stones*, in the UK.
May 29	The U.S. album version is released as *The Rolling Stones: England's Newest Hit Makers.*
June 1	The Stones arrive at Kennedy Airport for their first U.S. appearances, including Dean Martin's TV show.
June	At RCA Studios the band meets Jack Nitzsche; first U.S. tour, starting in San Bernardino; first encounter with sax player Bobby Keys in San Antonio; first U.S. recordings at Chess Studios in Chicago.
June 26	Back in England, their single, "It's All Over Now" (recorded at Chess) is released.
August 14	The second EP, *Five by Five*, comes out in the UK.
October	The second U.S. album, *12 X 5*, is released; first appearance on American television's *Ed Sullivan Show*; the band plays the *T.A.M.I. Show* in Santa Monica.
November	The UK single, "Little Red Rooster," goes to number one on UK charts (the only time a twelve-bar blues would do that); more recording at Chess Studios.

1965

January 15	The second UK album, *The Rolling Stones No. 2*, is released.
February 13	The third U.S. album, *The Rolling Stones, Now!* (*The Rolling Stones No. 2*) is released.
February 26	A single, "The Last Time," is released in the UK (U.S. version in March).
May	The band records "Mercy, Mercy" at Chess Studios and works on "Satisfaction," which they finish at RCA Studios in Los Angeles.
May 20	The Stones appear on an American musical variety show, *Shindig!*; introduce Howlin' Wolf and meet Son House.[2]
June 6	"(I Can't Get No) Satisfaction" appears in the U.S.
June 11	The British EP *Got Live If You Want It!* released.
July 30	The fourth U.S. album, *Out of Our Heads* released (UK version in September).
September 14	Brian Jones meets Anita Pallenberg in Munich, Germany.
September 25	U.S. single "Get Off of My Cloud" released.
December	The band begins recording "19th Nervous Breakdown"; *Aftermath* sessions begin at RCA Studios in Los Angeles;[3] the fifth U.S. album, *December's Children (and Everybody's)* released.

1966

February	"19th Nervous Breakdown" released, first in the UK then in the U.S.
March 6–9	*Aftermath* sessions at RCA Studios in Los Angeles continue; the band records "Paint It Black" and "Under My Thumb."

March	Richards purchases Redlands, his bucolic estate outside of London.
April 15	The fourth UK album, *Aftermath*, is released (U.S. version in July).
May 7	"Paint It Black" is released as single.
July	The Stones conduct their fifth and final tour of North America during so-called teenybopper era; Richards notes that they reconciled with Jones on this tour; Pallenberg joins the tour in Texas; tour ends in Honolulu.
August 3–11	Work continues at RCA Studios, "Let's Spend the Night Together" and "Yesterday's Papers" released;[4] Brian Wilson attends the session for "My Obsession."
August	Jones and Pallenberg go to Morocco for a vacation.
September	Jones starts composing the soundtrack for a West German film *A Degree of Murder* (*Mord und Totschlag*).
Late August–September	Recording for *Between the Buttons* continues at IBC Studios in London and RCA Studios in Los Angeles.
September 23	"Have You Seen Your Mother, Baby, Standing in the Shadow?" released as a single.
September–October	Final UK tour for the next four years; Jagger and Marianne Faithfull (invited to the show by Richards and Jones) get together after one of the shows at Colston Hall, Bristol.
December	The first live album, *Got Live If You Want It!* released; Jagger officially breaks up with longtime girlfriend Chrissie Shrimpton and starts seeing Faithfull.

1967

January 13	The single "Let's Spend the Night Together" with "Ruby Tuesday" on the B-side released; the Stones appear on *The Ed Sullivan Show* and Jagger is forced to change the words when they perform "Let's Spend the Night Together."
February 5	Jagger threatens to sue the British tabloid paper *News of the World* for alleging that he admitted to using drugs, when the paper had actually interviewed Jones.
February 11–12	After an acid-fueled weekend party, police raid Redlands after being tipped off by *News of the World* and finding some illegal substances that later led to charges against Jagger and Richards; Faithfull's reputation is sullied as she is found naked wrapped in only a rug.
February–March	The fateful trip to Morocco; while driving there, Jones is hospitalized in Toulouse, at which time Richards starts his affair with Pallenberg.
March–April	The Stones' Europe tour is the last of the era; they play in Warsaw, their first concert in a communist country; around this time Jones starts to give up hope that Pallenberg will return to him.
April	The West German film *A Degree of Murder* is released starring Pallenberg with a soundtrack by Jones; other musicians who played on it include Jimmy Page (guitar), Nicky Hopkins (piano), and Kenney Jones (drums); Brian Jones played a range of instruments, among them the guitar, Mellotron, dulcimer, and sitar.
May 7	Jones, along with other rock stars, attends a Jimi Hendrix concert in London.
May	Jagger and Richards formally charged for the February drug bust; Jones is set up in a police raid and busted for drugs; the band starts work on "She's a Rainbow" at Olympic Studios.

June	Mick Taylor joins John Mayall's group, the Bluesbreakers.
June 8	Jones records a sax solo on the Beatles "You Know My Name" at EMI Studios in London.
June 14–25	Jagger and Faithfull travel to Tangier, Morocco.
June 15–18	Jones attends the Monterey International Pop Music Festival, where he introduces Jimi Hendrix.
June 27–30	Found guilty for allowing cannabis to be smoked on his premises (Richards) and for illegal drug possession (Jagger), the two are jailed, then released on bail pending appeals.
July 2–22	The band forges ahead with recording at Olympic: "We Love You" single and *Their Satanic Majesties Request* (which continues in spurts throughout rest of year); Lennon and McCartney provide backup vocals on "We Love You." The band also records "In Another Land," written by Bill Wyman and the only song released by the Stones with him on lead vocals; "In Another Land" appeared later in the year as a single.
August 18	"We Love You" comes out in the UK (in September in the U.S.).
September 20	The Stones split with manager Andrew Oldham who was absent for *Satanic* sessions.
October	Jones jailed for cannabis possession; he appeals and is released on bail.
December	Eighth U.S. and sixth UK studio album, *Their Satanic Majesties Request*, released.
Late December	Holidays to exotic locations continue: Jagger and Faithfull to the Bahamas and Brazil; Richards and Pallenberg to Morocco; Jones to Sri Lanka; and Wyman and Astrid Lundstrom to Sweden.

1968

February–March	Rehearsals begin for *Beggars Banquet*; the band starts working with American producer and drummer Jimmy Miller.
March	Jagger purchases Stargroves, a country estate outside of London.
March 17	Jagger takes part in the first large-scale British protest against the Vietnam War at Grosvenor Square outside the U.S. Embassy.
March–April	Sessions for *Beggars Banquet* begin at Olympic Studios in London; "Jumpin' Jack Flash," "Street Fighting Man," "Child of the Moon" recorded; Jones absent for many sessions as his health worsens.
April 27–28	Promotional film shot for "Jumpin' Jack Flash" in London.
May	Mick and Keith meet Gram Parsons on tour with the Byrds.
May 12	The band plays live for first time in over a year at the New Musical Express Poll-Winners' Concert.
May 13–23	Work on *Beggars Banquet* at Olympic continues.
May 21	Jones is arrested for possession of cannabis; he temporarily moves into Redlands with Richards.
June 4–10	The band records "Sympathy for the Devil" among other tracks; while they work up this song they are filmed by Jean-Luc Godard for his film *One Plus One*.
July	Jones and Suki Potier arrive in Tangier, Morocco; on July 23 and 24 Jones records the *Master Musicians of Joujouka [Jajouka]*; Richards and Jagger do the final mix for *Beggars Banquet* at Sunset Sound in Los Angeles; the album is delayed due to dispute with Decca over cover art.
July 26	Jagger's twenty-fifth birthday is held at the Vesuvio Club in London; Watts, Faithfull, Lennon, and McCartney are there; at the party Jagger previews

	Beggars Banquet while McCartney previews the Beatles upcoming single "Hey Jude/Revolution."
August	Gram Parsons hangs out with Richards at Redlands; Jones learns about Cotchford Farm in Hartfield, Sussex (former home of A. A. Milne, author of *Winnie the Pooh*), which he purchases later in November.
August 31	The U.S. single "Street Fighting Man" is released.
September–October	Jagger shoots the film *Performance* in London; he is rumored to have had an affair with co-star Pallenberg; Richards moves into Robert Fraser's apartment with Pallenberg and starts experimenting with heroin.
September 26	Jones's trial in London results in a guilty verdict for possessing cannabis, and he receives a fine; Jagger, Richards, and Suki Potier are there for support.
October	The public learns of Faithfull's pregnancy with Mick; she miscarries later in the month.
October 30	Wyman and Lundstrom move into his newly purchased country estate, Gedding Hall.
November 16–17	*Let It Bleed* sessions commence at Olympic with "You Can't Always Get What You Want" and "Memo from Turner."
December 5	A promotional party for *Beggars Banquet* held at the Gore Hotel in London.
December 6–7	Ninth U.S. and seventh UK studio album, *Beggars Banquet*, released.
December 6–12	Rehearsals and filming commence for *The Rolling Stones' Rock and Roll Circus*.
December	Jagger, Faithfull, Richards, and Pallenberg set off for a three-week vacation in Peru and Brazil; in Brazil, Jagger and Richards write "Honky Tonk Women"; Jones and Potier go to Sri Lanka.

1969

February–March	*Let It Bleed* sessions take place; the band is joined by Ry Cooder who plays on "Love in Vain" and "Sister Morphine"; Faithfull adds a couple of lines (at least) to "Sister Morphine" for which she eventually receives a songwriting credit.
April	Jones starts seeing Anna Wohlin; Jagger and Richards write "Midnight Rambler" among other songs in Positano, Italy.
April 23	Jagger, Watts, Wyman, Hopkins, and Cooder record a jam session at Olympic, released later as *Jamming with Edward!*
May	*Let It Bleed* sessions continue; Mick Taylor starts playing with band (May 31, on "Live with Me").
June 7	Richards crashes his car near Redlands, with a pregnant Pallenberg as his passenger.
June 8	Jagger, Richards, and Watts visit Jones to inform him that he is to leave the group; a press statement is issued.
June 13	The band holds a press conference and announces Taylor as lead guitarist and that their free Hyde Park concert is set for July 5.
July 2	Jones is found dead in his swimming pool late in the evening at Cotchford Farm; the band is told about it while they are recording at Olympic.
July 5	The Stones perform their first full-length concert in over two years, a free concert in Hyde Park dedicated to Jones, and in his honor Jagger reads two stanzas from Shelley's "Adonais," an elegy written in 1821 on the death of John Keats.
July 7–September	Jagger and Faithfull fly to Sydney; Faithfull is in a coma for days following a drug overdose. Jagger is there to film *Ned Kelly* through September; he writes "Brown Sugar."

July 10	Watts and Wyman attend Jones's funeral in his native Cheltenham.
August 10	Pallenberg and Richards's first child, Marlon, is born, named for the famous actor.
September–October	*Let It Bleed* sessions continue, sometimes without Jagger present.
October 17–November 2	The Rolling Stones fly to Los Angeles to get ready for a U.S. tour; they put final touches on *Let It Bleed* at Sunset Sound and Elektra Studios, record "Country Honk" and "Gimme Shelter," the latter with vocalist Merry Clayton.
November 7	The Stones' 1969 tour opens with their first-ever appearance in Fort Collins, Colorado; they perform much longer shows to a serious, more mature audience during a tense time in U.S. history, with much anti-Vietnam War sentiment in the air.
November 8–10	The band performs concerts in Los Angeles, Oakland (first time), and San Diego.
November 18	The Stones give their sixth and last-ever performance on TV's *Ed Sullivan Show*.
November	The tour continues with performances across country.
November 27–29	Three concerts are held at New York City's Madison Square Garden (first time there); the performances are recorded and released on their live album *'Get Yer Ya-Ya's Out!'*; the band performs two concerts at Boston Garden.
November 29	The band's tenth U.S. and eighth UK album, *Let It Bleed*, is released in U.S. (on December 5 in the UK).
November 30	The band's U.S. tour ends in West Palm Beach, Florida, where they headline a music festival.
December 2–4	*Sticky Fingers* recording begins at Muscle Shoals Sound Studio in Sheffield, Alabama; the band records "Brown Sugar," "Wild Horses," and "You Gotta Move."

December 6	The Rolling Stones headline a free concert at Altamont Speedway near Livermore, California, attended by 300,000; the concert turns into a disaster when a Hells Angel acting as stage security murders a black man, Meredith Hunter, who allegedly threatened Jagger with a gun.
December 7	The group hurriedly returns to England, possibly to avoid any legal problems in the aftermath of the Altamont tragedy.
December 9–18	Recording for *Sticky Fingers* continues at Olympic; the band rerecords "Brown Sugar" with Eric Clapton, which is not released at that time; work starts on "Dead Flowers."
Late December	Jagger goes to Rome with Faithfull; after a brief time they break up.

1970

January–February	At Olympic and Trident Studios in London, work on live material is recorded in November; the band finishes "Wild Horses."
January 26	Faithfull is acquitted of cannabis charges, while Jagger is found guilty and fined; he starts seeing Marsha Hunt.
February 4	The Stones are shocked to learn that they must leave England for 1971 to avoid paying heavy back taxes owed all at once.
February 19	The band learns that through a sleight of hand, they signed away their publishing rights and recording masters to Allen Klein's own corporation in the U.S.
March–May	Sessions roll on for *Sticky Fingers* at Olympic and at Stargroves; at the latter location the band uses their Mobile Unit for recording for the first time.
March	Godard's *One Plus One*, retitled *Sympathy for the Devil*, achieves limited release in the U.S.

June–July	*Sticky Fingers* work continues.
July 20	The Stones begin their break with Decca Records and sever official ties with Klein; they make plans for their own Rolling Stones label with help from Atlantic Records.
August	*Performance*, starring Mick Jagger as Turner, finally comes out in the U.S.
August–October	The band tours Europe, their first time with a horn section.
September 4	A second live album, *'Get Yer Ya-Ya's Out!'*, is released in the UK, then the U.S.
September 23	In Paris, Jagger meets his future wife, Bianca Perez-Mora Macias, who follows the group on tour.
October 17–31	Recording sessions at Stargroves commence, with work on "Bitch," "Tumbling Dice," "Sweet Black Angel," "Hide Your Love," "Moonlight Mile," and "Sway"; Richards is absent for the latter two songs.
November 4	Hunt has Mick Jagger's first child, a daughter, Karis.
November 24	Jagger and Bianca travel to the Bahamas to attend Atlantic Records president Ahmet Ertegun's party.
December–January	Mixing and overdub sessions continue for *Sticky Fingers.*

1971

March 4–14	The Rolling Stones give their farewell tour of Great Britain, the first time playing there in four years.
March 26	The band performs at the Marquee Club, site of their first concert; the performance is broadcast on British television.
April 1	Rolling Stones Records starts, with the new lip-and-tongue logo. Wyman and Taylor with their families leave for Nice, France.

April 3	Richards and Watts arrive in Nice; Richards rents the Villa Nellcôte in Villefranche-sur-Mer on the French Riviera; Jagger and Bianca fly to Paris.
April 16–17	"Brown Sugar" becomes the first single on the Stones' new label.
April 23 and 30	Eleventh U.S. and ninth UK album, *Sticky Fingers*, is released first in the UK, then in the U.S.
May 5	The band has a first rehearsal upon setting up in France at Richards's place in Nellcôte.
May 12	Jagger and Bianca marry in St. Tropez, France; Richards claims the marriage is a blow to their creative partnership.
June 7–October	*Exile on Main Street* recording sessions with the Mobile Unit begin in the basement of Richards's rented villa.
July 6	Producer Jimmy Miller arrives at Nellcôte.
October 1	Richards's guitar collection is stolen from Nellcôte.
October 9	Rolling Stones Records releases *Brian Jones Presents the Pipes of Pan at Joujouka.*
October 21	Bianca and Mick Jagger's daughter Jade is born in Paris.
November 29	Jagger, Richards, and Taylor go to Los Angeles to work on *Exile*.
December 4–19	More overdubbing and mixing sessions for *Exil*e take place.

1972

January–February	*Exile* work continues.
March 26	Richards and Pallenberg fly to Switzerland to enter rehab for heroin addiction.
March 24–25	Final mixing for *Exile* at Wally Heider Studios in Los Angeles takes place, perhaps only Jagger is present.
April 15–21	The lead single, "Tumbling Dice," released.

April 17	Pallenberg and Richards's second child, Dandelion (Angela), is born.
May 10	The Stones settle disputes with Klein and his ABKCO Industries.
May 20	The Rolling Stones are back in London.
May 22–26	The twelfth U.S. and tenth UK album, and the first double album, *Exile on Main Street*, is released.

NOTE

Most of this timeline is derived from the website, Time Is on Our Side: Chronology, http://www.timeisonourside.com/index2.html.

INTRODUCTION

The Rolling Stones released their first, eponymous album in the spring of 1964. The album contained covers of American R & B (rhythm-and-blues) songs, seemingly at odds with the subtitle of the American release—*England's Newest Hit Makers*. Yet the subtitle proved prophetic, as soon their songwriting propelled the band from a national sensation to an international phenomenon. But with their original songwriting set to explode with their breakout hit "(I Can't Get No) Satisfaction," forgotten by later audiences was the ebullience of their early years of music making as a live, R & B cover band, as immortalized on their debut album.

Aside from the modernist tendency to prize originality, the artistic force of the Stones emerges fully formed on this first album. The lead-off "Route 66" announces the restless, youthful, and Dionysian energy that will define the group. Compared to the crooning and tame Nat King Cole version (1946), or the attempt at a rocking update by Chuck Berry, the Stones steer the song in a direction that stakes out the direction of 1960s rock.[1] They lift the three-note piano riff heard at the opening of Berry's rendition and transform it into a propelling guitar riff that circulates throughout the verse. Suspensions on the guitar decorate each of the three chords of the song, again, giving a sense of movement and variety to the unyielding and rigid twelve-bar blues progression. Richards's guitar solo picks up the busy, nervous energy of the guitar fills, and his bends and descending double-stops distance the song further from its jazzy, jump blues roots and go a step beyond

Berry's. Hand claps on the backbeat add to the rhythmic synergy. Finally, Jagger's whining, nasally vocal tries to locate the song in the smoky honky tonks of the American South, a place he could only imagine from London.

Perhaps the most primal moment on the first album is heard on the UK release, the Bo Diddley song "Mona (I Need You Baby)," dropped for the U.S. release in favor of their hit single, "Not Fade Away."[2] The Stones were fascinated at this time by the so-called Bo Diddley beat employed in both of these songs (more on this beat and "Not Fade Away" in chapter 1). For most British youth, "Mona" would perhaps have been an obscure song choice, a 1957 B-side on the Checker label (a subsidiary of Chess Records). Again, they rearrange the musical elements of the Diddley original to make it a better song, while providing a stronger, catchier rhythmic backdrop through the amplifier's tremolo effect and the animated percussion section (drums, with maraca and tambourine). Thus it was the Stones' focus on the groove element of a given song that would define their success, and nowhere is that better heard, perhaps, than on these early encounters with the Bo Diddley beat.

American cover songs served the Stones well as a live touring band, building their reputation and gaining for them a loyal fan base. Indeed, Stones concerts to this day still include an R & B nod to their origins as a cover band. For example, at the Ford Theater in Los Angeles on May 20, 2015, a warm-up for their summer Zip Code tour, they played Otis Redding's "I Can't Turn You Loose" to close the show. Moreover and as we shall see, these types of songs provide the template for the original songs in the Stones' sprawling catalog.

Every song bears the marks and traces of other songs. That is, a song will share basic music elements and motifs with songs that came before. In popular music genres, it is easy to ascertain how a common musical language underlies the material, as songwriters return to the same chord progressions, rhythms, bass lines, melodic ideas, and riffs. Sometimes songs are so close to another one that appropriation can border on theft or plagiarism. The Stones themselves have received such criticism in the last few years. For example, and as Richards admitted, "The Last Time" is a reworking of a gospel tune made popular and recorded by the Staples Singers. It is possible that they would not secure this song as an original in today's highly litigated climate. Furthermore, the originality of "The Last Time" is an especially thorny topic since the Verve were forced to reassign their hit, "Bitter Sweet Symphony" (1997), to include Jagger/Richards in the music credits (while former manager Allen Klein collects on the copyright, too). Most listeners perhaps did not hear any similarities between the two songs, as "Bitter Sweet Symphony" actually samples not the original song but a 1965 orchestral version produced by Andrew Oldham.

Coming back to "Satisfaction," the song is not only their breakout hit but also their most critically acclaimed—*Rolling Stone* magazine has it ranked as the number-two greatest song of all time, improbably (in my opinion) behind only "Like a Rolling Stone" by Bob Dylan. If "Satisfaction" is a good as its reputation demands, some of its greatness is certainly due to what the Stones learned about performance in their early forays into R & B.

Yet we can still reasonably ask, why does "Satisfaction" score so high on the *Rolling Stone* ranking list? And is it, as the ranking might imply, the greatest Stones song? Before trying to answer these questions, we can question the journalistic intent of *Rolling Stone* magazine's list making of at least the last decade. Put bluntly, rankings and lists like these attract a certain type of popular-music audience with short attention spans who are nonetheless hungry for knowledge. Recently, websites like BuzzFeed among countless others have become enormously popular by ranking everything and anything using superficial headlines. At the same time, a case can be made that the *Rolling Stone* ranking list actually does rock a great service, especially as streaming sites like Spotify recalculate the rankings based on their own algorithm of how many plays a song gets, completely skewing the results toward more contemporary pop music. This is also the misguided impression of any outside observer who looks at YouTube hits to judge a song's cultural significance, where recent pop hits easily generate hundreds of millions of views. Thus in its defense, the *Rolling Stone* ranking takes into account a wider range of factors over just views, clicks, or fleeting popularity and includes, for example, a song's historical context and its effective stylistic and aesthetic influence on the larger culture and on other songs.

So despite some reservations about the purpose of ranking songs, let us take a shot at dissecting why "Satisfaction" ranks so high. First, notice the year of its release, 1965. If one year represents a watershed, a before-and-after moment in popular music, a strong case could be made for 1965.[3] This is the year of *Rolling Stone*'s number-one song, Bob Dylan's "Like a Rolling Stone" (really, this is number one!). It is also the year Dylan went electric and when the Beatles delved into writing serious music beyond love songs, releasing their groundbreaking *Rubber Soul* in December. Youth culture became more assertive, self-confident, and omnipresent in 1965. Its artistic endeavors were no longer seen as fleeting and faddish but rather as an emerging political, cultural, and economic force to be reckoned with, reflected in the onslaught of criticism against the institutions and societal codes of the past. Finally, if we take the top ten songs from the *Rolling Stone* 500 Greatest Songs list, the median year is 1966, while the average is 1968 (taking out Nirvana's "Smells Like Teen Spirit"—the list's token youth anthem from the 1990s—puts the average back right at 1965).

Second, the magazine considers the originality of the song.[4] "Like a Rolling Stone" challenged the "artistic conventions" of its time, rewriting commercial music history at the same time with its "punk" (organist Al Kooper's word), "disorganized" approach to recording the perceived unfiltered poetic sentiments of Dylan. Although written and recorded before the Dylan masterpiece, "Satisfaction" tapped into some of the wavelengths emanating from Dylan songs. It is "bold" in its own design with its rant against American consumerism. (Ironically, it was this unbounded desire of consumerism that helped foster the musical careers of so many rock artists like the Stones.) Continuing, the song opened up the frustrations and aspirations of the generation gap in a way that had not been conceptualized: "It was the sound of a generation impatient to inherit the Earth."[5]

Third is the musical substance of "Satisfaction" and how it appropriates and elevates sound ideas that were current. Today the Stones have come around to acknowledge their musical sources for the song. The fuzz-draped guitar riff, which came to Richards in a dream, is based on a Motown song, "Nowhere to Run" (credited to Holland-Dozier-Holland, 1964). As recorded by Martha (Reeves) and the Vandellas, "Nowhere to Run" has as its head motive played by the horns the basic outline of the riff that Richards uses in "Satisfaction." Watts took his drumbeat from "Pretty Woman" by Roy Orbison, or some song like it. Watts says that the beat was in vogue at the time, mentioning Stevie Wonder's "Uptight (Everything's Alright)," which also has it (though Wonder's song was released later in the year and after "Satisfaction,"

Watts's point is well taken). And concerning the lyrics, which are similar in topical relevancy to the type of cultural critique that Dylan was engaged in at the time, Jagger himself says he may have "nicked" ideas from Chuck Berry's "Thirty Days," especially the line about not getting any "satisfaction" from the judge. Finally, the gutbucket performance of the song—Richards reports that he was "shocked" that Oldham released it in such an unfinished state—owes much to their live approach to covering R & B songs. Richards's guitar riff sets the tempo, and then the bass and drums follow, respectively. The rhythm is perfect in its imperfection, as the Stones have learned that having all the instrumental parts line up in exact sync is not what they are about—rather, they are devoted to reproducing the ineffable swing content of blues and R & B.

Though we can never again experience "Satisfaction" like those lucky first listeners in the summer of 1965, with historical distance, however, we can hear how the song becomes the template for their later songs—in fact, the Mixolydian-infused progression (quickly, using the chord a whole step below the tonic or home chord, so from E to D in this case) of "Satisfaction" generates the core idea of their most famous songs, like "Jumpin' Jack Flash" or "Sympathy for the Devil." By seeking out connections and similarities among songs like this, it is hoped that this book offers something new to the experience of listening to the Stones. Arranged chronologically, the central chapters of the book focus on albums starting with *Beggars Banquet* (1968). These albums capture the countercultural zeitgeist of the late 1960s, an incredible time of societal and cultural discontent, upheaval, and transformation.

In the course of research for the book I studied the guitar parts to the songs analyzed and others not included in order to appreciate how the Stones' songs fit together musically. Working through the various tunings employed by Richards has given me new insight into fingering possibilities on the guitar, and much admiration for his ability to create an original style grounded in traditional blues. In trying to explain the organic nature of the Stones' music I have had to rely on some technical language. In the text I tried to keep this kind of talk to a minimum and tried to put a lot of the music analysis in the notes. To this end, there is a glossary to help decipher some of these terms.

* * *

I thank my editors and readers, Gregg Akkerman, Bennett Graff, and especially Rob Weiner. They gave me encouragement and helpful feedback while writing this book. Rob shared his vast expertise of the Stones and popular music generally to make this a better book. I also acknowledge my family, Valerie, Sofia, and Joey, for their patience with me during the writing process. I dedicate this book to them. Finally, I thank the Rolling Stones and their associates, past and present, for dedicating their lives to creating what is in my opinion one of the most engaging and rewarding oeuvres in recent music history. It is truly an honor to engage with their creation.

1

THE EARLY STONES

From R & B and the Blues to Chuck Berry

What actually happened is that we turned American people back on to their own [African American] music. And that's probably our greatest contribution to music. We turned white America's brain and ear around.

—Keith Richards, *Life*, 159

As Richards tells it, it took a band of outsiders from England to give white America the ability to hear its homegrown black music. Though he credits the band in this regard ("we"), it was more precisely the vision and idea of the Stones' founder, Brian Jones, that African American blues and R & B could open the minds of the disenchanted youth of the day, and in turn change the world.[1] But the refashioning of this music as British did become the main cause of the Stones. Their music caught on immediately in England, yet it would be a couple of more years before the band conquered the States. When they did, their appropriative achievement dovetailed with the explosion of the rediscovery of the blues in America. This is appropriately symbolized in Jones's reverential introduction of Howlin' Wolf to American audiences on the teen television program, *Shindig!*, in May 1965, the first time most young people had ever encountered a bona fide Delta bluesman, albeit via Chicago.

Before the blues, however, rock and roll had already turned the Western world upside down a decade earlier. In its unexpected and brilliant arrival, rock's dizzying disruption to the status quo had prepared the way for the Rolling Stones and the youth-led cultural revolution of the 1960s. This first tidal wave of rock and roll had far-reaching effects on how music was conceived, created, and disseminated. It displaced the popular songbook of Tin Pan Alley with its attendant crooners singing in front of mannered band arrangements. The new music relied on simple arrangements drawn from American vernacular or roots music, with a direct, immediate, and raw approach to musical material. While its sonic orientation was so radically different, as we shall see, its cultural translation forever changed the role of music in society. Even so, at the time rock and roll was considered a fad, even by many of its practitioners, but its authentic, inner connection to the deep well of African American music—especially the blues—was not yet well understood.

One obvious thing to most observers of the phenomenon was rock's riveting and Dionysian effect on youth. In the 1950s and into the 1960s, rock (it lost the "roll" sometime in the 1960s, which without it generally denotes the broader hybrid style it evolved to) became the main marker separating the generations, what came to be called the generation gap. By addressing the emotional travails and rebellious attitudes of many young people, rock opened a new market for the music industry. But it also instigated a feedback loop, whereby the separation and alienation of youth from what came to be called "straight" society, or the Establishment, steadily increased.

Led by the Beatles and the Stones, the new music dominated the cultural scene into the late 1960s and beyond as it became central to the personal identity of the baby boomers. More so than the Beatles or any other band, the Stones capitalized on the generation gap through their own rebellious and irreverent manners. As they rode this oppositional stance of rock through the politically charged youth revolt of the late 1960s, the Stones became one of the standard-bearers of the counterculture.

Today rock is often thought of as a single musical style. But it was always already a multiplicity, a master signifier that gathered under its banner a myriad of musical genres. A good example of this is the Liverpool music scene from which the Beatles emerged, called "British Beat" or "Merseybeat" (note that the music journal devoted to this music was called *Mersey Beat*), which fused rock and roll, doo-wop, and R & B, among others. Though the Stones were not labeled a beat group per se, their style was strongly influenced by the sound of these groups. After the band attended their first Beatles concert on April 18, 1963, at the Royal Albert Hall, Brian Jones was smitten with their music; according to Wyman, Jones proclaimed, "This is what we like, this is what we want!"[2]

Even if they included early rock and roll covers in their set lists, the early Stones considered themselves an R & B group. Stones biographer Sean Egan documents how initially Brian Jones often wrote letters to the media emphatically stating that the Stones were an R & B outfit. Jones's definition of R & B is revealing considering the direction the band would take: R & B is the American Negro's pop music, whose impact is purely emotional.[3] Driving this point home, it is helpful to read one of the first published reviews (or as Egan puts it, the first important one) of the band by Norman Jopling writing in May 1963: "Despite the fact that their R & B has a superficial resemblance to rock and roll, fans of the hit parade music would not find any familiar material . . . [they] have achieved the American sound better than any group over here."[4] Prophetically, Jopling gives the Stones the sendoff that they will soon be the "leading R & B performers in the country." Finally, the British conception of R & B was similar to, yet different from, the American understanding of it. Keith Richards understands it as an umbrella term that included the "whole blues network," especially the "powerful blues jump bands from Chicago."[5]

While the Stones and Beatles, among others, were crafting a new sound based on American music, a youth movement throughout England was growing. In London, this societal revolution became known as "mod" culture, short for "modernist." The original mods, newly empowered kids from the working classes in and around London, became fashion trendsetters who reveled in music and art. Their original music was the traditional jazz (abbreviated as "Trad," based on classic New Orleans jazz of the 1920s and the stride and boogie-woogie bass/piano patterns) popular in England at the time, and they studied French and Italian cinema to define their fashion sensibility. But around the time the Stones started, the mod scene quickly gravitated toward the R & B and blues played by them, which was more conducive to the amphetamine-fueled, rave-up dancing in vogue at the clubs and small venues. Later, one of the most lasting outcomes of the mod scene was the predilection for bands like the Beatles, the Stones, the Kinks, and the Who to be thrust forward into the international spotlight. Rock critic David Dalton (an early writer on the Stones) writes that without mod culture behind these bands, "R & B might have become just another fad like 'Trad' [jazz] and skiffle."[6]

Thus, at exactly the moment the band was hitting the scene, playing their first gig as the newly minted "Rollin' Stones" on July 12, 1962, at London's Marquee Club, the stars were aligning in their favor. The emotional experience of their brand of ecstatic R & B seemed the perfect match for the existential aspirations of the mods. Indeed, music was set to become the prime catalyst for the largest youth upheaval in modern history, a force unleashed with the arrival of Elvis on the world stage in 1956, but whose legacy was not guaranteed until the Beatles and Stones made it happen a few years later.

SOME SOCIOHISTORICAL BACKGROUND: THE 1950S

Before we get into the heady 1960s and the Stones' role in transforming their time, let us first set the stage in order to see how unpredictable and radical all this in fact was and try to quickly summarize the seismic sociohistorical changes accompanying rock and roll's genesis in 1950s America: the hardening of the Cold War with its threat of the atomic bomb and planetary destruction; the growing sense of malaise at the threat posed by communism and the increasing power of the Soviet Union; the beginning of suburbanization, propelled by postwar prosperity and the G.I. Bill; the final glory days of the political and economic dominance of so-called WASP (White Anglo-Saxon Protestant) culture, with its attendant social and moral codes governing propriety and personal conduct; and, dialectically related to this last, the beginning of the civil rights movement and its challenging of authority.

In spite of the unease of doomsday thinking and the prospect of upheaval to the social order of the U.S. South, the belief in progress and the hope of a brighter future held the collective mood of the day, characterized as the American Dream. Parents expected that through education and hard work their children's futures were limitless, and that each succeeding generation would improve and build on the achievements of the last. This can be seen on late-1950s television shows like *Leave It to Beaver*, an optimistic celebration of the nuclear family with its sharply defined gender roles and moral codes. American exceptionalism and its attendant doctrine of capitalist prosperity resonated with the rising prosperity of the average American and were also general hallmarks of the Eisenhower era.

Countering this simplified, reductive worldview that sought clarity in seeing everything in black and white (democracy vs. communism, good vs. evil, etc.) was a burgeoning problematizing of American values that had been brewing at least since the Great Depression. This phenomenon would first appear in the creative realms and in the academy, and examples can be multiplied at length. J. D. Salinger's *The Catcher in the Rye* is often cited as one of the pioneering novels in this regard, as the protagonist resists the "phony" or inauthentic world of adults. Norman Mailer's essay "The White Negro" focuses on white hipsters seeking to emulate African American cultural trends like bebop. Mid-century abstract expressionists painters Jackson Pollock, Mark Rothko, and Willem de Kooning among others challenged the safe aesthetic of America's representational art. American Beats like Jack Kerouac, writing in the shadow of European existentialism, were among the first to question the validity of the American way of life, and films like *Rebel without a Cause* (1955) quickly followed up on this theme. (As an aside, Bill Wyman even compares fellow band member Brian Jones to the drifting personality of *Rebel*'s Jim Stark as portrayed by James Dean, as Jones impregnated girls without any plan for his life or work.) Allen Ginsberg's "Howl" sings of fellow travelers (the "best minds") of his generation who did not fit into straight America, many destroyed by drugs, and celebrates the deviant exploits of Beat legend Neal Cassady in particular. Furthermore, the Beat poets and writers were particularly enamored of the improvisational powers of bebop musicians, especially the wildest saxophonist of his generation, Charlie "Bird" Parker, who lived on the edge and died young at age thirty-four in 1955. Finally, academic critics like Jacques Barzun in *The House of Intellect* discussed democracy's recent cultural attack on intellect and thinking, as given in what he argued was America's reductive educational system, which sought to accommodate different opinions because of their potential value for generating more commerce rather than spurring critical, artistic reflection or engagement.

At issue in the Beat generation's artistic challenge to orthodox American values and culture was one of the most basic existential questions posed by Greek moral philosophy over two millennia prior—namely, how should one conduct a life? Thus as the 1950s wore on, the younger generation seemed to respond to the building zeitgeist of disenchantment and started to doubt the received political orthodoxy and social institutions of their elders, thereby opening the rift of the so-called generation gap. Embracing the fast-growing rock and roll movement, middle-class American kids who had never heard jazz or Beat poetry finally had an on-ramp to a cultural force that they could use to vent their frustrations. Later on, coming of age in the 1960s, the postwar boomers only opened this chasm wider, and it was rock music and especially bands like the Stones that helped them to do it. And as we shall see throughout this book, the Stones (among others) would still remain in artistic debt to the creative, oppositional opening of the 1950s Beats.

MUSIC AS REBELLION

Rock and roll's initial rebellious spirit captured the creative restlessness and disaffection for their parents' way of life of the nascent youth movement. The new music's rebellion against the perceived gray, authoritarian cultural backdrop provided escape from the geopolitical and social-justice urgencies of the day and articulated a party lifestyle where adult concerns and priorities were irrelevant. In this respect it was also a form of escapism. As a leading rock critic writing in 1971, Lester Bangs describes rock and roll as "the Party," in his own uniquely Beat-inflected prose:

> All those early songs about rock n' roll were successive movements in a suite in progress which was actually nothing more than a gigantic party whose collective ambition was simple [sic] to keep the party going and jive and rave and kick 'em out cross the decades and only stop for the final Bomb of some technological maelstrom of sonic bliss sucking the cities away at last. Because the Party was the *one* thing we had in our lives to grab onto, the one thing we could truly believe in and depend on, a loony tune fountain of youth and vitality that was keeping us alive as much as any medicine we'd ever take.[7]

In Bangs's conception, rock transcends its original function as youthful entertainment music, offering a way of life and an escape from the seriousness of life. In the same essay Bangs makes a plea for keeping rock simple, as it was in the 1950s, and sticking to what he calls its "apolitical" nature. As an example that extols these virtues, in the same essay Bangs highly commends the Stones for their live album *'Get Yer Ya-Ya's Out!'* (1970) from about the time of his own writing.

With roots reaching into black vernacular music and blues, urban R & B, jazz, as well as country, this new kind of dance and party music called "rock and roll" and led by the likes of Elvis Presley, Little Richard, Chuck Berry, Carl Perkins, Eddie Cochran, and Buddy Holly could drive teens into hysterics, while parental observers were left dumbfounded. Although initially propelled by small, independent labels and producers working in unsophisticated and less-equipped recording studios, the industry's major labels along with Hollywood eventually joined the act. They realized there was much money to be made from this new, younger consumer group, who, along with the rising tide of prosperity for the middle class, had some extra leisure time, unlike previous generations who worked at much younger ages. Too, much of the controversy at the time was not only over the musical sounds per se, but over the perceived overt sexuality of its performance, especially in the case of Elvis. With the new reach of television combined with radio and film, youth rebellion was packaged and sold and gradually taken up by the mainstream press as a topic for discussion. But with this new reach, by the late 1950s the rebellious nature of the genre had started to subside; with Buddy Holly's death in 1959 and Elvis conveniently ensconced in the army, two of rock's greatest practitioners were no longer able to lead. This was also the year of the payola (pay for play) hearings in Congress, the political strategy for the old guard to halt the rise of the new genre.[8] Yet the packaging of the "teenager" as a consumer group, a boon to Madison Avenue marketers, was now too lucrative to push aside. And the teens themselves took note of their new status. As Richards points out, there was a new self-consciousness that went beyond "clothes and cosmetics," and literature and music gave teens a new self-identity.[9]

Starting around 1956, American rock and roll was embraced enthusiastically by young people in Great Britain, also fueling the popularity of the British folk revival based on American music referred to as skiffle, whose leading representative was Lonnie Donegan. With strumming guitars out front, John Lennon and Jimmy Page were among those amateurs who sought to connect with American popular music via skiffle, and Lennon's foray into the style directly resulted in the formation of the Beatles. Furthermore, Keith Richards cites specifically his infatuation with Little Richard, Eddie Cochran, Buddy Holly, and above all Elvis, all first heard in England on Radio Luxembourg. The two biggest fans of 1950s rock and roll within the Stones were Mick Jagger and Richards, old classmates from their school days in Dartford, Kent, a place bordering greater London. Jagger had even managed to attend the Buddy Holly concert in Woolwich in March 1958. Throughout their career the Stones would return to these 1950s roots as they revisited classics by Chuck Berry and wrote songs directly inspired by him (see the following section).

At about the same time, a blues revival was brewing in London. Led by guitarist Alexis Korner and harmonica player Cyril Davis, perhaps the first club to feature the new rhythm-and-blues music was the Ealing Jazz Club.[10] Richards calls Korner the "daddy" of the scene, as it was Korner's band at Ealing, Blues Incorporated, that first brought everyone together. The Ealing was originally a Trad jazz venue, and as such the arrival of Korner and his band represents the changing of the guard.

Responding to new demand, some record stores catered to these blues collectors and stocked indie-produced African American music from labels like Chess and Vee-Jay and reissues from these and other labels through the British roots label, Pye.[11] Collecting obscure blues records in itself can be seen as an act of rebellion, as it often entailed for these listeners a new way of seeing the world through the prism of black oppression. For example, many youths read the liner notes about the harsh day-to-day circumstances of the contemporary blues singers in segregated America and immediately identified with their marginalized plight. Richards notes the significance of this collecting scene before the Stones were formed, as he and Jagger bonded over records, sharing identical tastes. Indeed, one of the band's creation stories has Jagger running into Richards at the train station for the first time in years, with some American blues records, including Muddy Waters, tucked under his arm.[12] As it was, Jagger had already developed his connections within the London record-collecting scene, which according to Richards was eclectic and included people of all types and ages.

RECEPTION HISTORY: THE STONES' NARRATIVE AND BRIAN JONES

Today most rock fans think of the Rolling Stones as the artistic achievement of Mick Jagger and Keith Richards, two of the most famous men in rock history. If they are Stones fans in particular, they will know the other founding members like Brian Jones, Charlie Watts, and Bill Wyman, or later guitar add-ons like Mick Taylor and Ronnie Wood. But the identification of the Stones with Jagger and Richards runs deep. With Jagger as the front man and Richards as the guitarist and musical director, the two have written nearly all the songs, and most of the band's lore and mythology revolves around their exploits. In this regard, the band's narrative as their story aligns perfectly with the conception of the band's first manager, Andrew Loog Oldham, who focused on the two at the expense of Jones and even fired an original member of the band, pianist Ian Stewart ("Stu"). Stu managed to stick around as road manager, but ended up playing with the band (though not as an official member) until his premature death in 1986.

Still, it was Jones who had the idea for an English R & B outfit, one that would be the first English one to play the Chicago urban blues. Bill Wyman clearly has this in mind when he writes:

> Through his vision of music and his lifestyle, Brian was the inventor and inspiration of the Rolling Stones. The band would not have existed without him. He never received that proper credit during his life and I intend to ensure he gets it now.[13]

Following up on Wyman's point in his revisionist biography of Brian Jones, Paul Trynka makes the case that Jagger, and to a lesser extent Richards, have downplayed the role of Jones as the band's true architect.[14] It is Trynka's contention that Jagger has essentially airbrushed Jones out of the picture of the band. He argues that Jagger and Richards essentially conspired to push Jones aside, assume leadership of the band, and then, in the cruelest twist, fully take on his personal attributes after his death.

In his account, Trynka surmises that it was Jones "alone who had a vision, that raw electric blues could appeal to the youth of Britain."[15] Furthermore, he maintains that when the band first started, Jones was the only one who had already paid his dues on the nascent blues and live performance scene and was by far the most accomplished musician. That is, Jones had gone further than anyone else in England in investigating the musical chemistry behind the styles of Elmore James, Robert Johnson, and Muddy Waters; Trynka concludes (here, perhaps exaggerated) that Jones "worked out their secrets—powerful and arcane knowledge in the spring of 1962. Knowledge that would sustain the Stones for decades, to the present day—to a more profound extent than any of the band's present members acknowledge."[16]

Thus in this new retelling of an old story, Jones's central role in assembling the band holds the key to understanding the Rolling Stones phenomenon. Again and as just indicated, it was the blues scene at the Ealing Jazz Club from which the band had sprung in early 1962. Jones performed at Ealing under the stage name Elmo Lewis, after Elmore James, a bluesman from the Mississippi Delta who recorded his hits in the 1950s in Chicago. Jones would sit in with Korner and often would play in between Korner's sets. Encouraged by the response of both audience and other players, he decided to form his own band. Jones placed an ad in early March 1962 in *Jazz News*, but as Trynka says, the notice was more an advertisement than a recruitment notice.[17] Note that not long after this, Jagger and Richards had their first encounter with Jones, as they watched Jones perform on slide guitar a rendition of Elmore James's version of Robert Johnson's "Dust My Broom" in late March at the Ealing.

Stewart was among the first to respond to the ad and join up with Jones. He reported that Jones wanted a band that could replicate the style and sound of Howlin' Wolf's "You Can't Be Beat" (1956), a song that had just come out in London.[18] The two practiced at the Bricklayers Arms in Soho. They rehearsed with various musicians, and Jones tried hard to recruit his friend Paul Jones (who went under the name P. P. Pond) as vocalist, who instead decided to stay in school. (Later Pond became the singer for Manfred Mann, another British R & B group similar to the Stones.) But Jones was already well aware of Jagger. A student at the London School of Economics with a bright future, at the time Jagger was the second-string singer for Korner's band, which at the time included "Long John" Baldry.[19] In May Jagger decided to commit to working with Jones, but he stipulated that he wanted his friend Richards in the group as well as the other guitarist. The competition between Jones and Jagger begins early, and in particular over the harmonica that both of them played. Jones was further along on it and had already figured out the blues or cross harp, generously sharing his knowledge with Jagger.[20]

As the Stones shed Jones's leadership and gradually morphed into a rock/pop band, Jones continued to assert himself as a fashionable pop icon and sex symbol. Because of his popularity and charisma, the band still needed him, and musically he made vital contributions to their recordings. Beyond his guitar and harmonica playing, Jones was also an amazing multi-instrumentalist who could learn a new instrument very quickly, and was the one who usually added an exotic dimension to their sound—the most famous examples are his marimba in "Under My Thumb" and sitar in "Paint It Black." These are iconic moments for the Stones' recorded legacy, and the two songs present some of the band's most memorable soundscapes.

Finally, even after the death of Jones in 1969, their quintessential classic-rock album triad—*Let It Bleed* (the last album with Jones on it, though minimally), *Sticky Fingers,* and *Exile on Main Street*—pays homage to those blues sources at the basis of the band's origins. Restated, in these golden middle years the Stones fell back on their own roots as blues aficionados, coming their closest to capturing the spiritual purity of rural blues, especially the Delta blues style of its greatest exponent, Robert Johnson. Indeed, Richards first encountered the music of Johnson via Jones. He writes:

> And that's where [Brian's apartment] I first heard Robert Johnson, and came under Brian's tutorship and delved back into the blues with him. I was astounded at what I heard. It took guitar playing, songwriting, delivery, to a totally different height.[21]

Thus from Richards himself we gather how his blues tutelage under Jones became one of the master templates for the band. Richards goes on to say how he realized that everything in the blues was connected; that is, it is all a variation on a theme, though it is not clear if that is his current view or if he discovered that back in 1962 with Jones.

THE NARRATIVE CONTINUED: THE EMERGING SOUND AND CULTURAL INFLUENCE OF THE STONES

The Stones' notoriously raw and raucous approach to sound was certainly modeled on the styles, bands, and artists they were covering and imitating, especially Bo Diddley, Chuck Berry, and Jimmy Reed. It is our task in this book to analyze this sound, to break apart its textures, especially in relation to its historical context. In popular music, it is above all historical timing—being in the right place at the right time with the right sound—that can lead to viral success. With their sound and stage act coming together in early 1963, just as the Beatles were opening the floodgates for the British beat sound in 1964, the Stones could not have had better timing. As we have said, British kids were eager to move beyond the gray and narrow societal landscape of the 1950s, and in turn sought out new and ecstatic emotional outlets, which they discovered, incredibly enough, in specialty record stores that stocked imported African American music. English bands led by the Stones were starting to pick up on these trends, most especially the urban blues, which ironically were not particularly in vogue for either blacks or whites in the United States.

Yet given that there were plenty of other bands from the Stones' native London, as well as the northern bands of the industrial Mersey area centered around Liverpool, it is quite startling how early the Stones managed to separate themselves from the pack and emerge as the menacing alter ego to the bright and sunny Beatles, an image that remains with them to this day. Part of this was in their infectious attitude toward making music in the mold of their heroes, the blues and R & B musicians of the Chicago school. Richards has said that their early sound came from studying and channeling Jimmy Reed, a contemporaneous Chicago bluesman and notorious alcoholic who came from Mississippi. But it was also in the insouciant and irreverent way they looked and carried themselves at a time when popular musicians were supposed to be nothing other than entertainers purveying songs.

What is it, then, about their self-described "raw" sound that distinguishes the Stones from the legions of other new popular and rock bands, including the Beatles, coming out of England in the early 1960s? And how did this sound open the hearts and minds of British youth, and then in turn do the same thing in the United States and the rest of the world? How calculating were the Stones (or their handlers) as they peddled rebellion, their bad-boy image, and the Party (following Bangs) to conquer the popular music market? Of course there are countless ways to tackle questions like these, and excellent books, monographs, and films have dealt with the main story quite well. So let us continue with the standard narrative about the band.

It goes something like this: The Stones delivered their music, inspired by R & B, in a more challenging, direct way, with a sonic punch focused on the primacy of rhythm, and thus was more authentic to its African American roots than other English bands. Originally led by guitarist and multi-instrumentalist Brian Jones, in his role as lead vocalist Jagger soon emerged as the band's front man; without an instrument to encumber him, Jagger established a direct, shamanistic connection to the audience, and he gradually became viewed as the leader of the band. However, despite the rise of Jagger, Jones was not wholly pushed aside, and his popularity and iconic stature with fans—especially his connection to girls—continued to flourish. But Oldham forever altered the dynamic and power balance of the band by pairing Jagger with Richards as the songwriting juggernaut of the band, modeling on the Lennon/McCartney partnership of the Beatles. Significantly, Jagger/Richards came to replace the band's compositional approach under the pseudonym "Nanker Phelge." Oldham marketed the band as the dangerous alternative to the Beatles, famously summarized in the slogan "Would you let your daughter marry a Rolling Stone?" As Jones's input diminished and his erratic behavior increased until he was eventually fired from the band, Jagger and Richards stepped forward as the stars of the band, backed up by the straight-ahead and solid rhythm section of Wyman and Watts, both of whom were also marginalized.

As the members of the Stones, especially Jones, helped to define the rise of the Swinging London set, so their lifestyles, drug use, and romances attracted intense and sensationalist media attention. The pairings of Brian Jones/Anita Pallenberg and Mick Jagger/Marianne Faithfull (and before her, Chrissie Shrimpton) were among the most celebrated relationships of the 1960s. Both Pallenberg and Faithfull became more than girlfriends and groupies for the band, serving as muses and in many ways creative partners for the band in the late 1960s and into the 1970s. And just as Yoko Ono altered the relationships among the Beatles, so too did Pallenberg among the Stones.

One episode in particular involving Pallenberg marks a major turning point for the band and had big repercussions down the road. It begins the final downturn of Jones and sets up the fraying of the friendship between Jagger and Richards. The episode also intersects with Morocco, which would become the Stones' psychological escape valve, playing a similar role to what India did at the time for the Beatles. Finally, it energized the debate about the role of drugs in society and whether rock stars were above the law.

The episode begins in February 1967. Jagger and Richards were caught in drug bust instigated by a tabloid newspaper *News of the World*. The drug bust was intended to have entrapped Jones, who instead was away that day while working on a score for a West German film (*A Degree of Murder*) that starred Pallenberg. Seeking to escape the potential fallout if the story broke, and probably worried about more police surveillance, the band embarked on a trip to Morocco. On the way there, Jones became sick and stayed behind in France recovering. Richards and Pallenberg began an affair as they continued their way to Tangier. Eventually, with Pallenberg and Faithfull's help, Jones reunited with the party in Tangier. After a bad fight whose violence is open to interpretation, Pallenberg left Jones for Richards. In a final act of betrayal, the group deserted Jones when they all left the country. Trynka writes that it was not only losing Pallenberg but also the "traitorous actions" of the men he loved that devastated Jones.[22]

Though not married, Pallenberg and Richards would remain together through the 1970s and had three children together (one died at ten weeks). Their relationship was severely tested when Pallenberg filmed some sex scenes with Jagger in 1968 for the film *Performance*, written and co-directed by Donald Cammell. Richards is certain the two had an affair at the time, while Pallenberg denies it. Whatever the truth is, Richards took it badly, and his relationship with Jagger suffered irreparable damage.

After some rocky times with Jones, the band finally let him go and renewed their sound with the addition of lead guitarist Mick Taylor, freeing up Richards to further explore his interest in playing a middle-ground role between the rhythm section and the front line. Tragically Jones passed away, drowning in his swimming pool, very shortly after being let go. Thus, as they entered a new decade, gone were Jones's sonic experiments in favor of straight-ahead, blues-based rock, the dominant classic-rock style of the early 1970s. The Stones fully burnished their outsider image when they were forced to leave the United Kingdom as tax exiles (though a disappointment for British fans), setting up a notorious drug- and party-fueled life on the French Riviera centered on the waterfront mansion, Villa Nellcôte, rented by Richards. There they created some of their grittiest music in a basement using their mobile recording studio. The final period was marked by another change in personnel in the mid-1970s, when Taylor left the band and they brought in their friend Ronnie Wood of the Faces as his replacement.

Again, the Stones owed much of their initial popularity beyond England to their playing the anti-Beatles role. As English pop music was put on the map by the Beatles and other northern, Merseyside bands similar to them, the London-based Stones were presented as the dangerous, surly, disrespectful alternative to the Beatles—longer hair, bad attitudes, street clothes, and an edgier sound—with music modeled more closely and directly on African American sources. In contrast to the Beatles, the Stones had to be coaxed into becoming songwriters by Oldham. Whereas the Beatles represented a pure pop phenomenon with an optimistic, unique but familiar sound, the Stones presented more of an enigma from the start. Though they too had their legions of teenage fans, the Stones also cultivated more sophisticated artistic bonds, as for example with the leading New York City artist of their generation, Andy Warhol, as well as one of the principal photographers of Swinging London, David Bailey, both artists associated with pop culture and its appropriation who were ironically and initially resistant to pop music.

And while Jones led the early Stones, Jagger and Richards had eclipsed him by the latter half of the 1960s. Even the early records often revealed the synergy of childhood friends Jagger and Richards as they continued to find ways to push Jones aside. Influenced by, but not limited to, the purism of blues enthusiasts, the band's visceral appeal emanated from their approach to African American soundscapes, as for example Jagger's soulful evocations that snake in and out of the often ponderous and heavy grooves laid down by the rhythm unit. Indeed, as crystallized on their 1964 cover of Holly's "Not Fade Away," it was the groove content of the music, especially the relationship of the vocal part to the rhythm section, which would define the band's approach as their career unfolded.

Thus the Stones' earliest recordings and first album reveal their initial objective: both to pay tribute to and to turn people on to their musical heroes, African American blues and R & B artists or their followers in rock and roll. With its cry of both pain and resistance, and its internalization of social injustices both past and present, the blues and its attendant genres often bespoke a multivalent repository of African American life in the Jim Crow South. The Stones and other aspiring musicians of their generation growing up in postwar England were drawn immediately to the perceived raw authenticity and direct emotional interjections of what was understood as an exotic, outsider musical genre. Because of the novelty of transplanting this music to England, the Stones were able to capitalize on and, in turn, lead a youthful wave of rebellion that recontextualized this marginalization of the African American experience into a cultural universal transcending the historical specificity of time and place.

WHY LISTEN TO THE WHITE COVER VERSION OF A BLUES SONG?

As Jagger once asked, why listen to the Stones' versions of blues when the originals are handily available? It is odd that Jagger even poses the question, given that the Stones were originally a cover band. It is not clear if this is self-critical honesty or another way of marketing what the band was doing.

But to try to answer Jagger's query, let us first take as an example the Stones' 1964 cover (recorded in January) of Slim Harpo's "I'm a King Bee" that opens the second side to their first, eponymous LP, the song to which Jagger was referring. Although the releases of the song were only a few years apart—Harpo's recording of it dates to 1957—the Stones' version stakes out the broad territory of the white appropriation of the blues, from simple tribute to again the nuanced remapping of the African American Southern cultural milieu.

Harpo's lyrics feature sexually charged double entendres that are well-worn clichés within the broader context of the blues. We learn in the last line that the woman already has a man, making Harpo's overture all the more provocative, even if it is typical of the blues by this time. Although the AAB lyrical scheme conforms to the standardized rhythmic delineation of the twelve-bar blues, Harpo's version adds a few extra beats to make it an irregular thirteen-and-a-half bar pattern and starts haltingly with the drum entering on the second beat of the measure.

But the power of Harpo's aggressive blues derives mostly from his urgent vocal delivery against a menacing and muddied rhythm section, led by a guitar that is almost overdriven, and some expertly placed upward bass glissandos, both of which evoke a heightened sexualized atmosphere, similar to the feeling a muted horn in jazz often imparts. The back-and-forth shuffle pattern on the guitar's lower strings departs from the standard blues back-and-forth rhythm (the 5–6 degrees of the scale) and moves into a more menacing, darker pattern (played off the tonic, degrees 1–b3). Despite Harpo's masculine stance, his vocal pacing is relaxed and mellow at times; more importantly, it is mannered, in his use of a subtle and fast (quasi-quivering) vibrato added to a nasal country-and-western style of singing perhaps influenced by Chuck Berry.

When the Stones interpret the song, they keep the musical details of the song mostly intact, even the half-bar insertion. They are also careful to follow the nuances of Harpo's version, down to the bass part's upward glissandos and the singer's exhortation to "sting it then" that elicits an instrumental response. We can hear that the Stones had really studied their source material and use simple two-track recording technology to capture what are live studio performances—according to Wyman, many of the songs on their first album were recorded in one take. Still, Harpo's version remains simpler, more stripped down than the one by the Stones. The Stones add an acoustic guitar and a more agitated electric guitar part with a fluttering, oscillating figure on the notes E and D, thereby expanding the E tonic chord into a dominant-seventh chord, creating at once a more luxurious and urban sound in line with the resonant R & B music of the early 1960s. Unlike in the 1950s era, when a lot of covers by white artists sped up the original, the Stones' version is slightly slower than Harpo's. The Stones' guitar solo, the response to "sting it then," is more vibrant than the single-note one heard in Harpo's—and actually, here both guitarists play. The Stones also add an instrumental flourish right before the "sting it then," when

Mick says, "well, buzz awhile," and Richards (probably) plays a tremolo on the note E in the surf guitar style popular at this time, consciously or not. Jagger also rehashes Harpo's harmonica or "harp" solo (the blues term for this instrument), as an outro. Finally, one big difference between the versions is the choice of key—Harpo's is in the key of F, while the Stones take it down a half step to E. E is the more natural key on the guitar with its ringing open strings supporting the chords and has the effect of clarifying the texture.

And yet something was radical about the Stones' cover versions of this song and others from their early period, even if only in retrospect. Since Elvis first sang songs like "That's All Right," "Mystery Train," and "Hound Dog," the recontextualization of African American music was simultaneously introducing a mostly younger white audience to a different approach to music while creating a growing market expectation for more of this style. This approach to covering R & B relied on black cultural tropes, stereotypes, and signifiers from the American South that had metastasized since slavery and the days of minstrelsy. But it is not entirely clear how aware young people were at the time of this wholesale appropriation of black culture. Richards states simply that for the band, black music was the future, and white music like what the Beach Boys were playing, the past. He goes on to say that the Stones were getting white American kids to listen to what was already all around them, which they had previously ignored. And if other British Invasion bands like the Beatles, Animals, or Kinks were keen on this approach, perhaps no other band took it as far as the Stones did; moreover, even the Beatles, at least in the early stage of Beatlemania, had changed direction for a more pop-oriented, less R & B orientation. Thus the door was left wide open for the Stones to fulfill what quickly became their destiny—white minstrels, as it were, searching for authenticity and communion with their R & B/soul/blues source material, or, as Wyman terms this source, "convict music." Finally, it is worth reiterating that the Stones were and still remain committed to their earliest musical heroes and influences. Much of their success was due to the fact that they were genuinely inspired by the music they were playing, and their marketing machine remained tightly and consistently focused around this idea.

LISTENING VIGNETTE: "NOT FADE AWAY"

Buddy Holly's "Not Fade Away" delivers a powerful African American sound—in this case a rhythm with very old roots—to young white listeners. Most immediately, Holly's song relies on the rhythm of what has become known as the Bo Diddley beat, based on Diddley's eponymous song from 1955. The Bo Diddley beat combined an old pattern (see below) with the rock and roll backbeat and the shaking of the maracas. Holly's experience with the beat stems from covering the song "Bo Diddley" earlier in 1956, which was only released posthumously as a single in 1963, charting in the United Kingdom. "Not Fade Away" was probably also influenced by the song "Party Doll" by Buddy Knox. The beat is part of a family of rhythmic patterns from Afro-Cuban music called "clave" that probably goes back to Africa and had been used in American jazz before Diddley became the first (apparently) to employ it in an R & B or early rock tune.[23] The particular beat of "Not Fade Away" uses an accented 3 + 2 pattern over two measures (simplified as um bop - bop : - bop bop -),[24] where the first three "bops" occur on off beats (not on the downbeat pulses [one and three] but in between those—the two, four, and the two beats, respectively). The phenomenon of emphasizing the non-regular pulses is referred to as syncopation, a major feature of all African American music and which continues in rock and roll. Note that the syncopated backbeat in rock and roll, with accents on the respective two and four pulses of the four-beat measure (instead of one and three), aligns with the Bo Diddley pattern. That is, the first three "bops" fall on the same pulses as the backbeat in an act of rhythmic concrescence. In this way, these two syncopated patterns can be viewed as part of the same rhythmic essence of rock and roll. Finally, Holly's version of the rhythmic pattern leaves spaces around the accents, which clarifies the rhythm but also gives it a stopping or hiccup-type effect.

The Stones recorded the song in January 1964 at London's Regent Sound Studio (a small, independent studio where later on Jimi Hendrix and groups such as Black Sabbath recorded) while working on tracks for their first album. At the time Oldham considered it the first song to represent the true Rolling Stones sound. They released it as a single in March, and it appeared on the American version of their first album (prophetically subtitled *England's Newest Hit Makers*) in May. Because it was a single in the United Kingdom, it was not released on the album there (common practice at the time), where a Bo Diddley song, "Mona," appears in its place. With its pounding guitar played by Jones baked in the warmth of a tremolo effect, "Mona" is much more primal than "Not Fade Away," but did not get as much play in concert as "Not Fade Away."

The song begins with Richards's solo twelve-string acoustic guitar playing the two-chord turnaround of the song, E - A - : - E E -, two times, where Richards lets the accented A chord (voiced on the fifth fret with the ringing high A note) hang in the air after a single and strongly articulated downward strum. When the song proper starts, Holly's halting rhythm is exchanged for the more fluent explication of the beat as practiced by Diddley. The Stones add maracas (played by Phil Spector) as were first used in the "Bo Diddley" song and a tambourine accent on the second part of the two-bar pattern. Clapping on the backbeats goes on throughout the song with a subtle but significant variation. On the second measure (-bop bop -), the clap is dropped on the second beat (or the first "bop"), probably because the main Bo Diddley pattern plays on that beat; clapping on the fourth beat of the measure fills out the rhythm of the bar and makes the song more fluid. Note that the use of a clap track was included on many Stones covers from this period that also appear on the first album—for example, "Route 66," "Walking the Dog," and "Carol," as are these added percussion instruments generally (see also "I Just Want to Make Love to You"). The clap tracks are significant for imparting to the songs the layered and concrescent rhythmic approach found in African American music that again can be traced back to West Africa and the Caribbean.

For the chord changes, the original "Not Fade Away" as recorded by Holly has only two chords, E and A. These are the first two chords found in a twelve-bar blues song, referred to as the tonic or home key (I) and the subdominant (IV), meaning below (sub-) the dominant (the V, the second strongest chord after the tonic). The idea of using only two chords in a song is part of the heritage of blues, R & B, and in turn soul music, where the singer will often create lyrics on the spot over a repeating pattern played by the band. The repeating pattern over the two chords (I–IV) can be referred to as a vamp. Indeed, although Holly himself does not do so, the simple lines of "Not Fade Away" can easily become vamp lyrical material, as Jagger himself starts to do at the end with the repetition of the line "well love is love and not fade away." To add some variety to a song with only two chords, the Stones cleverly throw in an extra chord, imparting more drive or forward motion to the song. The extra chord is a D, which relates to the E as its Mixolydian or bVII chord and parallels the main chord motion from E to A. Rhythmically the subdominant (A) articulates the first "bop" of the second measure of the pattern, which again occurs on the second beat. Later on, we will see that these three chords form a constellation, as it were, in songs from "The Last Time" to "Satisfaction" to "Sympathy for the Devil."

Still, why do these seemingly small musical details matter? The answer lies in the question posed by Jagger himself—why bother listening to a cover in the first place? Namely, the changes introduced in the cover version tell us much about the musical priorities of the band. By changing and rearranging the song, the Stones are adding a new interpretive layer to it, reinserting the rockabilly hybridity of Holly's "Not Fade Away" into the black R & B and blues mainstream. Holly's lilting, almost tongue-in-cheek vocal style, pleading with the girl at times, gives way to Jagger's confident swagger and incessant bravado. The raucous Bo Diddley rhythm as reapplied to the song by the Stones complements Jagger's aggressive vocal style. Finally, Brian Jones's amplified harmonica playing provides another instance of the timbral expansion of the song and also recontextualizes the song within the urban tradition of the blues. Jones's harmonica wailings respond to each of Jagger's lines, at the same time making the compulsive rhythm even more emphatic. Finally, in a fitting tribute to Holly's original and a wink at the title, the Stones use a studio fade-out to end the song, a technique that is actually common on their studio recordings from this period.

Now, what was it like in 1964 for a young American listener, hearing the Stones' "Not Fade Away" in the year it was first released? The Beatles had already primed the American audience for what would become the British music revolution, also known as the British Invasion, having begun their conquest of America with a groundbreaking appearance on *The Ed Sullivan Show* in February. By summer the Stones had followed suit by also appearing on TV, still the quickest route to success in the crowded music business. For many young people, music harbored a safe and welcoming refuge from the traumatic events of the time, especially the John F. Kennedy assassination in November 1963. With its sunny idealism and its bolstering of the momentous civil rights movement, the Kennedy administration had the solid admiration of much of the nation's youth, and the shattering of "Camelot" is often referred to as the end of an innocent time for youth. Still, in 1964 the fashion styles of the 1950s had not yet entirely receded—for example, girls often wore their hair teased, even though pony tails and shorter hair were becoming the rage. Indeed the youth scene in 1964 was not too far removed from the milieu as depicted by the film *American Graffiti* (1973), set in director George Lucas's 1962 Modesto, California, hometown with its hot-rod cruising culture and paean to 1950s rock and doo-wop.

Yet in the fast-moving and fickle world of pop, young American teenagers would likely not be aware of nor care that a particular song was a cover. As noted by Richards, the Stones' explosive and blues-powered energy was the opposite of the American pop scene, especially the Beach Boys' polite sound (again, what Richards considered to be part of the past) as heard on mellow tracks like "Little Surfer Girl" (1963), a song that included the classic triplet subdivision of the beat and inclusion of the ubiquitous doo-wop progression (I–vi–IV–V, here D–Bm–G–A). The Beach Boys played at the *T.A.M.I. Show* that will be discussed below, a live concert event that retrospectively has become a beacon of '60s pop music, as did singer Lesley Gore, whose finale was her 1963 number-one hit, "It's My Party," again in a pop arrangement very much at odds with what the Stones were up to on their first albums.[25] As we shall see, the Stones were not averse to participating in the softer pop trends and ballads of their time, which they managed to navigate on their own terms.

Imagine yourself as a young teenager from the Los Angeles area going to hear the Stones on only their second U.S. tour and on the cusp of national fame, in the fall of 1964. Unlike your older sibling who collects single 45s of her favorite songs, you and your friends prefer when possible to buy a complete album. You consider yourself an educated listener since you have been studying classical piano since you were seven. But your musical imagination has recently grown with much of the new music coming out. Your prized albums from this new year of what everyone is started to call the British Invasion are *Meet the Beatles*, *The Beatles' Second Album*, *The Animals*, *The Dave Clark Five Return!*, *The Rolling Stones: England's Newest Hit Makers*, and your latest purchase by the Stones, *12 X 5*. You are infatuated with the infectious music of the so-called British beat groups, and especially the harder R & B of the Rolling Stones. Although you heard about it later, you missed seeing the band's appearance on *The Mike Douglas Show* back in June, but you did get to see them perform songs from their *12 X 5* album, "Around and Around" (Chuck Berry cover) and "Time Is on My Side" (Irma Thomas cover) on *The Ed Sullivan Show* on October 25.[26] On this appearance, the Stones cashed in on the growing rift of the generation gap—that young people do not want to be told what to do by the older people in charge—much to the chagrin of Ed Sullivan and your parents and grandparents who watched the Stones with dismay. You were taken aback by their emotional rendition of what seems like a gospel song to you, their ballad "Time Is on My Side." (In fact, if one song can be pointed to as leading the way to the Stones' American breakthrough, it would be this ballad.) Your experience with soul music is very limited, and your true introduction to the genre would actually be through Stones covers, even though you do not realize it at the time. (Ironically, Richards has pointed out that although the band was known for high-energy rock and roll in the United Kingdom, in the United States the Stones first became known through their slower songs and ballads.)

It is a crisp, beautiful sunny day for the Stones' Sunday matinee concert at the Long Beach Civic Auditorium on this first day of November. They had just played a couple of nights prior to an enthusiastic audience in Santa Monica as part of the *T.A.M.I. Show*, which was filmed over two nights to showcase the growing cultural phenomenon of "teenage America." Included in the *T.A.M.I.* lineup were popular rock and also R & B artists such as James Brown, the Beach Boys, Chuck Berry, Marvin Gaye, and Lesley Gore; the Stones had the honor of being the final act to perform. At that concert, Jagger studied the dance moves of Brown along with his expressive vocality, both of which had an enormous impact on Jagger's live stage act. Determined that you were going to see the next big British act after the Beatles, you have bought tickets to the Long Beach show with great anticipation; you are also very excited to see the other headliners, Ike and Tina Turner, for the first time. (Again, at this formative time for the band's stage presence, Jagger was also careful to take in Tina's dynamic dance performance, another instance of the Stones' appropriation of African American performance practice.)

Dropped off by your parents with a couple of school friends, you have no idea that you are witnessing the beginning of a revolution in popular music history. The place is packed with about 13,000 teenagers and a few watchful parents; word is spreading quickly about the Stones. The old auditorium is like a gymnasium, and folding chairs are set up on the floor. As is typical for the era, there are a few warm-up acts, some with previous hit records. You are most familiar with the music of the Southern teen idol, Jimmy Clanton, and Dick and Dee Dee, both representative of the type of pop music that was about to be swept away with the onslaught of the British Invasion.

After a couple of acts the Stones finally take the stage to wild cheers; you have a great view of the band. They open with "Not Fade Away," as they often did on this tour, paralleling its use as the first track on the U.S. release of their first album. The rhythm from the drums, guitar, and bass is pounding, and you are quickly on your feet, as are the others around you. You cannot believe how much more vibrant, deep, and gut-driven the band's live sound is over their records, accentuated by the natural reverb of the hall. Brian Jones's harmonica playing is fun to watch, and Jagger is masterful as he uses maracas to work the audience into a frenzy on only their first number. The guitar amps are small, but enough to articulate the sound and announce that we are in a guitar-centered era. You look around and girls are already sobbing at the sight of the band, a Dionysian spectacle repeated at nearly every early Stones concert. Almost everyone in the audience is your age, with a few parents serving as chaperones. The band members are all very thin and each wears a different style of clothes in contrast to the uniform suits of other bands of the era. Keith has cowboy boots on and wears a vest over a white shirt; only Charlie and Brian are sporting ties. They all have long hair, and Mick's hair is particularly messy and unkempt as he tosses his head back to the music. You are particularly struck by Mick's stare into the crowd as he seduces the audience with his eyes in a way that draws everyone into the magic of their music making.

The beat of "Not Fade Away" resonates with something deep inside you, and following the other, tamer musical acts, you grasp how different the Stones actually are. You know the Buddy Holly original from both the radio and your older sister's record collection, but the Stones' rendition has a stronger groove. Looking around again, you notice that many girls have already fainted during the first song; this would be common at Stones concerts in the early years. After about eight or so mostly up-tempo songs in the R & B/soul style—you lose count—the band takes a final bow and waves off. They mention that in a few hours they are actually due to play in Balboa Park, San Diego, about a two-hour drive away, though they are going there by chartered plane. At home that night, you think about what you just experienced and what you will tell your friends the next day at school. As you are overwhelmed, you do not really have the words to put into perspective the life-changing event you witnessed.

CHICAGO BLUES

The Stones' knife-edged approach to early rock and roll songs like "Not Fade Away" comes from their journeyman years of trying to unlock the sound of the urban, or Chicago, blues. As mentioned earlier, before the Rolling Stones formed, Brian Jones was calling himself Elmo Lewis after Elmore James, the Delta bluesman. Note that Jones is usually given credit as the first British guitarist of his era to play slide competently. His slide contributions to the Stones are multifaceted and give their early work a unique timbre for the era, especially when compared to their main rival the Beatles. The early Stones' blues interest was not unique to them, as they were part of a growing contingent of London youth who were obsessed with American blues (as we noted above). Richards himself describes in his own memoir the blues sources of the Stones and how he and Jones would analyze and break down the records of the 1950s Chicago school of blues players. Furthermore, they tended not to favor the single-line soloing guitarists like B. B. King or Albert King, but instead preferred guitarists who played in pairs. These guitar teams were the masters of what Richards calls the ancient art of "weaving." He lists among his favorite "weavers" Jimmie Rogers/Muddy Waters, the Myers brothers (Dave and Louis) who in the early 1950s backed Little Walter, Hubert Sumlin (who backed Howlin' Wolf), Matt Murphy, and guitarist Jimmy Reed's two-guitar setup with Eddie Taylor (the latter not cited by Richards); we could add the recordings of Elmore James to the list as they also feature a guitarist behind Elmore's slide playing.[27] Chuck Berry was allegedly too thrifty to hire a second guitarist and so he would overdub his own guitar on his records; Richards cites Berry's song "Memphis" as one of his best in the two-guitar weaving style.

Although the early Stones, at least in the recording studio, turned their attention to other genres and away from the Chicago blues, in the fall of 1964 they made a calculated decision to release their recording of Willie Dixon's "Little Red Rooster" as a single, a song first recorded by Howlin' Wolf (1961) and then covered by Sam Cooke (1963). Often thought to be recorded at Chess Studios, the Stones' officially released version was recorded on September 2 at Regent Sound Studios in London.[28] This session followed up a recording session the band did back in June at Chess Studios in Chicago that led to the release of the British EP, *5 X 5* (five songs as performed by the five members of the Stones), which became the basis for the American album *12 X 5* that came out in October. The most successful song from these first Chess sessions was Bobby Womack's "It's All Over Now," which became their first number-one hit in England. There was some risk of a loss of commercial momentum involved in the choice of a traditional twelve-bar blues song like "Little Red Rooster" for a single. Note that in this period, singles were more important than albums to the commercial success and popularity of a band. But as Richards has stated, with their growing fame it was time to prove to that they could do what they had originally set out to do, namely, spread the gospel of the blues. As it turns out, the structure of "It's All Over Now" already shares much common ground with the twelve-bar blues, especially the chorus on "well I used . . . / but it's all . . . ," occurring over the crucial harmonic event of a twelve-bar blues, the dominant-subdominant (V–IV) chord climax or turnaround. Furthermore, the Stones shattered the commercial orthodoxy that the blues would not sell in huge quantities. Perhaps because of both savvy marketing and their steadfast belief in what they were doing, their November release of "Little Red Rooster" was highly anticipated in England; the song quickly became their second number-one hit there. The American release of the song did not occur until the next year on their third American studio album, *The Rolling Stones, Now!*, which contained many of the same songs as the second British studio album, *The Rolling Stones No. 2*. Finally, "Little Red Rooster" is also significant in that it is widely cited as being the only time a twelve-bar blues song topped the British charts.

Recorded at Chess Studios, Howlin' Wolf's rendition of "The Red Rooster" (written by Willie Dixon, probably with Wolf's input) presents a slower song, a self-conscious return to the rough-and-tumble rural Delta after the faster, high-energy urban blues emanating from the electrified Chicago scene. Of course the title and the song's lyrics recall the earliest coded sexual euphemisms of the genre, often in bucolic farmyard settings. The song is in the key of A and features a call-and-response between Wolf's lead vocals and the stabbing sounds of his slide guitar (tuned to open A). The band's instruments are also slightly out of tune, which ratchets up the tension to the dramatic effect of the call-and-response fills to Wolf's vocal part. Although in the general form of the twelve-bar blues, Wolf does not phrase it in the standard way for the first verse as he anticipates the usual phrasing by inserting bars of 2/4 into the 4/4 time signature of the song, singing most of the first line ("I have a little red rooster") to the subdominant (IV chord) instead of the standard home chord (tonic or I), which will inform the Stones' version. In Cooke's reinterpretation, retitled as "Little Red Rooster," a jazz-style combo featuring A-list Los Angeles session players complements his smooth, soulful voice, and the subdominant phrase at the beginning is also taken out. The organ (played by a young Billy Preston, with piano by veteran Raymond Johnson) substitutes for the slide guitar, also imitating the scratching, muted strokes of the rhythm guitar; the drums (played by Hal Blaine of Wrecking Crew fame) add a polite swing with whispering brush strokes that keeps the rhythm of the song moving forward, as distinct from Wolf's.

The Stones take elements from both versions for their "Little Red Rooster" and still manage to make the song their own. The most significant change they make is to take the key down to G. However, they retain the open tuning (now though in G) for the main guitar part and keep Wolf's phrasing on the subdominant throughout the song (in this case, a C7 chord). Jagger's nonchalant vocal delivery possesses a restrained Apollonian coolness matching the band's subdued accompaniment, surprising considering that during this period they were so invested in an exuberant, rocking performance aesthetic. Instead, Jagger delves into Cooke's brand of soul singing, a style Jagger would fully explore in the next couple of years, complemented with a phrasing approach with hints of rubato (a slight slowing of the tempo followed by a speedup). In other parts of his delivery, by contrast, Jagger returns to

Wolf's characteristic stress of the first word of the second bar, bringing out the words "too *lazy*" (verse 1), "*hounds*" (verse 2), and finally "*please*" (verse 3). The most significant change he makes, however, is to announce himself as the "little red rooster," a self-conscious appropriation that neither Wolf nor Cooke attempted.

Watts, self-admittedly influenced by Blaine, adds a triplet shuffle feel (12/8) to the backing rhythm, and Wyman's bass tone approximates the standup bass on the original, played by Willie Dixon. Richards's acoustic guitar playing is subdued in the mix, while Jones's electric slide guitar (in open G) provides the instrumental counterpart to Jagger and is instrumentally the linchpin of their version. Although the song was not recorded live—Jones overdubbed his part without the others present—Jones considered this one of his finest performances.[29] One notable addition of Jones to Wolf's original is a chromatic descending lick (starting at 2:27) that accompanies Jagger's straight-ahead harp riffs in the outro, which over a G chord starts on the dominant-seventh scale degree (F) and goes by half-steps down to the fifth (D), each note underpinned by a minor third. Although he relies on stock musical devices of the blues, Jones's impromptu response to Jagger's harp lick seals the legitimacy of the band's rehashing of the Wolf original, namely, that they are now conversing in the blues language. For listeners not familiar with the genre, the confidence of the Stones' rendering shines through in an outro like this, placing them within the timeless, mythical river of the blues.

As the Stones' reputation was made around their raw approach to sound, ironically in the cases of their blues covers they actually present cleanly executed versions. When they recorded "Little Red Rooster" in September, they had had some previous practice recording the blues at Chess Studios during a marathon two-day recording session in June, which in hindsight was clearly momentous for the band's future. For example, though not their best work, they laid down disciplined takes of Wolf's "Down in the Bottom" (Willie Dixon), Muddy Waters's "I Can't Be Satisfied" and "Look What You've Done" (a B-side); of these three, the latter two were released at the time. But the band was doing more than preparing tracks for records; they were learning their craft in the recording studio. Listening to much of what they recorded in 1964–1965, we hear a band that was quickly absorbing all that their new environment had to offer, and one that was metamorphosing from another British beat band into an international rock phenomenon. As noted in the introduction, nowhere is this better exemplified than on the song "(I Can't Get No) Satisfaction," which they began recording at Chess in spring of 1965 and which will be discussed in the next chapter.

Further, as these tracks and many others recorded in the States from these whirlwind years show, the technical impact of American recording and sound production techniques cannot be understated in the Stones' meteoric rise to stardom in 1964. The band was clearly trying to advance the boundaries of what could be achieved in the studio by the fall, and they were inspired by what they heard back. After the *T.A.M.I.* and *Ed Sullivan* shows in October, the group checked into Chess Studios in Chicago for the second time in November in the midst of the second leg of their U.S. tour; they would return one more time to Chess in May 1965. The Chess tracks were used on a number of albums released during 1964–1965, from *12 X 5* to *The Rolling Stones No. 2*. The Stones were amazed that here they were able to achieve the legendary urban-blues sound they had wanted so easily, and recording using four tracks instead of two as they were doing in London allowed them to shape better arrangements. Besides, the American sound engineers knew how to get the funky, in-your-face sound sought after by the Stones as they heard it on the original blues records. Band members have given credit for their success to Chess legend and sound engineer Ron Malo, who had already recorded many of the artists—from Muddy Waters to Chuck Berry—they were trying to emulate. Wyman further specifies that the American studios had the ability to record at a much louder volume than they did at that time in England; pushing the amplifiers to high volumes results in a fuller, punchier, and more brilliant sound.

SOUTHERN SOUL MUSIC

According to writer Peter Guralnick, soul music is the introduction of the "gospel strain into the secular strain of rhythm and blues."[30] He also distinguishes soul from rock, where soul music is built on "knowledgeable anticipation" and moments of quiet, and rock is more direct in its "let it all hang out" approach. Soul music builds up to the conclusion via moments of stillness, an emotional release or climax that everyone knows is coming, though we are unsure of when and where it will happen. The soul singer (as the gospel singer before) tests the audience, relying on the dramatic tension and release of their art to "tease" the audience until they literally erupt. Finally, much soul music developed outside of the major studio system in the Deep South. It was an exciting, though dangerous, time for African Americans as they fought for freedom from the strictures of Jim Crow segregation. As such the music recorded was based on earlier Southern forms, from the field holler and prison songs to spirituals and gospel, and yet the experience was also to a large extent self-invented, done with a regional pride that was lacking in much nationalized popular music by the 1960s. The Southern soul triangle—Memphis (Tennessee), Muscle Shoals (Alabama), and Macon (Georgia)—would later have a big influence on the Rolling Stones in late 1969 at a crucial juncture in their career and help burnish their image as outsiders to the mainstream.

If the essential 1960s soul singers are well represented in popular music history—artists such as Otis Redding, Wilson Pickett, and Aretha Franklin—the instrumentalists backing them are hardly known. Surprisingly, many of them were white—half of Booker T. and the MGs and the main studio bands from the Muscle Shoals recording scene. The role of the soul band goes beyond providing a solid accompaniment foundation, as in accentuating different aspects of the rhythm, and subtly responding to the rising-and-falling lines of the vocalist. And like the vocal style, soul guitar playing grew directly out of the gospel bands. When accompanying ballads, individual notes of the chord are plucked and are allowed to ring. Following the 1950s doo-wop progressions with its inclusion of a minor chord, many of the progressions use minor chords. Also, vamping on two chords, a typical gospel practice, is quite common. Probably following pianists, guitarists add in suspended and extra notes to the chords, especially the sixth, thereby creating a richer harmonic tapestry for the vocalist. Often, riffs are combined with chords, giving the sense that there is more than one guitarist playing at the same time.

As an example that utilizes many of these guitaristic features, let us take "Mercy, Mercy," a soul song the Stones covered during their second Chess session in November and definitively recorded at the third Chess session in May 1965 for their album *Out of Our Heads* (1965). The song is a forgotten classic that is deserving of more recognition today. The Stones themselves brought "Mercy, Mercy" back for their July 5, 1969, Hyde Park concert and have not played it live since. Richards has said that when they arrived in America that year, they would go into record stores buying up the latest soul records. Perhaps one of the songs they found was the single "Mercy Mercy" (originally it did not have a comma in the title) performed by Don Covay and the Goodtimers. Note that later on Covay was a member of the so-called Soul Clan.[31] Guralnick writes that the song initiated a style of guitar-dominated soul; this style had a formative musical impact on the Stones and especially Jagger. As it turns out, the uncredited guitarist on the record is in all likelihood Jimi Hendrix. Wilson Pickett also recorded the song, releasing it with another brilliant guitar part (evidently played by Chips Moman) on his groundbreaking soul album *The Exciting Wilson Pickett* (1966).

The Covay version begins with Hendrix's guitar flourish. Hendrix deftly combines chords with a melodic line in a style that later will come to full development in his classic "Little Wing." The chord progression and pentatonic-based riffs come from the blues, yet the frequent and minor-chord changes place the song also in the shadow of doo-wop and R & B. The tone of the jangly guitar sparkles as its fills and chord accompaniment drives the song's syncopation. With the outsize significance of Hendrix's guitar for late 1960s British rock, it is fascinating to ponder that the Stones—unbeknownst to them—are probably the first on this scene to make a direct connection with him, albeit one they were unaware of. And because it is in a style that approximates the improvised vamps of the so-called "chitlin' circuit" of the early 1960s, the part is difficult to replicate—guitarists working in black vernacular styles have always been vexed by the question, how much of the "improvised" aspect of the part should remain? And this is born out in the recorded legacy of the song. The first and unreleased version recorded by the Stones (November 1964) is played workmanlike and appears to be sped up on the bootleg release, *2120 Michigan Avenue: The Unreleased 1964 Blues Album*.

By the second version (May 1965) Richards had absorbed the guitar part, and he gives an original, strident, and more improvisatory interpretation of the Hendrix part, and one with more rhythmic confidence than his first take on the song. In general, with a slightly overdriven (distorted) timbre and daring verve, Richards takes the song in the direction of rock. Yet this rock version of Hendrix's laid-back introduction has upward melodic extensions (on scale degree nine) played quickly and on the beat, and the resulting harmony marks the intro as a hybrid between R & B and jazz. Richards dramatizes these extensions and connects them melodically as upbeat anticipations, setting a more urgent mood for the song. But probably the most pronounced difference is in the opening riff over the A chord. Hendrix varies the bass under the A chord, from A to E (the E is very subtly played, however), and also emphasizes the tonic A as the landing place for his pentatonic riff; by contrast, Richards takes out the low E and leaves it to Wyman's bass, while his part focuses on the dominant-seventh note of the A7 chord, G, as the climax note. With this change, Richards propels the song from the polite to the ecstatic. The chord changes are mostly the same, except that for one of the changes Richards takes out a minor chord, which again has the result of a more streamlined, direct drive in the perception of the song.

Many of the songs the Stones covered on their early albums begin with a guitar flourish like "Mercy, Mercy." For example, on *Out of Our Heads*, there is "Talkin' 'Bout You," "Oh Baby (We Got a Good Thing Going)," and "One More Try" (an original song, with harmonica). But the importance of these stylized guitar intros is that they could be transformed into the riffs that become the hooks of the songs with something so catchy that it catapults the song to the top of the charts. Perhaps the two greatest instances of that stylistic impulse as conceived by the early Stones are their originals, "The Last Time" with its opening riff serving as the song's ostinato (a repeating part that serves as the musical glue) as played by Jones, and of course "Satisfaction," with its more menacing riff played by Richards.

THE SONGS OF CHUCK BERRY

Given the large quantity of blues and R & B sources behind the early Stones, Chuck Berry stands in a category of his own as the band forged its musical identity. In fact the guitar intros in 1960s soul music bear much in common with Berry's from the 1950s, especially their pentatonic focus, themselves rooted in an earlier generation of songs by Louis Jordan, T-Bone Walker, and Muddy Waters among others.[32] Perhaps the most famous of these intros is his "Johnny B. Goode" (1957), played by the Stones in 1962–1963, though there are no studio versions that are as yet released. The Stones instead chose some of the less well-known songs written by Berry to play and record, as for example (in chronological order of their recording, with their Berry release dates): "Come On" (1961, also their first single), "Bye Bye Johnny" (1960), "Carol" (1958), "Around and Around" (1958), "You Can't Catch Me" (1956, with lyrics that informed "Come Together" by the Beatles), and "I'm Talking About You" (1961, the Stones retitle it as "Talkin' 'Bout You"). Later on, another (by then) semi-obscure song, "Little Queenie" (1958; also part of the Beatles' early club repertoire), became their go-to Chuck Berry song in concert starting in 1969. And in 1971, on the verge of their becoming tax exiles from England, they included a live version of "Let It Rock" (1960) as part of the B-side (with "Bitch") of their UK single release of "Brown Sugar."

All of these songs feature stellar, though predictable, guitar styling by Berry, and as Richards has readily acknowledged, his channeling of Berry became the foundation for the development of his own guitar style. With its double-stop guitar intro in stop-time as an obvious cousin to "Johnny B. Goode," "Carol" stands as one of the most successful cover adaptations for the Stones as featured on early TV appearances and released as a single in June 1964. Berry's version is in the key of C, and the Stones transpose it down to the key of B-flat, probably to take into account Jagger's vocal range. With its clap-track overdub emphasizing every beat, the Stones speed up the Berry original, as was usually the case in white cover versions of African American songs (178 BPM versus Berry's 158 BPM). By the time of their live performance of it in 1969 at Madison Square Garden, released on their live album *'Get Yer Ya-Ya's Out!'*, the song was in the more standard rock key of A, and the Stones had slowed it back down to 138 BPM, which gives the song more gravitas. Further, with its driving blues-shuffle rhythm part, it presents a great idiomatic guitar song for Richards to let loose on, especially its call-and-response with the vocal part and the stop-time solo with the characteristic double-stops that interrupt the song throughout. Finally, by 1969 and as a more experienced player, Richards's expressive range had widened considerably, and his rhythmic style assumes a freer improvisatory flavor than the earlier take.

Taking one more Berry cover, "Talkin' 'Bout You" (as titled by the Stones, though not to be confused with the song by Ray Charles) also departs from the original key, from C to A. On Berry's original, the hetero-rhythmic accompaniment animates the song, with its emphasis on the first beat followed by an eighth-note patter in the rhythm guitar and active bass that plays over the stop-time at the end of the verse. Although a backbeat can be detected, other rhythmic features offset it. Berry's guitar has its characteristic trebly, bright, and cutting tone that further clarifies while displacing the pulse. When he sings, "I'm talking about you," his guitar falls into the familiar shuffle pattern. Echoing the rhythmic caginess is the evasive vulnerability in Berry's delivery of the song, which is not overcome until the third verse, where we learn he is engaged to the song's idealized woman. Summarizing, the overall rhythm on the Berry version is complex and typical of the fabric of the golden era of African American R & B of the 1950s and 1960s, where often, and like the Bo Diddley beat, the effect of the inimitable rhythm seems impossible to quantify.

By contrast, the Stones slow the song down considerably and play it in a straightforward way with much more accented weight. Richards starts off the Stones' version with a transposed copy of the Berry guitar solo intro, deliberately executed and at once more menacing than Berry's. This fits in well with the band's straightforward approach to the song, where Jagger's voice bristles with confidence at what seems the inevitability of his winning of the girl. The band smooths out the rhythm to a more predictable, regular pattern, stripping it back down to its backbeat origins. Richards obliges by emphasizing the second and fourth beats and eschewing the shuffle pattern. Thus, unlike "Carol" or "Around and Around," or even later on in "Little Queenie" or "Let It Rock," the Stones in this case rewrite many of the touches of the Berry original.

CONCLUSION

The Rolling Stones stood at the vanguard of the British discovery of American blues and R & B and were able to meld a conscious musical appropriation with the burgeoning cultural stance of youthful rebellion that resisted authority and traditional values. Ironically, their fans and the media judged their covering of older and contemporary music—usually a conservative stance—as a radical innovation, probably because of the recent African American origins of the music. Marketed as the dangerous alternative to the Beatles, the early Stones burst swiftly onto the international scene with an uncanny ability to capture the increasingly oppositional social stance of young people. Their timing could not have been more perfect, especially as the Beatles paved the way for other British bands to enter the mainstream, but it was also the larger societal paradigm shift to more rebellious youth-oriented culture that mirrored the band's take-no-prisoners approach to R & B and the blues.

In the fabric of this conversation with African American music, the Stones also began to create their own music, some of it also mired in controversy. Even if they did not write blues per se, operating in the shadow of the blues their work was often criticized as crossing sexual boundaries or misogynist. This only added more fuel to the charges that they were corrupting the youth. And yet their aloofness from criticism became part of the band's mystique. Again, their timing coincided with a paradigm shift in the music industry, as songs by the Beatles and Dylan around 1964–1965 were becoming increasingly viewed as artistically innovative, precisely when the Jagger/Richards team started to develop as songwriters. Finally, as we shall soon see, as drugs begin to exert a powerful influence on '60s music, it seemed that with every album the Stones were reinventing their music, as were other bands we might add. Indeed in this era, the idea of the album as an artwork began to take on broad generational significance, uniting young people in a shared worldview, in similar ways that the Internet or social media sites do today. In the next chapter we will turn to the songwriting and album reorientation of the band's mid-1960s efforts.

2

TOWARD AN ORIGINAL DIRECTION

Aftermath to *Their Satanic Majesties Request*

Andrew Loog Oldham realized that the future of the Rolling Stones lay in songwriting. In this respect, he was perhaps the first to figure out that the Stones needed to start writing their own songs or risk not having enough material to sustain a career and their popularity. And the royalties from songwriting were lucrative. By 1964 the Stones already came across as seasoned performers, and their musical timing and ability to swing were improving rapidly. In the studio, their confidence was growing. But they still lacked a songwriting direction, a skill at which their main rivals, the Beatles, excelled. Their first efforts at songwriting were as a collective under the name "Nanker Phelge." There are a handful of songs still credited to this moniker, including "Little by Little" (along with Phil Spector) from the first album. Nanker Phelge gets its biggest credit though for "Play with Fire," the B-side to the early 1965 single "The Last Time." But with keen business acumen, Oldham surmised that as a duo, Jagger/Richards had the potential to develop and be marketed along the lines of Lennon/McCartney. The Stones had witnessed the creativity of the Beatles songwriters as they finished crafting "I Wanna Be Your Man" before their eyes in the studio, in what was a gift to the Stones that became their second single. Thus by calling for a songwriting duo in the mold of their rivals, Oldham seems responsible for the quick demise of the Nanker Phelge compositional entity.

It is astonishing in hindsight that within a very short time span Jagger/Richards would be writing most of the Stones' material. Seemingly overnight their songwriting transformed the Stones from an R & B cover band to an original rock and roll band. The albums exhibit this process most dramatically. The first albums simply gather what the band had already worked out and was playing live, mostly covers. By contrast, the songs for *Aftermath* came to life mostly in the recording studio. They underscored the significance of *Aftermath*'s creative break in another symbolic way sure to catch their fans' attention—that is, by only including songs composed by Jagger/Richards. Note that from this album onward the two had solidified their lockstep leadership of the band. In this way, the Jagger/Richards team marginalized Jones, whom they (Jagger, Oldham, and to a slightly lesser extent Richards) deemed unreliable as the band pursued the path of original music (albeit still sprinkled with carefully chosen covers).

While the birth of the Jagger/Richards partnership heralds the rise of the Rolling Stones as hit makers and beacons of popular culture, it also marks the beginning of the demise of Brian Jones's role and purpose within the band. In the days of Nanker Phelge, Jones often drove the sound of the band—his biographer, Paul Trynka, goes so far as to argue that Jones was the "architect" of the band's aggressive, trebly, distorted sound that served as a model for the countless groups of the American garage band movement.[1] For example, he writes that Jones dominated the sound and mix of "I Wanna Be Your Man," recorded in Oldham's absence. With Oldham's encouragement, and by the time of "As Tears Go By," a Jagger/Richards song penned for Marianne Faithfull, Jones's leadership would be sharply eclipsed.[2] In this competitive professional environment lacking emotional support, and perhaps with some disdain for writing pop songs, unfortunately Jones would never blossom as a songwriter. Richards maintains, against this view, that Jones simply could not write songs and that Oldham matched him and Jagger together only because the two were hanging out at the time.[3] Yet given the existence of some early Jones originals, and the fact that later on he did compose an original soundtrack, the idea that Jones could not write appears to be an unfounded myth.[4] Finally, Jones should have received credit for his work with Richards on "Ruby Tuesday," one of the central classics of the Stones' oeuvre.[5]

But there was one original song preceding and leading the way to *Aftermath* that propelled the band to superstardom. This was their monster hit "(I Can't Get No) Satisfaction," a song still synonymous with the band. Perhaps the most unfathomable story concerning the Stones' music surrounds the song's genesis. Sleeping alone one night in his apartment in St. John's Wood, London, Richards dreamed the song's main riff, waking up just long enough to play it into a tape recorder. After showing it to Jagger along with the line "I can't get no satisfaction," Jagger wrote lyrics to the song in Clearwater, Florida, which the band then recorded a few days later at Chess in Chicago. They rerecorded it at RCA Studios in Los Angeles for the released single version. Both songwriters felt the song unready for release, but were outvoted by the other band members and associates.

"Satisfaction" marks a watershed for the Stones in many ways. Indeed, if one song stands for the Rolling Stones, it is this seminal 1965 number-one hit. Most importantly, it thrust the band into stardom on their own terms, as the song's sound and lyrics come off as gritty, abrasive, and authentic in the best tradition of the blues. The song's meteoric rise caught Jagger and Richards by surprise as they were not so confident as songwriters. But follow-up hits written later that year, "Get Off of My Cloud" and "19th Nervous Breakdown," show how what we can call a "Satisfaction" aesthetic—a simmering, cool, reflective self-consciousness where rebellion, humor, and sarcasm alternate with one another to a hard blues soundtrack overflowing with desire—permeates their work going forward.

Indeed their first songwriting attempts do not quite hint at the raw power unleashed by "Satisfaction." Initially and surprisingly, given the band's live performance choices, Jagger/Richards wrote soft ballads such as "As Tears Go By," or plaintively soulful ones like "Heart of Stone," or alternatively, the band worked up R & B–style songs that were heavily derivative of other songs, as for example "Little by Little" mentioned earlier (based on Jimmy Reed's "Shame, Shame, Shame"). Perhaps intimidated at the idea of writing up-tempo blues in the style of their heroes, there was one song that does point in the direction of "Satisfaction" and the band's edgy, mature rock sound—their 1964 hit "The Last Time." Like "Satisfaction," "Last Time" coalesces around a short, ringing guitar riff, although in this instance with Jones playing it. Richards has admitted that the song, though, is not too original, essentially being a reworking of the gospel number as sung by the Staples Singers.[6] But the song's overall sound, with its trenchant groove and vocal energy reminiscent of earlier rock, gave the band a platform on which to build.

The power of "Satisfaction" derives from the interplay between originality and tradition, especially in blues and soul music of the mid-1960s, recalling Southern soul and especially the Stax sound, while again taking a cue from a Motown song for its riff. Because of this, it is easy to see how a disinformation campaign developed in the media a couple of years later, saying that Otis Redding had written the song and then sold it to the Stones at their insistence for ten thousand dollars. Note that Richards considered the song's recording a temporary placeholder because he envisioned the guitar part as stand-in for the horns, which would play in a similar fashion to a Stax head arrangement.

Yet in terms of mainstream popular music, the gritty sound of "Satisfaction," with its freewheeling guitar oscillating between clean and fuzz tones, transcends what was produced in its time. If its originality derives mainly from the timbral effect of the fuzz guitar riff, at the same time the riff happens to be one of the most recognizable ones in rock history. Indeed, in this regard it is the lead guitar's riff and chattering accompanimental dialogue with other musical elements that point to the song's success. The raging, tempestuous, and defiant stance of Richards's guitar complements Jagger's vocal that is simultaneously restless, searching, and poignant. Furthermore, we can contrast the guitar's rhythmic and melodic fluidity—almost improvisatory in its effect—with the driving, straight-ahead quarter-note hits on the snare, embodying a beat (as noted in the introduction) that Watts has said was popular at the time via songs by Roy Orbison among others. Finally, again showing the wide-ranging emotional content of the song, Jagger's breathy vocal timbre oozes with desire while modulating into an angry rant for the verse.

Following what has now become a cliché when talking about the Stones' impact on the popular imagination, "Satisfaction" captured the historical moment. Music, and especially rock, increasingly was expected to articulate the aspirations of young people. Lyrics responded to the restless zeitgeist, and fans expected unique and colorful new sounds to go beyond the generic templates of mass music. As we sketched out in the introduction, 1965 perhaps demarcates the beginning of a radical shift in the notion of a song's purpose in mass culture—

from mere entertainment to life-changing event, from craftwork to artwork. Besides "Satisfaction," examples of songs in this vibrant new category from this year are Dylan's "Like a Rolling Stone," the Beatles' "Norwegian Wood," the Byrds' cover of Dylan's "Mr. Tambourine Man," and the Animals' "We Gotta Get Out of This Place."[7] Songs like these, combined with the effects of drugs (especially LSD) now had the power to affect the generational trajectory, which they did in the latter half of the 1960s as embodied by the counterculture.

Lyrically, "Satisfaction" pushes all of the right buttons that would burnish the Stones' status as countercultural heroes, propelling the band out from the coattails of the Beatles to major international stars with their own stylistic voice. The song accomplishes the feat of grafting the outsider worldview of African American blues onto the rising youth rebellion against the institutionalized status quo. And again its oppositional force met and helped form the generational urgency that was growing stronger in 1965.

The previous year (1964) the Stones had recorded Muddy Waters's "I Can't Be Satisfied," which would seem the natural impetus for the song on some level. In fact, "Satisfaction's" conceptual source (according to Richards) was instead a line from Berry's "Thirty Days"—"I don't get no satisfaction." In Berry's song, the singer is simply trying to get the girl to come back home. By contrast, Jagger takes the concept of "satisfaction" to another level. Here the subject matter is quite specific to become a complaint about contemporary society, as in the alienation experienced from rampant consumer capitalism, along with the sexual frustration of travelling rock stars trying to make it with girls who are unavailable (i.e., having their periods, a point that was missed by the censors). Too, and like so many blues songs, the song's main plea of not finding satisfaction, or the insatiability of desire, can be universalized to address anything or everything, at both the individual and the societal level. It was this equivocal feature, its specificity and vagueness, that allowed the song to assume the role of a generational rallying cry, separating it from the complacency of the status quo while thrusting the Stones into their new role as leading musical representatives for the burgeoning segment of disaffected youth.

To maintain their hard-won popularity and to solidify their reputation amid growing competition on the popular music front, the mid-1960s Stones kept up the torrid pace of recording and touring also marking the early years, but now with a purposeful emphasis on writing and recording their own songs. As was common practice for bands during this heady and frenetic period, while touring they were writing the songs for the next album. The "on-the-road" mentality directly informs the band's lyrical content, yet as we have seen with "Satisfaction," the trick was to leave the content open and ambivalent enough that it could address a wide range of life experience.

As their early covers unleashed boundless sexual desire in their female audience, their originals carried that a step further. Indeed their songs followed the legacy of the blues, where a sexualized subject matter could also stand for something else, as in the social empowerment of the individual. Writing of the blues persona, sociologist Grace Elizabeth Hale maintains:

> The emphasis on personal performance in the blues in turn made sex the perfect subject and metaphor for its personas. Sex was a way of asserting the self in the world, of stealing some pleasure out of the grind of work and poverty. Sex too was about performance.[8]

In the Stones' original songs, the blues performative melded with a hyper-sexualized fantasy in ways that again drove young teenagers (especially girls) mad. For feminists of the era, the Stones and their music were seen as another instance of the subjugation and mistreatment of women. And yet a more nuanced view from today's perspective could interpret their music in the opposite way. Like the blues, it can be seen to empower women to embrace their passion and seek pleasure beyond their narrowly defined societal roles (more on this topic below).

With the changing dynamic and direction of the band that accompanied the marginalization of Jones and his original vision of the band, the Stones went from being curators of blues and R & B to a pop band on par (almost) with the Beatles. Still, as Jagger/Richards now assumed an unshakeable lock on the band's lucrative songwriting machine, Jones did not simply fade away. He remained extremely popular with fans. Further, Jones became a leading arbiter of fashion in the heyday of the mod-infused trends of Swinging London. And musically his imagination continued to expand as he developed into a master colorist with a wide array of instruments at his command. In his expanded musical role beyond the confines of standard guitar playing, prefigured in his slide work on songs such as "Little Red Rooster," Jones's addition of timbral warmth and colorful ambience cannot be underestimated and was especially needed to help the Stones keep up with the advancing studio techniques of their main rivals, the Beatles. Indeed, the identity of many of the era's songs is linked inextricably to Jones's parts. Some of the most recognizable of Jones's song contributions are contained on *Aftermath*, most brilliantly the sitar in "Paint It Black," twelve-string acoustic or sitar (with Richards also on twelve-string acoustic) on "Mother's Little Helper," dulcimer on "Lady Jane," and the marimba on "Under My Thumb."[9]

Aftermath was the crucial step for the Stones' conquering of the pop world and their much-needed answer to the Beatles' *Rubber Soul*. On the album Jagger and Richards apply their musical songwriting knowledge gleaned from years of song study and playing covers. The album's songs come off as more original than they probably are because of the hybrid musical style forged from the band's myriad sources— early rock and roll, the blues, R & B, soul, pop balladry, and folk rock. In fact *Aftermath* culminates the stylistic work the band had been developing since 1964. The recording circumstances were also favorable to the making of the album, both in the use of a familiar space and strong supporting cast of people with whom they already had made records. Recorded entirely at RCA Studios in Los Angeles at sessions in December 1965 and March 1966, the band's sound engineer was Dave Hassinger, who had recorded previous number-one hits for them such as "The Last Time" and "Satisfaction." Jack Nitzsche, an arranger and assistant to Phil Spector who had also previously played piano on Stones records, was also there to provide input and supply keyboard parts. In *Life*, Richards pays tribute to Nitzsche and his importance for the early Stones and tries to dispel some of the inflated and legendary status granted to Spector:

> Jack was the genius, not Phil. Phil took on Jack's eccentric persona and sucked his insides out. But Jack Nitzsche was an almost silent—and unpaid for reasons still not clear except he did it for fun—arranger, musician, gluer-together of the talent, a man of enormous importance for us in that period. He came to our sessions to relax and would throw in some ideas.[10]

But like the other unsung heroes of the 1960s Los Angeles studio scene with Spector/Nitzsche associations, notably the musicians of the Wrecking Crew, it can be difficult to gauge the exact significance of uncredited musicians' contributions to an artist or song.

As with all of the early albums, there exist two versions of *Aftermath*, the UK and U.S. ones, released a few months apart in April and June of 1966 respectively. And like the earlier albums, this release history adds confusion to the album's identity, as the American tracks depart from the UK tracks. The UK version came out only a month after the final session work. It is the more definitive of the two in that it represents what the Stones intended for the album. The U.S. version leaves off four of the tracks, including the leadoff "Mother's Little Helper," but compensates for this by adding the number-one hit at the time, "Paint It Black."

SECOND-WAVE FEMINISM AND "MOTHER'S LITTLE HELPER"

As discussed above, the Stones have often been cited as having an antifeminist or even misogynist streak running through their songs, and nowhere is that perhaps more in evidence than on *Aftermath*, with songs like "Stupid Girl" and "Under My Thumb." However, song lyrics in the blues and R & B tradition that the Stones came from can also be read in more than one way, and sometimes ironically. For example, it can be difficult to know the intent of a song—is it a caricature, as Jagger has said about "Under My Thumb"? He has claimed that the song was actually his response to overly pushy women and some failed relationships. Either way, these types of songs fed into the "anti-woman" stance of the band and fueled the media hype encompassing them and the perceived sexualized nature of their performance and music.

The timing of these songs coincides with the rise of modern or second-wave feminism. Betty Friedan's *The Feminine Mystique* (1963) shows how during the 1950s the feminine mystique of women as homemakers and mothers became the cultural ideal through TV, advertisement, and marketing efforts, coincidentally controlled by men. She argues that women need more than domesticity, children, and their husbands to define who they are, and they should seek a greater purpose in career or work to bring out their own sense of self—or as Friedan says, to become complete. She first sensed that there was a "problem" with the feminine mystique as a suburban housewife herself. Friedan writes:

> Just what was this problem that has no name? What were the words women used when they tried to express it? Sometimes a woman would say "I feel empty somehow . . . incomplete." Or she would say, "I feel as if I don't exist." Sometimes she blotted out the feeling with a tranquilizer.[11]

Friedan points out that around 1960 the media started to report on the "trapped housewife" phenomenon. Ironically, the problem was diagnosed as the product of too much education. In high schools and college settings, women were plunged into the world of ideas, which did not prepare them for the life of a housewife. The solution was for education institutions to offer home economics courses designed to prepare young women for the domestic life of running a household.

At about the same time as the feminine mystique of the 1950s housewife was coming under attack, "the Pill" came along. This opened up a whole new wave of feminist thinking—note that one of Gloria Steinem's first published articles for *Esquire* was on the Pill. In the early 1960s the FDA's approval of the birth-control pill helped to usher in the sexual revolution that rock came to celebrate and embody.

Against this conceptual backdrop of the trapped housewife and with the promise of sexual liberation of women offered by the Pill, the Stones' often misunderstood "Mother's Little Helper" offers a brilliant social commentary on the plight of millions of housewives in the advanced industrial societies of Europe and the United States. Indeed it is as though Jagger read Friedan, as he channeled her basic ideas. In his lyrics, mother needs a helper, the drug Valium, to "calm her down" through her "busy, dying day." Her anxiety and depression comes from the household demands made on her by her kids and her husband. Pop songs are rarely this realistic and specific about the category of the everyday; for example, instead of preparing fresh food to cook, she "buys an instant cake," and then "burns her frozen steak." Because men are "so hard to satisfy"—notice the use of the trope of desire again—she goes to her doctor for her prescription of tranquilizers, which will "shelter" her through the night. At the end, the narrator admonishes her to be careful, that she could easily overdose.

Intertwined with the subject of the depressed mother is the theme of aging: "What a drag it is getting old." This ties in with the era's generational tension of youthful rebellion. Instead of the old attacking the follies of the young, we now have the reverse. Here "old" no longer entails life experience or wisdom. And in a clever twist, the older generation needs a supplement, in this case, drugs, to ameliorate the damaging effects of the stasis of adulthood. Finally, without this witty line, it is hard to imagine one of the main British anthems of the counterculture, the Who's "My Generation," with its much harsher critique of the older generation—"I hope I die before I get old."

RAGA ROCK: "MOTHER'S LITTLE HELPER" AND "PAINT IT BLACK"

In the mid-1960s, as popular musicians were starting to view themselves as creators beyond their traditional role as musician-entertainer, so they asserted a greater independence in the studio, especially in their search for new sounds. As we have already seen, the use of a slide guitar differentiated the Stones from other pop groups like the Beatles. As the 1960s wore on, English bands turned to a myriad of sources for timbral effect and color, sonically mirroring the colorful mod clothing styles of Carnaby Street, the vibrant heart of Swinging London. With so many sonic choices available and rock still in its infancy, there was much to explore. Traditional orchestral instruments created a classical veneer, electronic effects imparted an avant-garde flavor, and non-Western, world-music sources granted a given song a sophisticated, cosmopolitan sheen and impression.

One of the great exotic eruptions in modern pop history is the so-called Raga Rock of the 1960s, closely tied to the British Invasion. As the name implies, Raga Rock combines a rock backbeat with an Indian-music aesthetic. The musical term "raga" denotes not only the scale, but also the way the notes combine in the scale and certain characteristics of the melody that impart a mood or atmosphere. Further, one of its musical features is the backdrop of a drone; that is, a single, held pitch often used in the East for meditative purposes but which also forms the tonal basis for elaborate improvisation. The static drone evokes a moment of stable, focused energy. It is perhaps the drone's ancient and powerful simplicity that awakened a primal response in the West, as musicians incorporated it into not only rock but also jazz improvisation.

But what early listeners probably noticed first about the Raga Rock songs was the exotic timbre—the buzzy, jangly sound of the sitar (possibly) or a guitar stand-in for it. In these songs the sitar will often play a simple and short riff in a tight range and one that repeats throughout the song. The first song to employ the sitar was the Beatles' "Norwegian Wood" (October 1965 release), incidentally a song with a folklike chord progression that does not use the drone principle. Also, in "Norwegian Wood" the sitar does not play an independent riff, as most of the songs of the Raga Rock genre do, but instead plays a sequential melody that is also the sung melody of the song. Thus in this first instance the sitar functions more timbrally as an echoing reinforcement of the melody.

But Raga Rock also thrives on sounds that approximate the sitar. For instance, a jangly twelve-string guitar or distorted, fuzz-toned guitar could also substitute for the sitar, and here there are some precedents to the Beatles—notably, the Yardbirds' "Heart Full of Soul" (June 1965) and the Kinks' "See My Friends" (July 1965).[12] In these songs, the guitar part plays an independent riff as a refrain that repeats throughout the song, or what is effectively an ostinato. Note that "Heart Full of Soul" was supposed to use the sitar, but guitarist Jeff Beck substituted a guitar part for it to thicken the sound. "See My Friends" also has a ringing guitar playing the simple main riff and melody of the song, with droning open strings. The song's simple main riff is mi–fa–sol–fa using solfège syllables.[13] The Kinks' song is also more Indian in style and substance than "Heart Full of Soul" with its reliance on the drone principle and Ray Davies's subtle vocal delivery in a whining "Orientalist" style with volume swells and slight glissandos.

Following in the path of the respective Yardbirds and Kinks songs, "Mother's Little Helper" (recorded in December 1965) also uses a guitar stand-in for the sitar. The Stones keep the guitar riff within a narrow range of a third, as do the Kinks, but start a step lower against the tonic—this time as re–mi–fa. The Stones also use a question–answer format for the phrasing of the riff, ascending re–mi–fa (question), and then following with an answer, mi–re–mi. Note that the "mi" resolves into the tonic chord. The Kinks phrase the riff part on the downbeats of the measure, while the Stones emphasize the weaker beats of the measure, granting the song a more syncopated feel.

In addition, the other glaringly noticeable feature of "Mother's Little Helper" is that it is in a minor key. Although Rolling Stones songs can use minor chords as part of the progression for a coloristic effect, it is not often that the band has a song in a minor key. Putting this into a larger perspective, minor keys are not that common in rock music. Here, though, the minor is used evocatively and atmospherically, setting up an emotional undercurrent of melancholy. Furthermore, the tonic E-minor chord strummed at the beginning and through half of the verse functions as the drone does in Indian music, creating a primal, mantra-like energy not usually found in pop music. Famously, minor-key songs particularly turned off one musical contributor of the Stones. Namely, the Stones' regular keyboardist (though not an official band member), Ian Stewart, was outspoken in his refusal to play in minor keys, perhaps somewhat influencing the band, as there are very few Rolling Stones songs in a minor key. Note that we will be tracking the use of the minor in the Stones' work throughout this book.

With a typical collection of chords commensurate with '60s pop guitar and the Stones' own style, still, there are some subtle touches to the progression that add to the exoticness of "Mother's Little Helper." For instance, when the verse cadences back to E minor, it eschews the dominant chord, substituting for it the bVII7 chord, here D7. The easiest place to hear the D7 chord going to E minor is in the chorus on the word "drag." Again, this bestows on the song a modal flourish, a feature of world music and a component of Indian raga. In fact, analysis reveals the song to be a mixture of two modes.[14] Finally, animating this progression is one of Wyman's best bass lines. Indeed, on "Mother's Little Helper" he picks up the pace where his stinging glissandos for "King Bee" left off, and his upfront performance further contributes to the song's exotic ambience.

As *Aftermath* is the first Stones album without covers, it is also their first that does not rely on songs that were concert tested. And its timing coincides with the rise of the album as the vehicle for serious pop art. Richards states that it was the Beatles and the Stones who made the album "*the* vehicle for recording and hastened the demise of the single."[15] He continues that at that point the album became a "statement," without being a collection of singles with filler material.

Along these lines, the side-one ending "Goin' Home" at over eleven minutes long exemplifies this. In a shortened form, it might have made a viable single. The song is a simple blues song in E, with a loud thumping bass that accompanies the jangly country-blues guitar part played by Richards, with Jones on harmonica. The song proper effectively ends at about 3:09, and they could have simply faded the song out on the E vamp with Jagger's vocal improvisation. But they extend the song with a blues jam in E, somewhat formless but with vocal repetitions and build-ups. There are only a few long jams ("Midnight Rambler," "Can't You Hear Me Knocking") in the Stones' studio repertoire, but "Goin' Home" does not look forward to these but rather back toward early rave-up style jams, for example their version of Bo Diddley's "Hey Crawdaddy."[16]

Indeed, as the album became the center of the pop world, the corollary idea spread that it should have a unifying theme or "concept" attached to it. In the concept album, a unifying story line underpins the songs. Thus it is more than a loose collection of songs but is analogous to a novel or a short opera in that it could follow a character or idea and present the narrative arc of a beginning, middle, and end. *Aftermath*'s UK release occurred right before Brian Wilson and Tony Asher wrote what has been interpreted as one of the first concept albums, the Beach Boys' *Pet Sounds* (May 1966), while the American release followed it. Concept albums partake of an underlying story or idea in varying degrees. For example, the Beatles' *Sgt. Pepper's Lonely Hearts Club Band* (1967) is on the weaker side of the spectrum, while the Kinks' *Arthur (Or the Decline and Fall of the British Empire)* (1969) the stronger. The Stones never did conceive a concept album around a single narrative, though the closest they came was a year later with *Their Satanic Majesties Request* (more below).

If the UK track listing for *Aftermath* corresponds to what the Stones (or at least Jagger/Richards/Oldham) had in mind, the U.S. release tweaked their vision. As the UK version hit number one, it seems surprising that the record label (London, the U.S. affiliate of Decca) would change anything; again this was standard industry practice. Most significantly, the album's lead track, "Mother's Little Helper," is taken off in favor of "Paint It Black," once again a similar song in the Raga Rock subgenre.[17] Three other songs are left off entirely, as American record execs felt that fourteen songs was excessive. As led by the number-one charting novelty-song masterpiece "Paint It Black," the U.S. *Aftermath* still achieved number-two chart position.

Unlike "Mother's Little Helper" that was recorded in December of 1965, "Paint It Black" was part of the album's main sessions in March 1966. The song is also in E minor.[18] It relies on many of the same chords as "Mother's Little Helper," especially the D, G, and A (although this latter chord is minor in "Mother's"). But the song turns on a two-chord oscillation between the tonic and its dominant chord, B (missing in "Mother's"), heard in the first line on the word "want." And like "Mother's Little Helper," the song is also a modal mixture.[19] Other similar touches are the sharing of the melody between the guitar riff and the vocal part, the acoustically strummed presentation of the E minor chord as a drone substitute, and the subject matter of depression. The cause of the depression in "Paint It Black" is the death of the singer's lover. The second verse depicts the witnessing of her funeral, as in the black cars containing both flowers and the departed.

The specific musical exoticism of "Paint It Black" embraces and extends beyond India. The main Indian feature of the song is Brian Jones's doubling of the vocal melody on the sitar. This appears to be the first Stones track to have a sitar, and Jones apparently learned the instrument quite quickly. But the opening guitar riff (also the song's melody), as commented on by Richards himself, is not necessarily Indian. Richards hears it as Jewish or Gypsy. And Jagger himself comments that the song has a Turkish groove to it.[20] Whatever the ethnic source, the point is that it was a change in direction from the blues and American pop, and in particular, a move toward something non-Western. Combined with the lyrics, the song can take on a sinister, satanic feel, especially during and after the swirling chanting section of the outro (starting at 2:15). The bass swells and rolls on the snare drum impart a fatalistic and perhaps militaristic atmosphere as the song fades.

Thus to summarize, the Stones' forays into Raga Rock and other experiments of the same period helped loosen the grip of R & B and the blues on the band's style. It also allowed them to change the typical blues and pop-music topoi, as darker and controversial lyrical ideas were broached. Last, it opened up new timbral dimensions for the band's sound, which would come to fruition down the road with *Their Satanic Majesties Request*.

POST-*AFTERMATH*: *BETWEEN THE BUTTONS*

The band got back to RCA Studios for recording sessions in the summer of 1966 and started work on *Between the Buttons* (February 1967), presenting their most "English" of albums. LSD and the psychedelic mindset were starting to spread and would impact the band the most on their next two albums. As Swinging London turned psychedelic—Richards notes that the band was away while this event happened—the Stones remained somewhat aloof from the new trend, yet they did allow it to impact their music. The main criticism of this period is that the Stones became reactive to current musical trends, especially psychedelic rock, and were no longer seeking to build on and develop their own bluesy sound. The Stones of this period do seem more indebted to or have more in common with what was occurring in the British music scene, in particular the nouveau Swinging London bands like the Who, Cream, the Yardbirds, the Small Faces, and the Kinks.

Further, with multi-track recording and overdubbing becoming de rigueur, some of the direct, unthrottled thrill of the Stones' live sound was lost on *Between the Buttons* and *Their Satanic Majesties Request*. That is, this style of multi-track recording and experiments in the studio did not complement the band's strength, the powerful synergy of a musical conversation grounded in a live, improvisatory aesthetic that is constantly changing and rhythmically flexible. Paradoxically, the band also responded by writing some of their most endearing songs during this heady time of rapid technological advance, including a couple of their all-time most popular songs, the quasi-ballads "Ruby Tuesday" and "She's a Rainbow." As well, their status as rock and roll rebel superstars only increased, as they came into trouble with the authorities over drug use and put on a defiant front that cast them as unfair victims and thereby increased sympathy for them.

Between the Buttons continues with the dual UK and U.S. releases. The UK version lacks the singles "Let's Spend the Night Together" and "Ruby Tuesday," both of which do appear on the American release of the album. The album is also significant in that it is the last time that Oldham was the producer, even if by this time his contributions were less than they once were. Thus the album demarcates the end of the Oldham era for the Stones. It was recorded at RCA Studios but finished up at Olympic Studios, newly located in Barnes, London, where Glyn

Johns was the engineer.[21] Note that Olympic would be the Stones' choice London studio for the next several years and was a cutting-edge studio for its time.

For some writers like Jon Landau of rock journal *Crawdaddy!* and *Rolling Stone* fame who became one of the first "serious" rock critics of the era, the album ranks as one of their greatest. Indeed Landau, a fan of the band, prefers the album to the classic, "golden period" albums of the late 1960s and 1970s, which he finds cluttered and overproduced. But reviews of the album have remained decidedly mixed, with recent critics still coming down hard on some of the tracks.

Again there remain charges of sexism and chauvinism in the songwriting. Jagger's "Yesterday's Papers" is cut from the same cloth as "Under My Thumb." Jagger sings about discarding a girl as one does a newspaper, since there are a million girls waiting in the wings. But there are some autobiographical details in the songwriting that perhaps mitigate these accusations, and again, a song can be read in different ways. Jagger was splitting up or had split up with ex-fiancée Chrissie Shrimpton, leaving her for his new girlfriend, the singer Marianne Faithfull. Indeed the latter personage hovers over the album, as it is ventured that Jagger has her and what she represents to him in mind in many of the songs. "Complicated" is a good example of this, with its clever juxtaposition of a girl who appears "simple" but who is actually complicated, which seems to be the result of her education. Heard within the rising tide of feminism, the song lyrics seem to be grappling with the new self-assured, educated young woman of the 1960s who wants to "have her own way."

Jagger also anticipates the sexual scandals that will come to roil the political establishment in the new era of sexual liberation. A piece of social commentary, "Back Street Girl" takes a direct look at the exercise of male and class privilege and its demeaning sexual fallout. The song does not appear on the American release of *Between the Buttons*, though it does on the seminal 1967 American compilation album *Flowers*. The song paints a desperate picture of a prostitute or a mistress, who is "common and coarse." The upper-class, married gentlemen addresses her in a condescending albeit honest way, telling her she will never be part of his world, but to accept his favors nonetheless. She is his possession, his "backstreet girl." And still there seems to be more to the seedy, clandestine story. He appears to be in love with her, or at least emotionally and sexually dependent on her, as expressed in the tender melody and accompaniment. The song's melancholy acoustic musical treatment looks back to a simpler, pre-rock era. Like the exotica of the Raga Rock songs, "Back Street Girl" transports the listener back to another world, to a style outside of rock. That is, the song is a musette, a sentimental waltz with nineteenth-century roots in French cafes, commonly played on the accordion. The instrumental break features the vibraphone playing of Jones over a lush backdrop of accordion, harpsichord, and acoustic guitar.

Other songs on *Between the Buttons* (all are Jagger/Richards originals) show the band writing, assimilating, and playing in a polyglot of stylistic influences, from Bo Diddley ("Please Go Home"), Bob Dylan ("Who's Been Sleeping Here?"), Chuck Berry ("Miss Amanda Jones") to the Kinks ("Cool, Calm and Collected" and the ironic music-hall revelry of "Something Happened to Me Yesterday"). "Connection" is a Richards song about drug use before he starting using cocaine and heroin, with an almost proto-punk sensibility that met with a positive reception. One critic suggests it was played too fast, noting that Montrose's slower version from 1974 brings out the latent soulfulness of the song.[22] "Connection" is also significant in that it marks the first time that Richards sang a lead vocal part, albeit with Jagger (playing the tambourine) doubling his voice. "My Obsession" is built around an incessant and syncopated drumbeat of Watts, which can be represented as 1 + **2** + 3 **+** **4** + (bold indicates cymbal accents). Richards's distorted guitar rumbles a low, swirling riff in the background that sets the song's dark demeanor. Present at the mixing of "My Obsession," Brian Wilson was so impressed with the song and the sound of the band that he rethought his approach to the album he was trying to complete at the time, *Smile*.[23]

LISTENING VIGNETTES: "LET'S SPEND THE NIGHT TOGETHER" AND "RUBY TUESDAY"

"Let's Spend the Night Together" was one of the first songs Richards wrote on the piano; on the recording though it is Nitzsche who plays the bouncy piano part that dominates the harmonic texture while Richards plays bass. Richards also confirms that the background vocal parts are derived from the chords that he worked out on the piano. Conceived as a single to accompany the British release of *Between the Buttons*, the band flew to New York in January 1967 to promote their new single paired with "Ruby Tuesday" as a double A-side. Notoriously, Ed Sullivan refused to allow the band perform the song that dealt with casual sex on his show; compromise was reached when Jagger agreed to substitute the word "time" for "night." Jagger and Wyman show their displeasure with the censorship as they roll their eyes on the word "time." But this gesture seems more the stuff of show business than outright, authentic rebellion; that they agreed to play it at all shows their complicity in the commercial machinery of the entertainment industry. Because of the immorality associated with the song, American DJs were also wary of playing the song, with the result that it did not chart well. Jagger tried to defend the song with a more nuanced view, that it is after all just a phrase, one that he would say when he met new people. Many have thought he was writing to his new girlfriend, Marianne Faithfull, whom he had only recently seduced.

It is January of 1967, and you have recently graduated from the Ealing Art College, taking a job at Decca working in the art and marketing department. You know that the Rolling Stones are currently their biggest artist, and you have been a fan of theirs since you first saw them play live many years past. Your other favorite band is the Who, in part because their lead guitarist, Pete Townshend, had also studied at Ealing. You have dabbled in the growing drug scene, but have yet to try LSD, of which you are aware. The London underground and psychedelic scene is in full bloom by early 1967, with weekly psychedelic events at the Marquee Club and the UFO Club complementing the colorful, youthful mod fashions of Carnaby Street. You have dabbled in the recent fashion styles but remain more conservative. Your girlfriend, who is a bit younger than you, is really into mod music and fashions and likes the new and harder groups such as Cream, Jimi Hendrix Experience, Small Faces, and Pink Floyd, currently the rage among the young and hip in London. But it is a big place, and the Beatles, Stones, Kinks, and Animals (with a new lineup) manage to hold their own even with the inevitable changing of the guard.

After leaving work in West Hampstead on a cold winter day you take the tube to Soho, where you find your favorite record store to purchase the much-hyped new Stones single, "Let's Spend the Night Together/

Ruby Tuesday." You take it back to your nearby flat where later on you, your girlfriend, and a few friends listen to it. The first thing you all notice about "Let's Spend" is the strong presence of the piano instead of the guitar. The doo-wop backing harmonies and call-and-response almost seem to overpower Jagger. But it is a great song to dance to, and the energy is unflagging throughout, even slightly increasing as it goes on. You don't know a lot about chords and harmony or progressions, but you all sense that there is more to this song than usual (there are more chord changes in this song than a typical Stones song). As a visual artist, you sense that they are working with a different palette than normal in this song—but then, you had come to expect that in pop music there is constant change as groups try to stay on top and current.

But what do you make of the lyrics? Is it a chauvinistic song? Your girlfriend and her friends do not seem in the slightest bothered by the title and its suggestion, in fact just the opposite. You are well aware that they have grown up with the newly minted sexual freedom of Swinging London—but will this thinking spread to other places? Is this another unfolding of the generational divide, or does the song go too far in its subversion of morality as the older generation interprets it? And you also notice upon repeated listening that Jagger is not so self-confident as the title might suggest. Although he seems bold as he's trying to seduce the girl, still, there is something vulnerable about Jagger's plea—he is turning "red," his "tongue is tied," he is "off of his head," and his mouth is "dry." He needs her so badly in the song that he sounds dependent on her—not exactly the image of the bold Lothario or Casanova that Jagger plays on stage. Later, when you learn about *The Ed Sullivan Show* debacle and the song's reception in America, it only confirms your puritanical view of that country.

Turning the record over, "Ruby Tuesday" seems very similar to many recent Beatles' songs. Another piano song, it is the use of what you believe is a cello (it is actually a double bass) that reminds you of Beatles songs like "Yesterday" or even more recently "Eleanor Rigby." The lyrics even seem to take an indirect dig at "Yesterday," a sappy song you can't imagine the Stones ever liking ("Yesterday don't matter if it's gone"). You all agree it is a break-up song unlike none other, with a powerfully joyous though melancholy chorus. The girl described is so ultra-modern in her independence; are these the kinds of girls the Stones encounter in their rarefied world of superstardom? You can't pin this type of girl down as she changes all the time in the pursuit of her own dreams.

"Ruby Tuesday" went on to number-one status in the United States (though not in the United Kingdom), and perhaps it was due to this proximity to the kind of songs the Beatles were writing at the time. Despite its leave-taking that begins on a minor chord (Am), with a descending bass line and chord progression similar to "Under My Thumb," the music for the chorus turns hopeful as it exuberantly confirms the tonic chord of the home key (C). A drumroll on the snare signals the transition out of the somber verse and into the uplifting section to follow. On the first word of the chorus, "goodbye," the band kicks into high gear to proclaim one of the most memorable anthems in pop history.

Richards wrote "Ruby Tuesday" with help from an uncredited Jones. Both are responsible for the unique timbre of the song—Richards bowing the string bass fingered by Wyman and Jones adding haunting notes played on the recorder. The song is a tribute to Richards's ex-girlfriend, the model Linda Keith. Richards recounts how Keith was a "powerful cultural force in West Hampstead," an area where Decca Studios was also located (near Broadhurst Gardens).[24] This fashionable area became the "stomping grounds" of Jagger and Richards during these years. But Keith's real importance to music history is how she figures into the discovering of Jimi Hendrix—after hearing him perform with Curtis Knight at the Cheetah Club in New York, she alerted Richards and then Chas Chandler (the former bass player for the Animals). Chandler heard him play at the Café Wha? in Greenwich Village and quickly became Hendrix's manager and brought him to London.[25]

PSYCHEDELIC TURN: *THEIR SATANIC MAJESTIES REQUEST*

For enormously popular bands like the Beatles and the Stones, the experimental side of psychedelic rock offered a refuge from the demands of constant touring. That is, it does not require an audience per se and can blossom in the confines of the recording studio. Sound engineers, arrangers, and producers (this last sometimes the musicians themselves) are vital to the process of creation. Because of multiple takes, meandering improvisations, and the penchant for experimentation in the search for new and weird sounds, albums started to take much longer to produce. Indeed, music executives were often wary of the albums of psychedelic rock, seeing them as ego-driven and self-indulgent. On the other hand, the genre was a necessary step for rock musicians to take in their quest to be taken seriously as artists and led directly to the progressive and classic rock of the 1970s.

The events encompassing the making of *Their Satanic Majesties Request* signal a turbulent period in the personal lives of the band members. First is the infamous drug bust of Jagger and Richards in February 1967 at Richards's newly acquired country estate, Redlands. As we said in chapter 1, the bust was in fact a carefully orchestrated setup by the media—*News of the World*, the same organization that finally closed in 2011 due to the phone-hacking scandal—in conjunction with the police. The trial and the threat of real jail time were devastating and nearly ruined the Stones. To escape the pressure, the band decided to meet up in Morocco. Jones and his girlfriend, Anita Pallenberg, Richards, and others took a trip driving through France and Spain; on the way there, while Jones was hospitalized, Richards ended up with Pallenberg, whom he would stay with for the rest of the 1960s and 1970s. Although Jones and Richards had recently begun patching up their friendship, this would be a final blow, and Jones never fully forgave Richards. Finally, while making the album, they made it clear to Oldham that they did not need him any longer and he resigned.

The standard interpretation of the album is that the Stones were trying to make a concept album in response to the Beatles' *Sgt. Pepper's* and failed to reach that level. Yet Jagger thought they should make a concept album well before *Sgt. Pepper's* was released (June 1967), and the original idea was a spoof of the British passport, which began "Her Britannic Majesty's . . . Requests." Despite this, they managed to put together a few standout songs—"She's a Rainbow," "2000 Man," and "2000 Light Years from Home." Also, the album is the beginning of their long association with another great session keyboardist, Nicky Hopkins.[26] And many of the experimental sounds on the album have held up well, especially on "2000 Light Years."

In defense of the charge of ripping off the Beatles, Richards is helpful when he writes that the Stones were often holding a mirror up to their times, and the Beatles were just one influence among many. Again, 1967 and its Summer of Love represent a changing of the times, as the oldest baby boomers began to reach adulthood and the hippie and psychedelic counterculture assumed mainstream status. By sticking to their roots in this year, they might have risked seeming passé to this new movement. Further, the number of psychedelic albums would only increase in the next couple of years. And from this perspective, the Stones album can be seen as more psychedelic and trip-oriented than *Sgt. Pepper's*.

As its name implies, psychedelic rock takes as its starting point the drug, and specifically hallucinogenic experience, from either or both of the creation and reception sides. Indeed, Raga Rock and the fascination with sounds associated with the meditative East might be its starting point. Extending the geographical metaphor, psychedelic rock takes the listener on a journey, transporting you to new, unknown, and unexplored areas of consciousness. The lyrics might be surreal, or juxtapose unlike things and images (parataxis). They might also reference the drug experience itself, or the strange connections of thought made while under the influence. Musically, there is an emphasis on exotic or unusual sounds and timbres; there might also be sections of free improvisation and rhythm, as structures and boundaries begin to decompose. Sound was no longer dependent on what instruments were available, as now engineers were able to work with tape tracks to manipulate sound, including flanging effects and the swirling stereo sounds heard on these records.

Their Satanic Majesties Request pulls off all of these attributes of the genre. "2000 Light Years from Home" is a highly regarded spacey piece, as the star traveller journeys farther into deep space while becoming more aware of the naked starkness of his isolation. Jagger wrote down the lyrics expressing his feelings of isolation while in jail, using it to avoid the confrontational topic of the police. The bulk of the song's recording occurred in the summer, also about the time of the release of Pink Floyd's first album and psychedelic masterpiece, *Piper at the Gates of Dawn*, with its own improvisational fantasy tribute to space travel, "Interstellar Overdrive." A working title for "2000 Light Years" was "Aftermath," and according to Wyman it was only in September that the band settled on the song's actual title.

"2000 Light Years" begins with an avant-garde, otherworldly intro in a free rhythm with Hopkins playing a tape-altered piano, recalling the prepared piano of the American avant-garde composer John Cage's oeuvre. Swelling, held notes vie with stabbing, pointillist blips of sound, ostensibly meant to represent the emptiness of space. The first swelling pitch heard is a B-flat, which contrasts with the tonic E major of the song. Note that the interval from B-flat to E forms the sonic equivalent of a tritone, a dissonant interval called the "Diabolus in Musica" ("devil in music"), in line with the album's title. Richards enters with a stark riff in E minor, which one writer compares to a Spaghetti-Western theme, probably because of the low timbre. Early outtakes of the song begin with this riff. Note that "Interstellar Overdrive" also begins with a guitar riff in E and uses similar pitch space as the Stones' song (A, B, and G)—it is beyond our scope here, but an interesting comparison could be made between the two songs. Richards's fuzzed-out guitar plays a second, blues-based, and syncopated riff throughout the verse, giving the forward momentum of the spaceship. As usual, Richards's riffs are narrowly focused on only a few pitches. But what makes the song so unique and psychedelic is Jones's ambient playing on the Mellotron, a small keyboard that generates its sound using tape. The Beatles had used one on "Strawberry Fields," among other songs. The multivalent Mellotron was a natural match for a multi-instrumentalist like Jones. In an instrumental break (2:05) where Richards plays a menacing rhythm over an E chord that could find a place in any classic hard rock song, Jones adds bubbles of futuristic sound using a theremin, an electronic instrument often used in movies to connote alien landscapes, with its most famous pop-song application perhaps being "Good Vibrations" (October 1966) by the Beach Boys.[27]

LISTENING VIGNETTE: "SHE'S A RAINBOW"

The most accessible song on the album, and also the first completed song for it, "She's a Rainbow" contrasts with the dark, satanic message of the album. Its lyric exudes a hippie worldview, and its conceptual apparatus might not be that original—it most likely takes its concept from a song by Love called "She Comes in Colors" (released on the album *Da Capo*, October 1966). Originally titled "Flowers" (remember that the idea of Flower Power was a political concept, slogan, and catchphrase for the hippies of the day), the song paints a celebratory picture of a woman, using flashes of color to describe her. The psychedelic experience could certainly heighten the perception of color, reflected in the bright and colorful clothing preferred by hippies, symbolized in the flamboyant tie-dye clothing of the era and also in the flashy colors found in the clothing boutique shops of Carnaby Street. In this respect the song's literary theme fits in well with a couple of other psychedelic classics from this era that rely on color, such as Hendrix's "Purple Haze" or the Beatles' "Lucy in the Sky with Diamonds." Unlike Jagger's allegedly condescending depiction of women we have been tracing, the female of "She's a Rainbow" is held up as innocent and pure. In this regard, note that both nature and the innocence of childhood were important subjects for the psychedelic mindset. Jagger ties these ideas together in another whimsical song finished in close proximity to "Rainbow," "Dandelion," which was released as a B-side to the single "We Love You" in the Summer of Love. "Dandelion" also uses descriptive flower imagery from a children's game. With backing vocals that include Lennon and McCartney, Jones plays an oboe solo on "Dandelion," unique for the Stones.

Structurally, "She's a Rainbow" alternates between a piano solo played by Hopkins, with added strings and a tambourine for orchestral color, and a traditional song part played by the band. The song begins with the chorus, with the suggestive line that again captures the spirit of the times, "she comes in colors everywhere." After a piano interlude, the performers repeat the chorus, and then another interlude. The piano interludes are in a neo-Baroque style, with lively string and orchestral accompaniments that become more abstract as the song progresses. Finally they get to the verse-chorus sections, and the song builds up around more psychedelic imagery with references to the sky and the sunset. Surely meant as a psychedelic sendoff, the song concludes with an off-key guitar chord (E) played by Jones (the song is in B-flat).

A lot more could be said about *Their Satanic Majesties Request* in the context of psychedelia. Given the amount of time they band spent on it, the fast-changing musical landscape of the time, and with the copious amount of outtakes that have been released (as *Satanic Sessions*), the album probably needs a re-evaluation that is beyond the scope of this writing. The accusation that the Stones abandoned their roots is also more complex than it first appears. Its reception history is complicated by not only the songs themselves—for example, the driving and pleasantly grungy "Citadel," which seems to fit quite well into the ideal type of a Stones song—but also with other material they had started to work on, such as "Child of the Moon (rmk)," a song associated with their next roots album, *Beggars Banquet*, to which we now turn.

3

SUPERNATURALLY CHARGED BLUES

Beggars Banquet (1968)

A major part of the Stones' mystique has been the group's uncanny ability in concert to elicit the deepest emotional response in their audience. It began with the crazed teenage (and younger) girls wetting themselves at concerts in England, followed by the male, testosterone-fueled violence when they toured abroad. At first this seems to have surprised the band. But with each tour there was a building momentum, a snowball effect as it were, and with hit records added to their live repertory they bounced off audience energy in a feedback loop as the frenzied response only mushroomed. When they stopped touring in 1966 and retreated artistically to the recording studio, they also lost that visceral, personal, emotional connection with their fans and audience. This might have taken some toll on their inspiration. Thus by the time they finished *Their Satanic Majesties Request*, their final studio album without the support of a tour, the band had run out of gas, as Richards puts it.

But then, what followed has been touted as one of the greatest artistic turnarounds in popular music history. In the spring of 1968 at the recording sessions for *Beggars Banquet*, the Stones' creative imagination caught fire once again. The cathartic opening that their music gave to their audience seems to have now been redirected at them. And it was on two levels—both in their music and lyrics. They secured arguably their best producer, Jimmy Miller, an American who was also a drummer, who guided them in the studio to achieve their thickest and most groove-oriented sound to date, while Richards relearned his way around the guitar neck as he played in alternate open tunings. Jagger wrote lyrics that addressed the negative events and energy politically dividing the time, while still offering up a resistant, rebellious outward stance—a defiant attitude that in the 1970s was taken up under the banner of punk.

THE RIFF TO "JUMPIN' JACK FLASH"

While working on *Beggars Banquet*, the Stones also recorded "Jumpin' Jack Flash," one of their finest blues and proto-punk masterpieces. Lyrically inspired by Richards's gardener in Redlands, the song was released as a much-needed single in May 1968, going to number one on the UK charts. It was their answer to "Satisfaction" and perhaps their greatest song, at least in their own judgment and in terms of audience reception. Using only acoustic guitars recorded through a cheap cassette player (more on this lo-fi process below), Richards achieved the dirty, sticky quasi-electric sound he had been trying to achieve for some time.

Unlike most other Stones riffs, the genesis of the main riff to "Jumpin' Jack" is open to dispute. In his autobiography Richards says that the "magic discovery" of the riff "just came," and is a blessing—if he had to choose to play one riff for life, it is this one.[1] But it is still not certain that he wrote it, and he does not go out of his way to refute one of the bombshells of attribution in the Stones' music to come out in Wyman's *Stone Alone*. Wyman claims to have played the main riff first on an electronic keyboard one day while jamming in the studio with Watts and Jones, and that Jagger and Richards acknowledged it and then took it as the basis for the new song.[2] Speculating, the riff itself does sound like something a bass player would come up with, and Wyman had been writing in this period. Richards counters that the song itself is part of a universal, quasi-mystical tradition back to "the archaic, classical, the chord setups you could only hear in Gregorian chants or something like that." But he does not refute Wyman's claim. Furthermore, note the intrusion of the category of exotic world music in his commentary, something we have seen before and will be tracking later in this book:

Richards contends that the "allll-right now" has an Arabic quality to it, echoing ancient music that "you don't even know." Perhaps what he is saying, though rather elliptically, is that whether or not Wyman had the kernel of the riff—that is, perhaps its note content and rhythmic shape—still, the expressive-technical execution of the riff, its performative unfolding, points to something else entirely—another universal realm as it were. After all, Richards plays it using an alternate tuning (see below), and its final voicing on the studio version is very unorthodox; the sonic result does seem to depend in part on the way it's fingered on the guitar.

SUPERNATURAL BLUES

But what explicitly caught listeners' attention in this song and the *Beggars Banquet* material was the creation of a new kind of blues, what *Rolling Stone* has called a "supernatural" blues (the full phrase is "supernatural Delta blues by way of Swinging London," a wonderfully evocative and catchy formulation).[3] It is a blues that is qualified in some hard-to-quantify respect. For example, in his contemporaneous review of the album, Jon Landau reiterates that the Stones were a *rock-and-roll* blues band from the beginning (his emphasis).[4] And now armed with experience gleaned from years in the studio, the Stones were able to extend their technical knowledge of sound reproduction to the blues music that they had started with and studied for years. In what becomes a rebirth of his approach to the guitar, Richards became obsessed with how to capture the thick sound for the guitar he heard in his head. His obsession resulted in some of the most singular, unique, and stripped-down recorded guitar sounds in rock history. He articulates how they wanted the instruments to melt into one another and what they were aiming for:

> What you're looking for is power and force, without volume—an inner power. A way to bring together what everybody in that room is doing to make one sound. So it's not two guitars, piano, bass, and drums, it's one thing, it's not five. You're there to create one thing.[5]

"Jumpin' Jack Flash" captured this aesthetic, possessing not only a new guitar timbre, but also a sonic blending unlike anything the Stones had yet achieved. Solidifying this blend on this song and other songs on *Beggars Banquet* is the pronounced groove element, credited to the input of producer Jimmy Miller that picks up where their earliest R & B recordings had left off. Yet even with this hot rhythmic injection, a calm, steady coolness pervades the album's atmosphere, in part due to the acoustic and laid-back country vibe to the songs.

In *Beggars Banquet* the Stones employ the album's subtitle and packaging to engage the receiver/audience directly in a performative speech act. As *Their Satanic Majesties Request* parodied the British passport's request—or demand—for safe passage for the bearer, so too *Beggars Banquet* invites us to the event of a medieval feast requiring an RSVP. Further, both albums' entreaties turn traditional concepts on their head. The *Satanic Majesties* album transfers the sovereign's domain from Britain to Satan; *Beggars Banquet* asks that we attend a feast, albeit one thrown by decadent, tattered minstrels (as shown in the inside picture spread that imitates a seventeenth-century painting; the session photographer was Michael Joseph). In effect, both albums operate on dual semantic levels, with descriptive contents on the one hand that, on the other, ask for responses from us.

Though we could find much common ground between the two albums, musically and otherwise (especially the occult glosses), the media used *Beggars Banquet* as a pretense to proclaim the greatness of the Stones and their comeback. With the release of the single "Jumpin' Jack Flash" a few months prior to the album's own release, the press was enamored of the idea that the band was going back to basics, to the "supernatural blues" cited above, reviving the roots and blues music that had initially got them going. And the Stones were fortunate to have had their formative years during the birth of serious rock criticism and journalism, embodied in Jann Wenner's aptly titled and celebrated fan magazine, *Rolling Stone*.[6] Indeed, the discourse of aesthetic rebellion represented by the Stones was now intertwined with the left-wing leanings of college-educated or well-heeled baby boomers, ironically in what became a respectable literary outlet. The type of rock criticism practiced by *Rolling Stone* and similar journals in England, notably *New Musical Express* and *Melody Maker*, helped situate the Stones as the musical voice of the time and generation, a position they held at least through 1972. Furthermore, it is in the period beginning with *Beggars*

Banquet that they finally surpassed the Beatles as rock's standard-bearers, finalized with the Beatles' formal breakup in April 1970.

The Stones' lineup for *Beggars* includes Brian Jones, yet by this point his input was minimal. The one song he did contribute to significantly was "No Expectations," where he played slide guitar. Along with "Sympathy for the Devil," this was a Jagger favorite from the album. By this point Jones was out of step with the direction the band was heading, in that he had wanted to continue to explore electronic and experimental sounds as he had on *Satanic Majesties*. Furthermore, Wyman states that Jones's electronic interests were effectively blocked by Jagger, who himself was trying to learn the Moog synthesizer in order to write film music for his upcoming role in *Performance*, a British gangster film that used the single "Memo from Turner."[7] Near exhaustion, psychologically unstable with frequent mood swings, and suffering from generally poor health for many years, a highly publicized and devastating drug bust in May 1968 (his second) nearly put Jones over the edge. In the summer a field trip to Morocco to record native master musicians did rejuvenate him, but not for long. In September, though, he faced a trial for the drug charges with the possibility of jail time. Jones was fortunate that after a jury found him guilty of the drug charges, a judge let him off with only a fine. Although he would still appear on a couple of tracks on *Let It Bleed*, his status as a Rolling Stone took a blow for his minimal input on *Beggars*.

Picking up the slack for Jones, nonmembers of the group made important contributions to the album's unique sound. Nicky Hopkins joined the band on keyboard, playing both piano and organ. A drummer from Ghana, Rocky Dijon (Dzidzornu) added percussion, most notably the congas on "Sympathy for the Devil." Ric Grech, Dave Mason, and the Watts Street Gospel Choir also made appearances that we will discuss with their respective contributions below. But it was Jimmy Miller, an American drummer turned producer, fresh from work on Traffic's first two acclaimed albums, who gave direction to the band and helped them bring their sound into focus. Miller would stay on with the band through their next period that includes their most critically celebrated albums, through *Goats Head Soup* (again, like *Beggars*, it too lacks an apostrophe).

In terms of video/film presentation, television appearances with the band performing (either for real or miming) or in interviews were all that the Stones had done. They had not acted or made movies such as *Hard Day's Night* the way that the Beatles had. Peter Whitehead had shot a documentary film of a brief 1965 tour of Ireland, *Charlie Is My Darling*, but this was not fully released until 2012 and had received only partial and limited screening prior to that. Michael Lindsay-Hogg (who had frequent collaborations with the Beatles) had done a couple of short song promotional videos with the group for *Satanic Majesties*. Lindsay-Hogg continued with a promo for "Jumpin' Jack Flash" with the group in face paint (except for Richards), and he did continue to work with the band for the entire 1970s. But with three film projects in 1968, the Stones seem to have realized the potential of the cinematic genre for marketing, although one of these, *Performance*, only involved Jagger.

GOOD VERSUS EVIL: "SYMPATHY FOR THE DEVIL"

We shall start with one of these films, the Jean-Luc Godard film *One Plus One* (or, *1+1*), also known as *Sympathy for the Devil*.[8] The film documents the studio genesis of "Sympathy for the Devil," juxtaposing band rehearsals at Olympic with various avant-garde tableaux. In particular, Godard intersperses his footage of the Rolling Stones with stark scenes of armed Black Panthers reading out loud from Amiri Baraka's *Blues People (Negro Music in White America)* among other texts in a Battersea scrap yard; white women in white robes are brought in and subsequently killed. In a bucolic scene shot in Hyde Park, a film crew interviews a strange woman named Eve Democracy (played by Godard's young wife, the actress Anne Wiazemsky) who only answers "yes" or "no" to questions; there is also another scene of the proprietor of a bookstore reading *Mein Kampf* while patrons browse pulp fiction and girlie magazines. Note that Richards considers these elements of the film "a total load of crap."[9] As the other tableaux combine an avant-garde aesthetic with ideology drawn from Marxist perspectives, it is difficult to reconcile how the scenes of the Stones' music making for profit fit into the ostensibly Marxist direction of the film as a whole. But responding from Godard's perspective, the point might be to interpret all of these unrelated vignettes, rock music creation included, as part of his critique of bourgeois culture in his effort to promote a far-left-wing, anti-capitalist, revolutionary agenda. In this respect Godard attempts to inscribe the Stones and their songs into a narrative of class struggle and the critique of unbounded capitalism.

Even if the Rolling Stones as a subject seems incongruous to the film's agenda, it is fortuitous that Godard captures on film the evolution of "Sympathy of the Devil," arguably one of the most unique, original, and compelling songs in the Stones' catalog and possibly in rock history. In a straight documentary style that has the camera pan through the room, Godard shows the struggle and the creative growing pains the band went through to get the rhythm and instrumentation right in the song, and their eventual arrival at an iconic sound and hit record. It provides an insider's peek at how the Stones work up a song in the studio, and especially of the power dynamic of the band. Wyman and Watts emerge as weak, passive sideman, barely necessary for a song's creation—as we shall see, the actual sideman, Hopkins and Dijon, offer more. Godard also captures Jones's downfall. At the beginning Jagger is interested in teaching Jones the song. By the end Jones is in an isolation booth, strumming away on an acoustic guitar that does not seem to be heard in the song's final mix.

It is also quite remarkable to witness the transformative changes the song undergoes in the film. It starts as a folk ballad, with acoustic guitars strumming a typical rhythm with the song's chord changes as Watts searches for a beat to complement the country-blues feel. Next we see Richards on his late-fifties black Les Paul custom guitar, the one with three pickups and the recently done psychedelic moon-scene paint job that allegedly he and Pallenberg did. (This guitar can also be heard on the *Rock and Roll Circus* live-filmed version of the song.) He lets out a flurry of licks that are the seeds for what becomes his most famous guitar solo. Hopkins plays the organ. In the next scene, Richards has switched to bass, the instrument he will ultimately play on the studio version of the song. The song's tempo is still quite slow (ca. 96 BPM), with Watts playing a halting awkward groove (with snare accents on 2 and the "&" of 3 and 4) while Wyman accompanies him on a West-African style gourd shaker (listed as a maraca on the credits). The loud organ in this mix gives the song a churchlike, gospel vibe. Jagger expresses his frustration at Watts—"Try to make it a bit more live, it's a bit dead, you know? Not clipped enough somehow." In the film the band's personalities are on display, as we see the emotionless Wyman and

Watts, who are perhaps concerned about their continued roles in the band, while the animated Richards and Jagger are clearly the center of it all. Jones, again, is essentially absent even in his presence.

In terms of the song's meaning, multiple and contradictory interpretations are possible. At the time some Christians viewed the song as satanist in intention, that is, as a celebration of the Devil's works. On this interpretation, Jagger identifies himself with the Devil and invites us to do the same. In fact, coming off the heels of *Satanic Majesties* (an album that actually does not contain any lyrical references to Satan), the band was thought by some Christians and others to be devil worshipers or at least black-magic occultists.

Though on the literal surface there seems to be some truth to the above characterization that the song is satanist, this judgment based on its literality is actually off base. First, it can be argued that the Stones are simply using the demonic and its shock value to sell records and boost their own rebellious notoriety. Differently put, the Stones are producing music within the hyper-commercial pressure cooker of the entertainment industry, and as such the band latches onto the Devil/rebellion theme to maximize profits and sell more records. Further, what better way to burnish a defiant reputation than through the appropriation of the Devil and distinguish their product from the Beatles (who recorded perhaps their most harrowing song in July 1968, "Helter Skelter," also thought to be satanic but which actually names an amusement park ride).

As has been known for centuries, the artistic presentation of the dark side sells. Indeed the subject of the Devil has a proven track record of popular artistic commercial success. The musical fascination with and depiction of the Devil and the demonic signifier has a long and venerable place in music history—quickly, some famous works include Tartini's "Devil's Trill" Sonata for violin, Paganini's "Devil's Laugh" Capriccio (op. 1 no. 13) for violin, Meyerbeer's grand opera *Robert le diable* (*Robert the Devil*), the numerous settings of Goethe's *Faust* in nineteenth-century opera (especially Gounod's, upon which Bulgakov partly based his book, more below), and symphonic literature (especially Liszt's *Faust* Symphony) and Stravinsky's *Soldier's Tale*. Plus there is the legend of Paganini selling his soul to the Devil in a Faustian bargain to become the greatest violin virtuoso the world has ever known. And perhaps more directly to the point with the Stones, the demonic literary trope figures in the blues, albeit filtered with an African-derived sensibility of the Trickster, a figure who turns the social hierarchy on its head. Famously, Delta blues players wrote songs about the Devil and some even claimed to have sold their souls to the Devil, as for example Robert Johnson.

And in the aftermath of "Sympathy" the Devil continued to sell; among the numerous songs about the Devil we can cite the Grateful Dead's "Friend of the Devil" (1970) and Van Halen's "Running with the Devil" (1978). Furthermore, as Jagger notes, the entire heavy metal genre is indebted to the Devil and his imagery, as in Black Sabbath ("Black Sabbath"), Iron Maiden ("Number of the Beast"), Mötley Crüe ("Shout at the Devil"), and the innumerable metal bands in their wake. In essence, the mysterious, dark force of the Devil seems to be in league with the force of music itself, in that both can easily ignite our imagination and elicit strong emotions. Thus on this reading, the Stones are participating in a long-standing tradition of representing and interpreting the world from the demonic side, while at the same time opening the floodgates for a new variant of hard rock.

Further, a closer look inside the song's genesis reveals that there is much literary nuance embedded in the song. The circumstance for its composition also negates the view that the band was directly putting forth a specifically satanic message. Jagger modeled the lyrics on a satirical book he had just read on recommendation from Faithfull, *The Master and Margarita* by the Russian writer Mikhail Bulgakov (1891–1940), itself based on Gounod's operatic setting of Goethe's *Faust*.[10] The historical references in "Sympathy" cover much of the same terrain as the novel. Jagger has also stated that the song comes from his reading of Baudelaire (a few lines at least) and that he was writing in the open-ended poetic mode of a Bob Dylan lyric. For an example of a line from Baudelaire that resonates with "Sympathy," the poet meditates on where beauty comes from and musingly writes: "From Satan or God, what difference?"[11] In addition, another of the nineteenth-century poets that influenced Bulgakov was Mikhail Lermontov (1814–1841), who also struggled with the question of good versus evil. This equivocality of good versus evil sets up a similar motif to "Sympathy," as we shall see. Finally, Dylan's songs of this period often trot out a series of historical characters that can cluster around a moral topic—see, for instance, "Desolation Row" or "Sad-Eyed Lady of the Lowlands."

Yet what led perhaps to these contradictory readings of the song is that Jagger sings from the first-person point of view, with the Devil as the storyteller. Again, its literal interpretation seems to lead to charges of satanism. But another argument against this, beyond the commercial and literary ones, is the way art achieves its effect. Namely, the performing arts are able to work their magic because we as the audience suspend reality—for a moment, we believe that what we are experiencing through the artwork is "true" or reality. Thus although Jagger as the singer is proclaiming himself to be Lucifer, he is also role-playing, much as an actor does when he assumes a character. Through the lens of artistic presentation, we believe in him as such.

In this context we should mention that the filmmaker Kenneth Anger tried to enlist Jagger to portray Lucifer in his film *Lucifer Rising*. The film was not realized until 1972; the film starred Bobby Beausoleil, a member of the Charles Manson family who was convicted of murder; for more on Manson see the next chapter.[12] But Jagger did score another Anger short film of the time, *Invocation of My Demon Brother*, employing in his avant-garde scoring a Moog synthesizer and electronic effects including white noise.[13] Toward the end of *Invocation*, Jagger and Richards appear very briefly in a whirling montage of a satanic ritual; Anger takes the film clips from their Hyde Park, London, concert, July 1969.[14]

Finally, we can take note of what Richards has said about the song. For him, the song simply acknowledges the evil present in the world and that the demonic is a force that we must constantly confront. In other words, both good and evil in the world exist and what matters is how we choose to deal with it. Or put another way, the song uses the Devil to call attention to the persistence of evil in world events. Richards also sees the song as part of its own historical time of turmoil, coming off the revolutionary fervor that swept the world in spring 1968, culminating in the Paris student riots and the Soviet crackdown in Czechoslovakia in May 1968, and finally the assassination of Robert Kennedy that occurred while the song was being recorded. Indeed, the lyrics were adjusted to accommodate this last tragic event.

The song starts with the speaker introducing himself as a man of "wealth and taste," just as Professor Woland, as the Devil, appears in

Bulgakov's novel. Jagger states that his purpose is to steal a man's "soul and faith." He then affirms the historical existence of Jesus Christ, something that Woland also does in the novel against the Soviet atheists. Even Jesus had a moment of "doubt and pain," when the narrator insinuates that, for a brief moment, Jesus almost caved in to him. The song's next reference to Pontius Pilate also follows from the second chapter of the Bulgakov novel. For the chorus, the Devil wonders if you can guess his name, a question that becomes more emphatic as the song progresses.

From there, the song picks out dark world-historical events that imply radical evil—the assassination/murder of Czar Nicholas II and his family, the Nazi blitzkrieg, the Hundred Years' War, and the assassinations of the Kennedys. These events are the Devil's "game," yet for this last event, the Devil proposes that "we," too, are culpable. The only puzzling line in the song concerns the troubadours who are murdered before reaching Bombay. Some have said that this vague reference could be a metaphorical reference to the Beatles' sojourn to India. Whatever its actual meaning, this is the only "game" of the Devil that does not seem to refer to a definite historical event—perhaps Jagger was trying to introduce an element of ambiguity at this point in a song that devastates lyrically in its historical precision.

Next, in a reversal that jarringly takes leave of the historical narrative, the Devil states that cops are criminals, and that sinners are saints. The part about the police seems to be drawn from Jagger's libertarian perspective with his mistrust of institutional power. For the line about sinners as saints, there is precedence for this in Bulgakov's novel, where upon Pilate's questioning, Jesus says, "There are no evil people in the world."[15] But this idea, when held up against the earlier part of the song, presents a contradiction: Are we complicit in the world's evil, or free from it? The song leaves us hanging with this question of moral culpability, of good versus evil, and does not resolve the contradiction of whether we are guilty or free from sin.

After these reversals—"as head is tails"—the speaker reveals his name, Lucifer, for the first time in the song itself. Here it is worth digressing on the use of this word in the Bible and its tenuous, ambiguous relationship to other proper names, such as Satan and the Devil. The word "lucifer" in Latin literally means "bringing light" and was used to designate the morning star, or the planet Venus; significantly, it was not originally applied to Satan. The Hebrew word for "morning star" that was translated later as the Latin word "*lucifer*" (not yet a proper name) only appears in the Bible once, in a passage comparing the King of Babylon to the falling of the star (Isaiah 14:12). At a later time the word as a proper name was transposed onto Satan (with roots in the Old Testament; Satan has stronger ties to the New), a telling and incontrovertible hermeneutical error. Note that in the Abrahamic tradition, Satan or the Devil appears to originate as a fallen, rebellious angel. As with the word "lucifer," the Biblical exegesis of these words is also complicated and equivocal and also historically evolves and changes meaning. Thus whether Jagger intends to or not, the proper name "Lucifer" as a possible revealed name of the title's "Devil" further blurs the line separating light from dark, good from evil. Perhaps this idea is captured in the song's lyric—that if you call him "Lucifer," it will help to restrain him or limit his actions.

Coming back to the song proper, Lucifer then implores the listener for sympathy. One aspect of sympathy is having pity on or sorrow for someone's situation. Seemingly a simple trope, yet sympathy's literary, philosophical, and historical dimensions are quite massive. For the German poet, playwright, and theorist Gottfried Lessing, sympathy or compassion (*Mitleid*) is a key component of art, allowing us to experience the cleansing (catharsis) of tragedy. This asking for sympathy, in particular for the Devil and his evil works, furthermore, completes the reversal we analyzed earlier. Once again, the whole notion of sympathy for the Devil seeks to equivocate the root cause of evil in the world.

This section leads to the churning, turbulent final section of the song, a blues-styled outro that Jagger sings in a falsetto in a call-and-response patter with the lead guitar and chorus ("whoo whoo"; more on the outro below). Over the verse chords that morph into a vamp, Jagger-cum-Lucifer now takes on the role of seducer. He addresses his beloved as "baby," "honey," and "sweetie," as he teasingly implores, "what's my name?" But the question turns into a demand, as he wants her to acknowledge who his actually is, as if she has forgotten the earlier revelation that he is Lucifer.

Turning to the music, "Sympathy" marries an African groove and the blues. Although the blues has its spiritual roots in West Africa, it combines with its source groove in a propulsive, impetuous synergy that lifts the lyrical content song. Thus the idea of "supernatural blues" cited above—especially given the demonic lyrical content—is an apt description that could carry over here, as it captures the aesthetic orientation of this hybrid rhythm. Finally, it should be mentioned in this context that the Stones' various trips in Morocco would have exposed them to the complex and interwoven rhythms prevalent in the music making there (more on this when we discuss "Continental Drift" in the last chapter).

And, as noted above, the tempo at the song's inception was slow. The final BPM of the song is faster, though still slow compared to the typical rock song (ca. 117 versus the more typical 130 BPM; note that Traffic's "Dealer" is about 134 BPM, while Santana's "Soul Sacrifice" is about 130 BPM). The song does have a slight tempo increase, a common occurrence in songs that do not use a click track. Although Jagger had conceived it on the slower side, during the recording process he wanted to liven it up.

It would be this primal groove that sealed the song's reputation as demonically inspired. The groove does not follow a typical rock beat, but has an ancient, timeless quality to it—nicely matching the historical dimension of the lyrics. Jagger has described the groove of "Sympathy" as a samba. For example, at the July 5, 1969, Hyde Park concert, Jagger goes out of his way to introduce the song as such, where on this epoch day the band had a full African drum ensemble play the song with them. With its multi-layered, syncopated rhythm, whether or not it is samba (strictly speaking), the percussion section certainly evokes West African and Afro-Brazilian drum circles. Like the Raga Rock they had explored, this world-music element imparts to the song an exotic veneer. More specifically, Jagger thinks that white people associate this non-Western rhythmic style with the sinister. Here is the quote from his landmark 1995 interview with Jann Wenner published in *Rolling Stone*, where Jagger specifically addresses the song as such:

> Plus, the actual samba rhythm is a great one to sing on, but it's also got some other suggestions in it, an undercurrent of being primitive—because it is a primitive African, South American, Afro-whatever-you-call-that rhythm. So to white people, it has a very sinister thing about it.[16]

To animate the percussion section in this primitive direction, they brought on Dijon to play the congas. The rhythmic stratification can best be heard at the opening of the song—first Watts's drums and hi-hat, followed by Dijon's conga entrance, and finally the shaker of Wyman. When they added congas to the percussion section of the song, there was not much immediate precedence for it in a rock context other than Traffic's eponymous debut album (especially the song "Dealer"). In this regard it is perhaps no coincidence that Jimmy Miller was also the producer of Traffic. But the rhythm track for "Sympathy" goes beyond what Traffic was doing in featuring the percussion, insofar as it starts with the percussion, bringing it to the front of the mix where it sticks throughout the song. Also note that this was more than a full year before the Latin-rock explosion that Santana initiated with the conga-and-percussion introduction to "Soul Sacrifice" at Woodstock. On the Godard film there are some Middle Eastern and African drums that the band was experimenting with, no doubt from the band's trips to Morocco; it seems that Watts is utilizing one of these. The percussion introduction to the song is then made more primal when added to it are Jagger's screams and what sounds like electronically manipulated laughs (probably Pallenberg and Faithfull). Lastly, the percussion ensemble will play unabated, without rest or fills, for the rest of the song, similar to a ritualistic drum circle in Africa.

Despite its primal percussive attack, the Stones' arrangement is organized hierarchically, and the seemingly disparate musical elements coalesce into a cumulative unity. That is, over the percussion foundation, the band layers other sonic elements in a highly organized fashion, with a snowballing compulsion by the song's end. But what seems like an effortless arrangement was the result of trial and error. After much experimentation in the practices leading up to the song's recording, the instrumental accompaniment was reduced to a quite straightforward arrangement, which allows for the primacy of the groove and vocal part to come through.

The piano (Hopkins) and bass (Richards) begin with Jagger's vocal entry. Although Wyman had started off playing the bass for the song, in the practice sessions he was soon relieved. Apparently Richards had a different conception in mind and so he took over this part, and not for the first or last time on a Stones recording. Richards plays loudly in the mix, and his aggressive, anxious playing anticipates his later overdubbed guitar solo. He stabs at the instrument in a way that Wyman rarely does in this period, and his hard-picked articulation certainly gives the song its forward-moving power. In contrast to the syncopated percussion section, the piano and bass start by holding a single chord and note respectively on the downbeat of the measure. By starting in such a simple fashion, the verse's basic four-chord pattern is established at the rate of one chord per measure.[17] But this simple version lasts for only two lines; for the line "I was around when Jesus . . . " the bass starts its incessant cross-rhythmic dialogue with the percussion. This active and provocative bass line will carry for the rest of the song, and later on the piano will join in the rhythmic revelry.

The song's verse-chorus alternation conforms to the stylistic pattern of the blues. If the verse is constructed over a four-bar vamp on E played four times for a total of sixteen measures (plus an extra measure of E thrown in as a transition to the chorus), the chorus at "Pleased to meet you . . ." moves to the dominant chord of B, substituting for the typical blues turnaround of the V–IV. Instead of playing the turnaround once as is done in the twelve-bar blues, the melodic line of this chorus instead restates the dominant chord, and Jagger sings over it again ("But what's puzzling . . .").

Continuing to probe the idea of a multi-layered approach to the sound palette, at the song's third verse ("I watched with glee . . .") a chorus enters, singing a response of "whoo whoo" that overlaps with Jagger's part. Originally the "whoo whoo" idea came from the control booth from either Miller or Pallenberg; in either case it was on Miller's insistence that they ran with the idea that, along with the percussion, makes the song unique. Note that in Godard's film, Pallenberg and other women in the Stones entourage[18] (Faithfull), along with other band members and Glyn Johns, can be seen recording this backup vocal part in the studio. Yet it is not entirely clear if they actually present on the final mix of the song at Sunset Sound in Los Angeles, when the part may have been re-recorded with only band members.

In addition to the "whoo whoos," Richards's wailing guitar solo brings another singular sound and style that adds to the song's vitality. Played over the verse chords with the same measure count, his overdriven tone is blistering and bright, very different in tone and style than earlier or later solos he recorded. The solo adheres to the blues style of the song, with Richards carving out a series of licks based on a couple of different rhythmic motifs. Given the architectural unity of the solo, with descending licks answered by ascending ones organized into paragraphs, as it were, Richards also leaves rests (silences) in the solo, especially where the "whoo whoos" poke through. Indeed, the carefully wrought phrasing using only notes starting from the most classic of the blues scales—E-minor pentatonic (E, G, A, B, D)—compact in its efficiency is in the same league as the era's best single-line solos from blues artists such as Hubert Sumlin, Albert King, or Buddy Guy. The punched-out notes of the staccato attack build up very quickly and into the solo's highest range (in the fifteenth position, with the first finger starting on the fifteenth fret and with the highest note [B] on the seventeenth fret on the E string) when he cuts the solo short, abruptly, leaving the listener wanting more. He puts an exclamation mark on the solo with a strongly attacked and growling chord (B) on the downbeat of the chorus, with a descending glissando that elides with Jagger's reentrance.

Because in this single-line solo Richards seems so far from his stylistic element, there are rumors that it was actually Jimmy Page who played the solo. And there was some precedence—note that Page was one of the most in-demand session guitarists in the London studios, and he had played the guitar part on a demo of "Heart of Stone." However, in the Godard film, you can see the genesis of the solo in Richards's hands as he bursts out many of the iconic licks and pieces of the solo as he warms up. If anything, perhaps, there are some solos that Page did with the Yardbirds that could be seen to have influenced the staccato blues style of "Sympathy," especially "Happenings Ten Years Time Ago" (a single from 1966) and "Think about It" (released March 1968 as a B-side). Further, Richards plays the solo live on *Rock and Roll Circus*, though he only appears to go to the fifteenth position once and without as much fiery energy as the studio version, with the bulk of this filmed solo staying around the twelfth position licks of the studio version and then improvising around a couple of notes (E and D) in the much lower fifth position. The playing in the fifth position does not figure into his studio solo.

The guitar solo will return in the outro (starting at 4:30), answering Jagger's pleading to "get on down." Jagger complements the guitar interjections with some tasteful scatting. He then jumps into the falsetto range for his seductive calling out of "what's my name." Finally, this outro can be compared to the one from "Goin' Home." Recorded about three years apart, both outros share similar musical features with the main focus on expansion through improvisation, yet it is instructive to hear how much the stylistic purview of the Stones has changed in "Sympathy": from an R & B, rave-up style rooted in Southern soul, to a modern, edgy hard-rock one based on the Chicago electric blues.

ON GUITAR CHORDS, TIMBRE, TUNING, AND THE TONAL/MODAL UNITY OF *BEGGARS BANQUET*

Songs in the American and British vernacular tradition ranging from folk, country, R & B, and on through rock and roll tend to rely on chords that are easily fingered on a guitar. Thus, most songs in this tradition will contain chords that have open strings—especially the E, A, D, G chords, and to a lesser extent the B chord. Note that these chords correspond to the bottom (lowest) five notes of the open strings, respectively, of the guitar and are playable in first position. Furthermore, guitarists can easily play other chords in first position, such as the C chord, that relate to these chords and also have open strings.

Most songs have one chord in particular that is their home chord, usually where the song starts and ends. Referred to as the tonic, it is usually the place where the song feels at rest. Other chords wander away from the tonic, sometimes building tension as in the case of the dominant chord and to a lesser degree the subdominant (literally, the chord below the dominant), other times substituting a similar-sounding chord to the tonic or one of these. In most popular music, even blues, there are only a few chords for each song, usually the tonic, dominant, and subdominant, which clearly articulate the main structural points of the lyrics. Note that just knowing the six chords cited above, a guitarist is able to play in four different home keys the tonic, dominant, and subdominant; if a chord from outside of these three is used, it adds color to the progression.

For example, in "Sympathy," the verse employs a four-chord sequence or progression (E > D > A > E), while the chorus uses only two chords, centering on the dominant and its resolution back to the tonic (B–E). Thus, with the ability to play only four chords—E, D, A, and B—a player can make his or her way rudimentarily through the chord progression of the song. Finally, note that in traditional music theory, chords are represented by Roman numerals derived from their scale steps, counting E as one, hence the tonic becomes I, the subdominant,

IV (A is four steps up from E), and the dominant, V (B is five steps up from E). Understanding how the D chord fits into these chords is fascinating but requires more explanation, and we will return to this below. But again, it is not necessary that a vernacular or popular musician and/or songwriter grasp the functional reasoning behind these chord progressions. Thus it can be argued that there was an intuitive grasp of how these chords fit together in a tonal scheme by the great songwriters of '60s pop who were not trained—of course, British ones like Lennon/McCartney, Jagger/Richards, Ray Davies (the Kinks), and Pete Townshend (the Who) would be at the top of this list—based on their rudimentary understanding of guitar chords. Because the same chords form the basis of popular music, a collective grammar built up over time, where songs relied on the same arsenal of chords, and listeners and musicians came to have certain expectations about how a chord sequence should sound.

As can be gathered from this brief overview of the music theory behind popular songs, because you only need a few chords there is an amazingly fast learning curve to being able to perform as a rock guitarist. But with greater competition in the music industry as the '60s wore on, guitarists sought to push the envelope as it were, developing new ways of distinguishing their part from what everyone else was doing. Riff-centered rock was one way—for example, songs like "Day Tripper," "Pretty Woman," or the Stones' own "Satisfaction." Another was to incorporate different voicings of the chord. This was done by fingering the chords in different locations on the guitar neck and not in the usual first or open position of folk guitar. Indeed, rock guitarists tend to rely on barring the chords in the upper positions; that is, laying the first finger across all the strings and then fingering the upper chordal notes with the free fingers.

Still, what if fingering these same idiomatic chords limits one's musical imagination, especially if rock songwriting is so closely tied with the guitar? In other words, how could a guitarist reach beyond these standardized fingerings and create new sound worlds for the instrument? Around the time of *Beggars Banquet*, Richards had become bored with what he could do with the guitar and struggled to move beyond what had hardened into clichés in his technical approach. Perhaps this struggle was prefigured in his turn to songwriting from the piano that we saw earlier with songs like "Let's Spend the Night Together." Speculating, it seems that if he could not find a forward through this artistic impasse, the very success of his songwriting partnership with Jagger would be threatened, and in turn the continued relevance and even existence of the Rolling Stones.

Richards found two paths to move forward that reignited the Stones in the late 1960s, both of which would have long-range implications for the sound and musical identity of the Stones as they moved from the 1960s to the 1970s. The first was through timbre. As much musical exploration in the late 1960s began to rely increasingly on what could be done in the recording studio, Richards sought new possibilities for the tonal color of a guitar. He claims that he became obsessed with replicating a particular sound that he heard in his head, and on "Jumpin' Jack Flash" he figured out how to achieve it.

The second path was his discovery of the harmonic possibilities of open tunings. This provided a much-needed inspiration for both his songwriting and his guitar setup for live music making. Open tuning (a special type of scordatura) refers to a pitch deviation from the standard tuning of the guitar, or EADGBE (from the lowest to the highest strings; usually strings are numbered 6, 5, 4, 3, 2, 1), that results in a sounding chord. Common open tunings are in D, G, and E and using a capo can further modify each of these. Refer to table 3.1 for a summary of some common open tunings.

The beauty and economy of these open tunings is that they each produce a chord with only the open strings. To play another chord, all that is needed is to bar the strings across the same fret with the first finger. Richards relates that he knew about open tunings early on in his career, in particular Don Everly's use of them on "Wake Up Little Susie" (open G, with capo; more on this tuning below) and "Bye Bye Love" (also open G with capo).[19] Open tunings, and especially D and G

Table 3.1. Open Tunings for Guitar

Open tuning (= open strings sound a chord)	Strings (6, 5, 4, 3, 2, 1)	Example
E	E, B, E, G#, B, E	"Salt of the Earth"
E-flat	Eb, Bb, Eb, G, Bb, Eb	"Jumpin' Jack Flash"
D ("Vestapol")	D, A, D, F#, A, D	"Street Fighting Man"
G ("Spanish")	(D), G, D, G, B, D	"Honky Tonk Women"

for the Mississippi Delta tradition (open G is often referred to as "Spanish" tuning), had always been popular among slide guitarists (Brian Jones, for one), since, once again, the slide substitutes for the first finger bar chord and frees the other fingers to play upward chordal extensions.

Richards claims he had never seen open G until he met slide guitarist Ry Cooder. Note that this seems like a bit of selective memory on his part, especially given that Jones had played in open G for his slide guitar part on "Little Red Rooster," but he did record at a separate overdub session apart from the group.[20] According to Richards, Cooder was using open G for his slide work. Cooder was at the start of his career but he did have professional experience, having played with both Captain Beefheart and Taj Mahal. It might have been Nitzsche who brought Cooder to the attention of the Stones. Cooder went on to do some session work for the Stones in the late 1960s and the early 1970s, playing guitar for the *Performance* soundtrack as well as on *Let It Bleed* and *Sticky Fingers*. He also did an album (more of an outtake session) with the Stones (Jagger, Watts, and Wyman) sans Richards, released as *Jamming with Edward!*[21] Richards did not show up for some recording dates because of Cooder's presence; Cooder was there at the request of Miller to add to the guitar parts.

Besides "Little Red Rooster," alternate tunings were not standard fare for the early Stones. But there are other effective ways to change the guitar timbre. For example, they did experiment with lowered tunings, notably on "Tell Me," with its twelve-string acoustic tuned down a step and a half, or "Gotta Get Away," also with the guitars tuned down a half step.

Closely allied with alternate tunings in changing the timbre of the guitar is the application of the capo, a device that clamps onto the neck and fingerboard to shorten the string length. This adds more tension to the sound of the open strings, giving the guitar a brighter, punchier sound. A song that effectively uses the capo with a vibrato/reverb effect for a typically jangly '60s texture is the song "I'm Free," with its capo on the third fret of the rhythm guitar. (As an aside, when they brought back "I'm Free" as a live song for the 1969 comeback tour, they played it without the capo, transposing the song from its original C down to A.) The studio version of "Paint It Black" uses a twelve-string guitar that is capoed on the third fret for its distinctive sound; when they first played it live in the 1960s they also took it down without the capo that in turn changes the key. That is, "Paint It Black" was altered from the sounding F minor studio recording, which we analyzed in E minor in the previous chapter (following how Richards plays it now, with a capo on the second fret), to D minor live (without any capo). *Beggars Banquet* does not use the capo, although its associated single, "Jumpin' Jack Flash," does in its live version, namely at the fourth fret.[22] Finally, as we shall see in the next chapter, *Let It Bleed* is where the capo makes a pronounced entry into the Stones' music.

Significantly, beyond capo usage, open tunings were impacting the Stones' sound on *Beggars* for the first time. Richards reports that after *Satanic Majesties*, he had become bored with playing guitar. He was listening to a bunch of blues recordings from the 1920s and 1930s when he realized how many of these songs were in open tunings and it occurred to him to do the same. Once again as stated above, many of these songs used open tunings to facilitate the use of slide, which basically requires the open tunings so that chords could be fully voiced.

Perhaps the first open tuning Richards explored is the so-called Vestapol tuning. In this tuning, the guitar's strings are tuned to an open D chord (D, A, D, F-sharp, A, D), and historically it probably predates slide playing. Vestapol was a very common parlor guitar tuning during the nineteenth century; the name Vestapol comes from the title of a popular song called "The Siege of Sebastopol" that is played in open D, a reference to the Black Sea port fought over during the Crimean War. Vestapol tuning is related to open E, achieved easily by tuning all the strings up from D a whole step.

Now, *Beggars Banquet*'s focus on open tunings, especially open E, drives not only the sound of the album but its tonality. For the tonal unity of the album, refer to table 3.2.

Still, it is once again E—the key of "Satisfaction" and so many other Stones' classics—that signifies perhaps the most distinctive and prominent key for the early Stones, so it is no surprise to see the band working in this key. Indeed, four of the album's ten songs are in open E. Furthermore, "Jumpin' Jack Flash," once again the single that precedes the album, uses a guitar tuned in open E-flat, which is the same tuning relationship among the strings as E, just down a half-step. "Jumpin' Jack Flash" also utilizes another guitar in "Nashville" tuning (see the discussion of "Wild Horses" in chapter 5 for more on this tuning). It turns out

Table 3.2. Keys and Guitar Tunings of Songs from *Beggars Banquet*

Song	Key	Tuning
"Sympathy for the Devil"	E	standard
"No Expectations"	E	acoustic slide—open E
"Dear Doctor"	E	standard
"Parachute Woman"	E	standard
"Jigsaw Puzzle"	E	acoustic—standard electric—open E
"Street Fighting Man" (side 2)	C	open D
"Prodigal Son"	E	open E
"Stray Cat Blues"	D	open D
"Factory Girl"	D	standard
"Salt of the Earth"	E	open E

that more than half of the album's songs (a total of six) use open tunings. Finally, the B-side of "Jumpin' Jack," "Child of the Moon (rmk)" (started during the *Satanic Majesties* sessions but completed later) uses open D tuning. Interestingly, Richards does not yet use open G on *Beggars*. In chapter 5, we will see how open G will transform the Stones' sound and tonal direction in a radical way beginning with the album *Sticky Fingers* and will define Richards as a guitar player moving forward from there.

Perhaps because of this newfound fascination with open tunings, the tonal orientation of the album taken as a whole exhibits remarkable consistency and seems to be part of a master plan. For example, the five songs of side one form a suite in the key of E, as it were. Side two provides the tonal contrast, and with "Street Fighting Man" the band finally introduces a key change, to C. This song also ends in a different key than what it began in, with an outro in D. After a Delta blues cover song in E ("Prodigal Son"), the next songs take up the key of D, and the album finally concludes in E with the anthem "Salt of the Earth." Thus to characterize the larger tonal architecture of *Beggars Banquet*, the album moves from E to C to D and back to E, with that central brief, though significant, dalliance on C. Indeed it is quite a refreshing lift when listening to the album as a whole to hear the sparkle of the key change to C—even if listeners do not grasp the intellectual idea of what a key change is, they can feel the timbral change and pressure lifting of the song. In this fashion, too, the central tonality and shift from E in "Street Fighting Man" can be compared to the middle movement of a symphonic work, which often gives a contrasting key to the work's main one.

Summarizing, at the macro-level of tonality the album moves from E to D and back to E, again with C smack in the middle. Mirroring this at the local level is the actual progression of "Sympathy," where the first chord change of the verse (cited previously) is from E to D. The tonal relationship of E as a tonic chord and D is important for understanding the harmony of the Stones' music and 1960s pop generally (a good example would be the Beatles' "Norwegian Wood"), and here we will try to offer an explanation.

A LITTLE MUSIC THEORY: ON THE SIGNIFICANCE OF THE MIXOLYDIAN CHORD

In tonal music, there is a leading tone, a note that is a half-step lower than the tonic—in the key of E it would be a D-sharp. We hear the relationship of these two notes in the chord progression of the tonic (E) to the dominant (B), where the D-sharp note is a member of the B chord, pulling, as it were, toward the tonic note E, where it resolves or finds completion. Now, in folk, jazz, and other vernacular (i.e., non-classical or art) musics, the leading-tone note is often relaxed to the note a half-step below it, in this case D. This D could be analyzed in a couple of different ways. First, it could be seen as a modal note, that is, a note outside of the major scale that instead comes from a modal one. For example, in the case of E, the D could be part of the Mixolydian mode; that is, the seventh-scale degree of an E scale with a lowered leading tone. Note that the modal scales have ancient roots, predating the major-minor system by centuries (if not longer), and its use in religious and secular folk music never went away despite the triumph of the major-minor system in classical or art music. Second, another way of understanding this note is tonally, that is, to keep it within the major system. In the context of E, D is related to one of its subsidiary chords, the subdominant or A chord; D is the fourth scale degree of A.

Continuing, if the D is made into a chord where it is also the root or bottom note, then in the key of E, the D chord can be understood either modally or tonally. Using the Roman numeral analysis, D would be designated as bVII if Mixolydian, or a IV chord of the IV chord (represented with a forward slash, or IV/IV) if understood as a tonal relation of A. Thus, representing the chord progression of the verse of "Sympathy," E > D > A > E, we could have it as either I > bVII > IV > I, or as I > IV/IV > IV > I. The former or Mixolydian way is more elegant and relates to the minor-blues scale we mentioned above, where D is also the (lowered) seventh note. Further, the main problem with the IV/IV designation is that the latter IV chord, on A, becomes another tonic, which is surely not the way or how we experience this sequence of chords.

While we are on this progression and before turning to the rest of *Beggars*, let us mention the use of E > D > A in earlier Stones' songs leading up to "Sympathy." In "The Last Time," the only three chords used are E, D, and A, and the basic riff heard in the intro is layered over the E > D > A progression. In the riff itself, the most important note is D, which is the third note in the sequence. "Satisfaction" is another E > D > A sequence, and there the fifth and highest note of the riff, also the most important of the riff, is the note D. Further, other significant songs in the key of E that go to the D chord are "Get Off of My Cloud" and "19th Nervous Breakdown." "Get Off of My Cloud" uses the familiar I–IV–V–IV (E–A–B–A) chord progression as found in songs like "La Bamba" (original key of C) or "Wild Thing" (original key of A).[23] The D chord occurs during the chorus of "Get Off of My Cloud" on the line "Don't hang around."

Finally, the progression of "Jumpin' Jack Flash" is of particular interest in its use of the bVII idea. The intro plays with the three chords I, IV, and bVII, but instead of the I > bVII > IV idea of "Sympathy," the performers reverse the last two chords to get I > IV > bVII. The chords are B-flat > E-flat > A-flat in the studio version, using a guitar at the opening tuned to open E-flat; in concert Richards plays it a half-step up in key of B, using a guitar tuned to open G with a capo on the fourth fret, for a vastly different sound. This puts it in a more familiar, rock-and-roll key, where the intro and verse chords become B > A > E; as expected for the chorus at "all-right," on the "all," they shift to D (bIII). As a final thought, these chord areas of "Jumpin' Jack" and the other material are also the root notes of the minor pentatonic scale and thus can also be heard as stopping points of longer-range "mega-riffs," for lack of a better term.

UNPLUGGED: THE STONES' ACOUSTIC TURN

Since MTV's famous TV series blew up in the 1990s, the term "unplugged" has been used to refer to the relaxed, informal music making with primarily acoustic instruments (even if miked). Artists known for their hard-rock performance practice—from Aerosmith to Nirvana to Eric Clapton—forsook their signature electrified sounds and recast their songs in the perceived pure light of acoustic guitars. The reception was enthusiastic and positive, as listeners felt they were hearing the true emotions of the band and that the music was somehow more authentic without the alteration of the sound signal through effects, distortion, and the ever-higher wattages of modern amplifiers.

Though never marketed as such, the 1960s had its version of the unplugged movement. Side by side with the burgeoning electronica of psychedelic music, the folk atmosphere of acoustic music provided another contrasting outlet for expression. As Dylan was the primary inspiration behind much of the acoustic adaptation in rock/popular music, it was ironic that as acoustic instruments were making inroads in rock he was switching to electric instrumentation in 1965, at the precise moment of his greatest influence on pop music. But his move to front a Chicago-style, electric blues band reflected the trendiness of the contemporaneous folk-rock movement, with groups like the Byrds and the Animals scoring major hits playing acoustic music with electric instruments.

In any case, prominent rock groups like the Beatles, Stones, and even the up-and-coming Pink Floyd were already incorporating acoustic sounds in their music, whether as a layered texture or as the primary sound, and showing a willingness to release pure acoustic, unplugged music in much the same way the singer-songwriters both then and later did, and certainly anticipating the acoustic prominence in groups like Crosby, Stills & Nash; the Grateful Dead; or Led Zeppelin. On *Aftermath* alone, the Stones already had four songs effectively making use of the "unplugged" acoustic style, as it were, namely "Lady Jane," "High and Dry," "Take It or Leave It," and "I Am Waiting" (this last with its harpsichord reminiscent of "Play with Fire"); note, too, that plenty of other early songs by the Stones had acoustic guitars in the mix (especially "Little Red Rooster" and "Not Fade Away," as we have already seen). But *Beggars* took this to a new level. So dissatisfied with the chaotic studio manipulation of the source signals on *Satanic Majesties*, the Stones retreated from the wide-open palette choices of erratic psychedelic display with its swirling admixture of instruments and emphasis on electronic effects, as Richards and Jagger pushed the Stones in the direction of simpler, layered acoustic textures with Mississippi Delta roots. In *Life*, Richards maintains that live in concert, the Stones of course are a rock and roll band, but in the studio, as albums like *Beggars Banquet* shows, they were anything but:

> You can't say apart from "Sympathy" or "Street Fighting Man" that there's rock and roll on *Beggars Banquet*. "Stray Cat" is a bit of funk, but the rest of them are folk songs [. . . .] And also it [the slow, acoustic songs] made the up-tempo numbers stand out even more, against a lovely bedrock of really great little songs like "No Expectations." I mean, the body of work was not to smash you between the eyes. This was not heavy metal. This was music.[24]

But in making and recording these new folk songs, still the band did not work like folk artists and brought to bear on these songs their prior experiences in the studio. Even if the thick, distorted sound of Chicago blues remained their goal when making rock, what they learned in the making of *Satanic Majesties* did change their concept of what was possible in terms of creating new sounds. Finally, although Richards now hears "Sympathy" as a rock song, this was an arrangement it took on very late in its genesis; note that if "Sympathy" had stayed in its original conception, the entire first side of *Beggars* would have been acoustic.

The album's second song, "No Expectations," is a personal favorite of Jagger, in part because it is the last song that Jones contributed to in a significant way. Through the years the song has not been played live very much; when they played it live (with electric guitars) for the first time at the Hyde Park memorial concert for Brian in 1969, also known as "Stones in the Park," it was as a tribute to Jones. The song's intro features Jones on slide guitar playing the song's melody, finishing with upward five-note chordal flourishes that take advantage of the E open tuning. Furthermore, the flourishes add emphasis to the chord change we analyzed above in "Sympathy." The flourish begins on the upbeat leading to the chords that have asterisks, from E > D* > A* > E*. Coloring the song's languid melancholy is the use of the A major-seventh chord at the start of the verse; this can be heard at "take me to . . ." That is, the addition of the major-seventh note gives the chord progression a jazzy flavor, but to pop listeners from the 1960s, the major-seventh sound would be recognizable from another melancholy song about heartbreak by Gerry and the Pacemakers, "Don't Let the Sun Catch You Crying" (1964). Further, the "No Expectations" scene of the ending of a love affair, along with its reference to a train and station, anticipates the poetic conceit and lyrical content of the Robert Johnson cover they did the following year, "Love in Vain."

The next three songs are highly stylized; that is, they take their musical cues from clichés and codes shared with other genres. "Dear Doctor" parodies a country waltz with its story of a wedding day gone wrong told in Jagger's imitative drawl of a poor white Southerner. Giving the song its jangly ring is Nicky Hopkins on a tack piano. Tack piano is a type of prepared piano where tacks or small nails are inserted into the felt hammers, giving the timbre a metallic edge. These types of pianos were used to play ragtime-styled pieces in the honky tonks of the South and also appear in Hollywood Westerns in saloon scenes featuring beaten-up and old upright pianos. The tack piano will return on "Wild Horses," another song evocative of the old Southern milieu. In the same year and months after the "Dear Doctor," the Beatles recorded the honky-tonk infused "Rocky Raccoon" with a tack piano solo performed by producer George Martin.[25]

Harmonically, "Dear Doctor" presents the by-now familiar E–D–A chord sequence within the verse, over the lines "Can't you please tear it . . ." But the song would have been too monotonous to keep to the key of E, especially with the repetitive waltz rhythm they set up. So, after a brief acoustic guitar solo that has an idiomatic, ascending blues riff in triplets leading to an E7 chord, they use that E7 chord to pivot to the new key of A. After the chorus in A, the new key can be recognized when Jagger sings the third ("I was tremblin'. . .") and fourth ("Darlin', I'm sorry . . .") verses. In the fourth verse Jagger uses a falsetto voice to assume the character of the woman who is leaving him on his wedding day. To end the song, the guitar plays the ascending riff, but now transposed up to A. Dave Mason added guitar on this track, so it is not clear who is playing these blues riff interludes, but it is most likely Richards.

The next song is a driving twelve-bar blues song, "Parachute Woman," again paying homage to the boisterous, braggadocio lyrics of one of the Stones' heroes, Muddy Waters. Seemingly fixated on the relationship of E and D, the intro plays off of these two chords, with D on the upbeat leading to E, which they will also use in the verse. With its much harder, edgier sound, "Parachute Woman" owes its unique timbre to how the backing (rhythm) tracks were recorded, which we will discuss below with "Street Fighting Man." A sullied acoustic guitar (perhaps) solo line imparts a dirtier blues overlay to the verses, as does the powerful harp-led outro (ca. 2:20; it is not clear if it is Jones or Jagger playing this, probably the latter).

Finally, closing side one is "Jigsaw Puzzle" (spelled on the album as "Jig-Saw Puzzle"), a song written by Jagger that pays homage to Dylan. The singer trots out a series of characters before turning to the depiction of the band members; for example, playing off their outlaw/rebel image (the word "outlaw" describes the gangster of verse two), the "damaged" guitarists have been "outcasts" their whole lives. The last verse inexplicably finds grandmothers protesting their pension payments, with the Queen offering her blessings. Jagger refuses to complete the puzzle, and his passive withdrawal in the chorus seems postmodern in his refusal to tie the various tableaux into a narrative.

The verses' music loops four chords at the rate of one per measure in a predictably patterned way that Dylan does in countless similar songs like "Desolation Row." The third chord (an F#7, heard over the line "tryin' to waste his time") is outside of the key of E, adding coloristic relief to what would have been a mundane sequence of chords. Wyman performs one of his best bass lines to date, an active part that he develops with bits of the song's melody through the long six-minute song. Not often noticed are remnants of sonic fragments from psychedelia, overlaid on the otherwise traditional acoustic guitar and piano playing (Hopkins). Jones (most likely) plays on the Mellotron, accompanying a wild and at times erratic slide guitar part, apparently played by Richards.[26] There is a solo section at about two minutes into the song, where the two parts play in tandem a line that is timbrally reminiscent of their space music on *Satanic Majesties*. Many outtakes of this song survive, which show that the song was worked up quite deliberately and is sonically in no way as straightforward as any Dylan song from this time.[27]

LISTENING VIGNETTE: "STREET FIGHTING MAN"

From the rebellious stance of the blues ("Satisfaction"), to an exotic pop-art dirge ("Paint It Black"), to a psychedelic depiction of space travel ("2000 Light Years from Home"), the Stones now expand their lyrical range to violent revolution in "Street Fighting Man," the lead single from the *Beggars Banquet* album. Despite its censorship and limited airplay, "Street Fighting Man" transformed the Stones' image yet again. They, along with their audience, were now fully grown up and participants in the protest politics of the day. Although other songs on *Beggars* do not engage with the political per se as much as this song, the idea of resistance to authority proclaimed in the title of "Street Fighting Man" effectively colors the whole album. Ironically, "Street Fighting Man" is an equivocal political statement and does not seem to make a clear argument for social action one way or another (more on this below).

When they decided to return to their musical roots on *Beggars*, Richards was searching for an earthier sonic direction as he heard it on old blues records. The solution they came to was unique for the time, combining lo-fi and hi-fi recording techniques, acoustic and electronic effects, and multi-tracked layers of various instruments for texture. The lo-fi part was the most intriguing as they recorded guitars and other instruments (sitars, etc.) into Richards's portable cassette player, which were then played through an amplifier and rerecorded back using another microphone onto a professional multi-track tape machine in the studio.

Although allegedly recorded only on acoustic guitars though with electric bass, the three songs "Street Fighting Man," "Jumpin' Jack Flash," and "Parachute Woman" all took advantage of this unorthodox recording method to achieve their knife-edged soundscapes. Along with the open tunings, this new way of recording would open up for the Stones the possibility of moving forward to realize a paradoxically simple yet complex sonic carpet for the blues-rock music they were developing. Restated, their conscious return to the musical simplicity, authenticity, and directness of the blues style was matched by a novel recording technique Richards had hit upon specifically to capture the halo of raunchy blues purity.

Showing continuity with *Satanic Majesties*, the layered recording process for "Street Fighting Man" shares much in common with the psychedelic music they were trying to leave behind. It appears to be the first song to use the cassette-recorder method mentioned above with respect to "Jumpin' Jack Flash," with Richards playing acoustic guitar and Watts playing on a 1930s practice drum kit, a very small, portable contraption often used by jazz drummers for live gigs precisely because of its ease in carrying it. The lo-fi tracks recorded on a portable Philips player were then remixed into the final studio (hi-fi) tracks.

Richards first wrote the music for "Street Fighting Man," and the song was recorded in February and then in March with very different lyrics as "Pay Your Dues" (its working title was "Primo Grande"). Despite wanting a more simplified sound, the original backing tracks have piano, sitar, shehnai (a Persian or Indian double-reed oboe), and viola on them; although the viola does not seem to be present on the final mixes of the finished song, the other instruments could still be heard along with the tambura (added by Jones; it is a plucked stringed folk instrument from Southeast Europe). Richards has said that there are many instruments on the backing tracks playing along with the guitar; their goal was to create an "eerie" space. He no longer knows what is on the track, maintaining that what remains on the track might be likened to "fairy dust."[28] The exotic instruments can be heard especially at the chorus when the sitar breaks through and with the other instruments in what is in fact an exposition of psychedelic music for the outro jam.

The final lyrics grew out of the growing social unrest of the spring of 1968. On March 17 there was a large anti-war protest in London that started in Trafalgar Square and ended violently in Grosvenor Square, the location of the American Embassy. Opposed to the war, Jagger was there to show his support for the anti-war protest, though he apparently left before any real violence occurred. But the protests left a mark on him personally, and he sang about them in his lyrics for "Street Fighting Man" and "You Can't Always Get What You Want."

The band finished recording "Street Fighting Man" in the middle of May, at a time when what began as student riots in Paris nearly became an actual revolution. But they did not release the song until September after the Beatles released "Revolution," a very different perspective on the same turbulent events. Once again, the close proximity of similar material caused comparisons between the two bands to be drawn. This time the Stones came out on top and were seen as representing societal change and revolution, while the Beatles disappointed with their cautious stepping back from recent events and condemnation of violent revolution.

Yet as has been pointed out, the lyrics for "Street Fighting Man" did not really advocate or support street fighting and violent revolution per se; the singer does not see a clear path forward. Retreating from the revolutionary demands, at the end of each verse Jagger reiterates that all he can do is to continue to create, to sing in his rock and roll band. For this he blames his environment, citing London as a dull, conservative place ("sleepy") where the new ideas will not find traction. In a final plea Jagger injects himself into the scene as the personification of "Disturbance." This role-playing is similar to the change of perspective to first person in his embracing of the name Lucifer, as we have discussed earlier in "Sympathy." But it does not work, for even as Disturbance threatens to kill the king, who can be interpreted as a metaphor for the Establishment, the complacent reality of London reasserts itself in the end.

When released as a U.S. single in August 1968, "Street Fighting Man" was well received by the Left and was feared for advocating a perceived radical position by the authorities. In the run-up to the Democratic convention in Chicago in the fall, the authorities banned the song there and subsequently in other cities, further burnishing the band's reputation as challengers to the status quo. The original record sleeve showed riot scenes depicting police brutality; with only a few printed, the sleeve was quickly pulled by Decca and is now a collector's item.

You are a twenty-year-old male student at Northwestern University in Chicago, studying political science, and you hope to be a writer someday. You are not as radical as some students you know, but you do not support the Vietnam War. You had applied for draft deferment as a conscientious objector and amazingly received it; you consider yourself fortunate. To fit in with your friends and other students, you try to dress in the hippie fashions of the day. You have not had a haircut for a few months and have dabbled in smoking pot, which seems to be everywhere you go. Musically you listen to mostly rock and a little bit of jazz. Growing up you experienced the British Invasion and loved both the Stones and the Beatles. Lately you were particularly drawn to "Jumpin' Jack Flash," which had become your favorite song over the summer. There was an emotional undercurrent of anger in the song's performance that seemed to reflect the times well; the assassination of Robert F. Kennedy in June has shaken some of your faith in the immediate prospects for a more peaceful, prosperous America. Race riots are still a common threat to civil order, even with the movement in disarray with the assassination of Martin Luther King Jr. in April.

At the local record store you learn that the Stones have just released a new single, "Street Fighting Man" (with "No Expectations" as the B-side). You buy it on the spot, along with the competing record by the Beatles, "Hey Jude" with "Revolution" as its respective B-side. Listening to these records gives you sense of freedom, and you realize how blessed your generation is to have been granted this great music. But not only that, the lyrics of the songs challenge you to think about the events of the year, especially the (Chicago) race riots after the death of Dr. King back in April that you witnessed firsthand. Being from a small town in the upper Midwest, this had been your first real encounter with societal and street violence. It seems that over the last few years large protests are a fact of American life. You have come to think that the country is on the brink of revolution itself, which has become a hot topic on your college campus.

So the new songs by the Beatles and Stones get you thinking once again . . . can violent revolution ever be justified? Or should we turn inward and "free our minds instead" as Lennon pleads? And Jagger's portrayal of the "street fighting man" haunts your mind—is this the best way to change the world? And most challenging for you is the idea of the end of capitalism—what system will come to replace it, and will it be better? One thing you know for sure is that coming of age in these morally fraught times will inform your perspective as a writer.

By the late 1960s, rock music enjoyed tremendous topical and cultural prestige among the youth. The songs and bands could initiate conversations, as young people grappled with the escalating violence both domestically and internationally. Both "Revolution" and "Street Fighting Man" addressed the burning issue of their day of how far to take the protests that were calling for deep institutional change generally and an end to the Vietnam War specifically. Coming off his meditation studies in India, Lennon is clear that he will not support change through violence, but rather through the peaceful transformation of the mind. Yet Lennon's music for the single version of "Revolution" is anything but peaceful. Initiated by a Chuck Berry–stylized guitar intro followed by an overdubbed scream of McCartney, the groove and accompaniment to "Revolution" is loose and sprawling, with the two overdriven guitars (run directly into the board—i.e., without amplifiers) creating a swirling, almost mad scene. Lennon assumes the voice of a teacher as he instructs his audience on why he thinks the revolution will not affect the right kind of change.

By contrast, "Street Fighting Man" assumes a different strategy in its approach to the ideology behind the violence. As stated above, the original musical accompaniment actually was paired with a very different lyrical conception, which can be heard in the outtake "Pay Your Dues."[29] It is not entirely clear what this rather enigmatic song is about, but it evokes tribalism, taboos, and the idea of paying tribute. Jagger does seem to hint at the insidious havoc wrecked by disorder and dishonesty on the world. Whatever the interpretation of these equivocal lines may turn out to be, they are still a completely different thematic conception from the topic of the final song. From this it follows that the music does not speak to revolution per se, having been conceived without a lyrical theme. But it is fascinating how once the new lyrics are grafted onto the song, the music's semantic content changes. At once the music itself becomes a clarion call for revolution, tone painting a scene of violence, street fighting, and social disruption. As we shall soon see, this is in marked contrast to their music moving forward, which does not revisit this topic. In this respect, Jagger has often been criticized for opportunism, tapping into the generational zeitgeist to sell more records—in the late 1960s, social unrest, and in the 1970s, hedonistic escapism. But for the young listeners of the era, most of them were sold on the sincerity of Jagger's lyrical expression.

And the music does represent the topic of revolution quite well, despite its not having been intended as such. Indeed the taut acoustic strumming and overdubbed, pounding drums at the opening have an unyielding quality that bristles with the ferocious insistence of a street march. The tight guitar sound comes from the high barring on the guitar (at the tenth fret, producing a C chord in the open D tuning). At the end of each verse and chorus, on the word "man" in "street fighting man," they play a D chord, over which Richards layers a descending minor-pentatonic bass riff (as on "Sympathy," Richards plays bass again on this song) that is one of the main signatures of the song, before and after Jagger says "No." D is not part of the key of C, and yet from D they abruptly move back to C, without preparation. In the outro, a compressed version of the chord progression unfolds as the song fades out on D, with a shehnai solo (the Persian double-reed instrument played by Dave Mason) over a layered psychedelic carpet of sound.

In live concert the Stones relax this tension and transpose it down to B major (down a half step), with Richards using five-string open G tuning and a capo at the fourth fret (the opening strings will now produce a B chord; again this is the same tuning setup as "Jumpin' Jack Flash"). For live music, this performance practice is one of Richards's preferred setups. And when they play "Street Fighting Man" in concert, the guitarists use a distorted effect, which more than compensates for the lowered key and tuning, as can be heard in the November 1969 Madison Square Garden live version released on *'Get Yer Ya-Ya's Out!'* For the outro, they jam in C-sharp (a half-step down from D), but then return to the tonic of B for the close (again they do not return to the tonic).

The Left's embrace of the song seems not to have been too bothered by Jagger's insistence that all that he can do is to sing in the band; it was enough that he played the dark force of Disturbance who wants to kill the king—or once again, end the current status quo. It also helped the band's credibility that Jagger sent the lyrics to Tariq Ali, the activist/revolutionary who apparently inspired the song and who repaid the favor by publishing the lyrics in his leftist journal just before the album's release in December.

ROUNDING OUT *BEGGARS BANQUET*

As if to counterbalance the demonic force of "Sympathy," "Prodigal Son" tells the parable of redemption from the Gospel of Luke. Robert Wilkins wrote the song and the Stones follow his version faithfully; the song as such first appeared on Wilkins's 1964 album, *Memphis Gospel Singer* (Piedmont Records).[30] Wilkins was from outside of Memphis and played in the same Mississippi Delta blues tradition as the better-known Son House and Robert Johnson. Further, Wilkins originally wrote the song with a different set of lyrics. Recorded in 1929, "That's No Way to Get Along" was about another "poor son" who was returning home after his mistreatment by "low-down women." He tells his friends to inform his mama that he is coming back home. Later on Wilkins found religion and became a preacher, hence the rewrite of the lyrics, which keeps the same concept of returning home after doing something wrong ("that's no way to get along"), though this time to the father (i.e., God). And as noted by Wyman, another fascinating connection between the Stones and Wilkins is that Wilkins appears to be the first to record the song "Rolling Stone" in 1928, over two decades before Waters's version for which the Stones got their name.[31]

"Prodigal Son" marks the return of the Stones to doing cover songs, their first released one since 1965 and first traditional blues since "Little Red Rooster." In reaching back to the 1920s, the song can be interpreted as a manifesto of their embrace of the blues at its source. On the Stones' version, according to Wyman, Cooder joins on guitar with Richards, possibly his first appearance with the Stones on record.[32] Cooder first officially receives credits for his work on *Let It Bleed* (or at least some of it), but he was present at some of the *Beggars* recording sessions, despite not receiving any album credits. Note that in the 1960s it was standard practice to not include all the session musicians in the recording credits. Indeed, as with many of the Stones' recordings from this period, it is not always clear who is playing what on a given track; although Jagger is emphatic that it is Jones playing slide on "No Expectations" (and most seem to think so), still some have felt that it is Cooder's take on the album, and it is at least possible that it is his playing.[33] And as we shall discuss in the next chapter, Richards may have learned more from Cooder than he lets on in his autobiographical *Life*.

"Stray Cat Blues" is the most forceful song on the album and breaks with the acoustic domination of the collection. Musically tying in with the subject matter of an underage groupie, the song oozes with seediness, especially in the vocal style. Jagger has said that his prime influence was Velvet Underground's "Heroin"; comparing the intros to both songs, the similarity can be heard (although "Heroin" starts on the tonic in a different key, D-flat, the result of having the instruments in lowered tuning, while the Stones start on the dominant seventh chord of D, or A7). Beyond Jagger's snarling vocals on "Stray Cat," it is the raunchy sound of the electric guitar in open D tuning that determines the transgressiveness of the song and how it plays the two-bar progression that repeats throughout the verse. With its inevitable, cyclical repetition, the verse progression effectively tells the tale of the groupie and her coming seduction. The scene intensifies in sordidness when Jagger finds out she has a friend.

The progression can be reduced to the same as in "Sympathy," now in the key of D. And yet the difference is in how this progression is voiced. The bass line, again played by Richards, descends in "Sympathy." In "Stray Cat," the line rises and then falls, from open D to the tenth fret (C chord) back down to fifth fret (G chord). Often with a big leap such as this, going from open position to the tenth fret, a player will fill it in with a passing or intermediary chord. Richards does this, playing the F chord (on the third fret), on the way up to C and on the way back to D (down from G).

The elegance of this progression with its passing chords over the open D tuning can be designated by the frets of the sequence: 0–(3)–10–5–(3) (back to 0 where it starts over again), which represent the chords D–(F)–C–G–(F). Note that to play a given chord, the player bars the first finger (index) on the given fret, while the open strings sound the notes of the D chord (i.e., the major triad). Thus even though it is basically the same progression as "Sympathy," with the voicing the resultant sound is totally heterogeneous. Each chord is symmetrically voiced—we feel the same vertical ordering of notes from low to high. Finally, in standard tuning on the guitar, the awkwardness of voicing of this exact progression becomes apparent when we watch Richards play it as such at the 1969 Hyde Park concert. Jagger seems thrown off by the thinness of the sound, with Richards forming standard chord positions in the upper-part of the guitar neck. Fingered in this way the song's progression becomes finicky, especially as the passing chord F becomes an awkward stop on the way and not something filling in the leaps. In other words, in standard tuning the progression loses that effortless rise-and-fall and the parallel, symmetrical force of the open tuning. They did their best to correct this during the 1969 American tour where Richards plays it in open position and leaves out the first F chord—the result is surprisingly close to the 1970s Lynyrd Skynyrd classic "Sweet Home Alabama," another D > C > G song (I > bVII > IV).

Just as "Heroin" dealt with a taboo subject, "Stray Cat" crosses the line into a morally conflicted subject matter. Of course, when read within the larger context of blues and rock history, drugs and underage girls have always been a part of it, not to mention contemporary literature, with Nabokov and his popular *Lolita* tackling the subject of pedophilia head on. Now, the Stones were certainly out to shock, in order to keep current their rebel/pariah status—they were not about to let "petty morals" bog them down. And the topic of underage girls would continue to be exploited in rock music from the '70s on, as a quick search of songs on the Internet using the term "jailbait" reveals—the Police's Nabokov-inspired "Don't Stand So Close to Me" among the most suggestive. In concert, Jagger would often change the age of the girl from the studio version of fifteen (a full year under the British age of consent at sixteen—note that the Beatles' own "I Saw Her Standing There" from a few years earlier has a girl of seventeen) to thirteen, as can be heard on the version on *'Get Yer Ya-Ya's Out!'* Yet in the 2003 version (the last time it was played live), they upped the girl's age to sixteen, as can be heard on the official release on YouTube. Here we are left to ponder why—was this because of the constant downbeat of feminist criticism? Or would the sight of a sixty-year-old man singing about a young girl be too morally disgusting in a time when pedophilia scandals, from priests to noted public figures, seem an omnipresent and depressing part of the news cycle? It is one thing for a twenty-five-year old to sing about fifteen-year-old groupies, especially in the permissive late 1960s era, but wholly another matter for a sixty-year-old to do so today. The times changed, and even if the song was originally meant to be an ironic take on the groupie situation or an updating of an old blues trope, the topic of "Stray Cat Blues" with its implied statutory rape is no longer welcome in our politically correct climate.

And the album's last two songs also can invite controversy. "Factory Girl" picks up the theme of social commentary on the plight of the working class, where "Back Street Girl" trails off. The image of this hard-working girl is none too flattering and suggests the band was dismissive of the lower classes. The lyrics were written too quickly in the studio and do not go beyond the description of the girl with her curlers, fat knees, and broken zipper on the back of her stained dress. At least in this song the narrator seems to be of the same social circumstances, unlike “Back Street Girl.” In keeping with the timbral dimensions of the unplugged aesthetic, the song features some traditional acoustic instruments, just as “Back Street Girl” does. And it is actually an interesting array of instruments, which includes fiddle (Ric Grech), mandolin (Dave Mason), conga (Dijon), and Watts playing tabla (classical Indian drums), but with sticks instead of his hands.

“Salt of the Earth” concludes the album in a grand, majestic way. The title comes from Jesus’s Sermon on the Mount (Matthew 5:13), where he refers to his disciples as the “salt of the earth” that must remain so if they are not to be “trampled underfoot.” The expression “salt of the earth” has come to refer to the everyday, unpretentious, common person, a kind of noble savage, as it were, of the working-class world. The Stones in part appear to intend the song, with its sing-a-long style anthem, as a thank-you and tribute to the people who have bought their records and made their career and lifestyle possible. And the religious allusion of the line remains present, as in the expression “say a prayer for.”

Yet the song is also not without controversy. After Richards sings the first verse, Jagger takes over, and sings a bridge that might call into question his sincerity—he sees “a faceless crowd” that doesn’t look “real to me.” Adding to the gloominess of this part is the use of the minor key, with its traditional association of melancholy or, here, despair. But still, it is not clear exactly what is intended with the bridge. Is this distancing critique, or something to be overcome in the pledge to drink to the working class? In the fourth verse Jagger sings about “gray-suited grafters” who are locked into an unscrupulous life, forced to choose between two terrible options, “cancer or polio.” But all this is smoothed over, with its majestic, if extraneous, chorus at the end. That is, when they did the final mixes for the album in July at Sunset Studios in Los Angeles, they added an overdub of the Watts Street Gospel Choir. The choir is most effective in the outro vamp. The outro signals the band’s return to their familiar R & B style, with its typical two-chord vamp on E7 to A that goes to double time.

Furthermore, “Salt of the Earth” marks another very rare instance where the band had to change a word for a particular live performance. In Richards’s first verse he sings, “Raise your glass to the good and the evil.” The word in question is the “and,” which means we are saluting the evil. This brings back the full sentiment of "Sympathy"—that there is good and evil in the world, and that sometimes we must acknowledge both of their influences over our lives. On a studio album, it is one thing to say what you want, but in a live performance matters are perceived differently—take the example of "Let's Spend the Night Together." After Ed Sullivan's censorship of their song "Let's Spend the Night Together" where they were forced to changed "night" to "time," the Stones vowed to never change their lyrics again. But sometimes, political circumstances intervene and do dictate a change. When Jagger and Richards (not backed by the other band members) performed it at the Concert for New York, a benefit for the families of the September 11 terrorist attacks, the "and" took on another significance. With so much national and audience anger and outrage directed at Osama bin Laden and al-Qaeda, it would have been a difficult line to swallow especially for those in the audience grieving for relatives and friends who died in the attacks. Richards wisely changed the line for the occasion to "good *not* the evil," where he made a gesture on the "not" to reinforce the fact that he had changed it; a populist touch that respected the solemnity of the occasion but at the same time destroyed the song's moral ambivalence and its original intention. Despite this populism, the song has hardly been performed live in concert, and this was a rare instance for it to be played; when they did perform it again in 2003 (the last time they have), the "and" returned, though quite garbled on the recording.[34]

CONCLUSION

Beggars Banquet transformed the Stones from an R & B/pop band into a full-fledged rock phenomenon. Wyman observes that 1967 was the watershed year dividing pop from rock, where the latter took its cues from a "virtuoso musicianship" instead of singles.[35] The Jimi Hendrix Experience and Cream were the new bands at the top of the rock scene at this time (though both groups would prove short-lived). But the Stones managed to bridge the pop and rock camps and still focused on putting out high-quality and craftsman-shaped singles in the coming years, their most highly regarded rock period, while satisfying the rock audience's demand for the longer-range listening experience of the album.

Relying on the same types of chord progressions and ones related to the blues, the Stones now expose the fantastic possibilities of the inherent riffs and guitar voicings that could be derived from these simple progressions. And of course, as we have seen, this sonic tendency lurking in the material is made possible by the open tunings that reawakened Richards's guitaristic imagination. Further, these open tunings would finally give him his identity as a guitarist straddling the traditional roles of lead versus rhythm player. He would now assume both roles at the same time, with a weaving style very different from another player like Hendrix, who had accomplished the same feat by different means.

Beggars Banquet also represents Jagger's leap as a songwriter, as he now handled wide-ranging, richer, and more complex topics. History, theology, revolution, and the working class were all fair game; yet he still probed the pain of heartbreak and took macho, posturing stands, with a sincerity tempered with irony and parody.

With all of these elements in place, and with the coming demise and weakening of the Beatles, the Stones were finally ready to assume their place in popular music history as the "world's greatest rock and roll band," as it were. At the very least, this would be their marketing for their tour supporting next year's record, *Let It Bleed*, to which we now turn.

4

"THIS RECORD SHOULD BE PLAYED LOUD"

Let It Bleed (1969)

As the 1960s were winding to a close, the Stones capitalized on the perceived turnaround they instigated with *Beggars Banquet.* The album's momentum gave them a renewed creative focus that they would in turn ride to the top of the music business. Probably the height of the Stones' generational influence came in 1969, as their musical vision addressed the times and they undertook an American tour that reestablished their live performance prowess and outlaw status. Two 1969 songs in particular burnished their rebel image: the anti-war "Gimme Shelter" and the incomparable song about a sadistic, murderous rapist, "Midnight Rambler."

Significantly, 1969 also represents the first watershed in the band's history. They had their first personnel change and experienced their first real tragedy as a band. Their founding member, Brian Jones, was found dead in his swimming pool after he was let go by the band two weeks prior. His replacement, the twenty-year-old Mick Taylor of John Mayall's Bluesbreakers, was quickly assimilated to the group. He underwent a trial by fire, as it were, contributing an overdubbed guitar part to their last number-one single in both England and the United States, "Honky Tonk Women," within days of joining the group. Taylor then played with the Stones at their free Hyde Park concert on July 5.

This was the Stones' first real public concert since their 1967 European tour, and it became an emotional memorial and tribute to Jones.

As they geared up to tour America as the "world's greatest rock band," they realized that they were stepping onto an entirely different continent than when they had last toured there in 1966. Their original audience of innocent screaming kids had morphed into older teenagers and college-age young adults. With drug use rampant and the hippie lifestyle now common, many of these young adults were also politically engaged, challenging institutions with their rage over the Vietnam War. Jagger echoed their feelings by wearing an anti-war omega shirt for the 1969 U.S. tour. Further, many viewed music as the social conscience of the day, as a force that could change the world—the belief that music underpinned social change perhaps peaked at the successful Woodstock Festival in August. Generally, in 1969 the existential stakes of playing and creating rock music were probably as high as they would ever be. The Stones did not exactly participate in activism per se, maintaining that they were only musicians, but they did not reject the appropriation of their music with the student and leftist political movements of the day.

But then things started to sour for the public reputation of the Flower Power movement, and a backlash was forthcoming. Attempting to replicate Woodstock on the West Coast and to deflect criticism from their high ticket prices, in December the Stones set up and played a free concert at the Altamont Speedway near Livermore, California. After a day of violence fueled by angry Hells Angels acting as "security," near the end of the Stones' set a terrible tragedy occurred. The horrific event was also caught on film. Hells Angels' members beat and stabbed to death Meredith Hunter, a young African American man.[1] The media pounced on the horrible spectacle of the Altamont Free Concert as a metaphor for the failure of what was being hailed as "Woodstock nation," and the end of the Age of Aquarius. Adding fuel to the media criticism was the breaking story about a hippie family cult's murderous rampage that began in the summer, led by the crazed Charles Manson. Manson was a failed musician who had worked with Dennis Wilson of the Beach Boys. He claimed that the Beatles' music, in particular the *White Album* and "Helter Skelter," predicted the end of the world that he had been preaching about for years, an apocalyptic battle that would begin as a racial war.

Into this hailstorm of media scrutiny and building backlash against the hippies and left-wing activists, in December the Stones released *Let It Bleed*, their darkest-sounding album to date. Recorded mostly in the spring, one year after *Beggars*, the album replicates much of the bad faith hanging in the air at the time. The violent images of war were unescapably present on television, as well as the anti-Vietnam demonstrations, the campus unrest, and the still-simmering racial tension in the States.

Marianne Faithfull unequivocally states that *Let It Bleed* is her favorite Stones album.[2] This is ironic given that her relationship with Jagger at this time was rapidly deteriorating. But her reasons for it are both historically grounded and mythically resounding. Jagger was starring in Donald Cammell's film *Performance*, a gangster noir film, and allegedly having an affair with Anita Pallenberg. Richards channeled his anger toward Jagger into the music that became *Let It Bleed*, providing a "mythical take on where we were all heading."[3] On Faithfull's interpretation of the album, she writes how the Stones' work amplified the intentions of Cammell's film: "*Let It Bleed* allegorized the themes of *Performance*. Took its toying with the occult and made it into Satanism and turned its flirtation with the gangster netherworld into anarchy."[4] Furthermore, the album was "of-its-time"; after Altamont, "'Gimme Shelter' was so in sync with the zeitgeist that it seemed almost supernatural."[5]

And as already stated, *Let It Bleed* continued the primal energy of *Beggars Banquet.* In particular, the directness and simplicity of *Beggars* had not only rejuvenated the Stones' compositional drive but also returned the band members to a place where they could start performing again. Still, following up a career-redefining, successful album like *Beggars* with new music is no small task. Especially for a band like the Stones, who, after the first couple of albums (which again, were not albums per se so much as collections of songs), operated by shifting their style with each new album to match the prevailing trends of the day. But with *Beggars* the band had distilled an approach to the blues and its expansion into rock that could serve as a foundation, as it were; it in fact did for the next few albums, and perhaps beyond.

Their new approach to the rock-country blues meld they had achieved in *Beggars* centered on the shuffle-derived, soul guitar playing of Richards backed by a rhythmic drive centered on, once again, hard-hitting groove pockets. According to their producer Jimmy Miller, Richards stepped up his guitar playing in order to compensate for the loss of Jones. Jones was present at some of the sessions and even contributed small bits to the album, but his creative contribution was now uneventful and minimal. Richards had effectively assumed the role of band leader, and his riffs from this juncture are some of the most iconic in the history of rock. His trumped-up role emerges quite distinctly in their single from the *Let It Bleed* sessions, "Honky Tonk Women."

Let It Bleed's first song erupts with political rage, the anti-war "Gimme Shelter," with its startling and terrifying cries proclaiming the words "rape" and "murder." The band continued its homage to the Delta blues tradition that they had initiated with "Prodigal Son," covering Robert Johnson's delicate and devastating "Love in Vain," which begins with Richards's exquisite acoustic playing. Richards's arrangement is more than just a tribute to the blues and Johnson. It speaks volumes about his ability to hone an original interpretation of a blues masterwork that invents new figures and riffs for the guitar that are idiomatic and yet sound completely new. And the album does contain some humor, the campy, tongue-in-cheek caricature of country music, "Country Honk," which they later reworked into their funky and catchy single "Honky Tonk Women." "Live with Me" picks up the raunchy theme of "Stray Cat Blues." "Live with Me" is also their first song with saxophonist and West Texan Bobby Keys.[6] "Monkey Man" returns the group to an updated, rock version of Southern soul that harkens back to the band's earlier days. The album concludes with an a cappella choir singing the first verse and chorus in a classical arrangement of their anthem "You Can't Always Get What You Want."

But in terms of a tonal plan, *Let It Bleed* does not follow in the path of *Beggars*. Indeed, every song changes to another key without any kind of pattern. And Richards does not experiment with open tunings as much, with only three of the nine songs in an alternate tuning, in this case open E. Associated with the album, "Honky Tonk Women" is his first song to use open G, but it was released as a single well in advance of and apart from the album. See table 4.1 for the keys of the songs on the album.

But Richards does use a capo on the majority of the songs. Guitarists will use capos to be able to use open strings in distant keys that do not use open strings. It also becomes easier to play in these nonidiomatic

Table 4.1. Keys, Tunings, and Capo Usage of Songs on *Let It Bleed*

Song	Key	Tuning
"Gimme Shelter"	C-sharp	rhythm guitar in open E
"Love in Vain"	B-flat	standard, capo on third fret
"Country Honk"	G	standard
"Live with Me"	A	standard
"Let It Bleed"	C	standard, capo on third fret
"Midnight Rambler"	B	standard, capo on seventh fret; slide part, open E
"You Got the Silver"	F	open E, capo on first fret
"Monkey Man"	C-sharp	standard; second (slide) guitar in open E, possibly with capo on second fret
"You Can't Always Get What You Want"	C	open E, capo on eighth fret

keys. For example, most beginners can easily finger G, C, and D chords; by placing a capo on the third fret of the guitar, fingering the same chords in the same way relative to the capo results in B-flat, E-flat, and F chords, respectively. Now, because the tension of the string has tightened relative to the string's shortening by the capo, the timbre of the guitar assumes a whole new color. And this seems to be the real intent behind Richards's capo use, to create a unique ambience and layering of string color for each song.

Finally, the capo usage and the open tunings explain why cover-band guitarists' attempts to replicate the Stones falls flat. That is, playing the chord progressions to a given Stones song is usually not enough. As guitarist and Richards's X-pensive Winos bandmate Robert "Waddy" Wachtel has put it: "Because growing up and playing guitar, you're learning Stones songs to play in bars, but you know there's something wrong, you're not playing them right, there's something missing."[7] He is talking about the open-G tuning specifically, but his general idea of learning to play the Stones in the wrong manner is also predicated on having the capo in the right place.

Along these lines of setting up unique soundscapes for each song, the Stones continue to expand their sonic range in *Let It Bleed.* Without the multi-instrumentalist Jones, in this period session musicians take on even greater significance. Indeed, this album featured their most beefed-up lineup of session musicians to date, allowing them to mint songs in arrangements with singular features. In short, the identity of certain songs resonates with their arrangements. There are clear precedents for this unfolding in the Stones' past repertoire, as in the marimba on "Under My Thumb" or the sitar on "Paint It Black."

On *Let It Bleed*, we can immediately point to two songs where additions to the arrangement profoundly inform the listening experience: Merry Clayton's vocals on "Gimme Shelter," incidentally the first female vocal solo in a Stones' song, and the London Bach Choir's singing and Al Kooper's French horn performance on "You Can't Always Get What You Want." Furthermore, every song on the album has something singular about its respective instrumentation, and cuing in to the altered ambience made by these contributions can amply reward the listener. Thus in a way, it can be argued that these extra, supplemental parts—all overdubbed—start to inhabit the essential identity of each song, and it is hard to imagine these songs existing without them. Even on their fiftieth anniversary tour, 50 & Counting, the band managed to find live choirs and French horn players able to perform "You Can't Always Get What You Want" as it appears on the studio album.

A GUITAR MANIFESTO EMBEDDED IN A TRIAD OF LYRICALLY CHALLENGING SONGS: "GIMME SHELTER," "MIDNIGHT RAMBLER," AND "MONKEY MAN"

Let It Bleed's major steps forward in guitar playing are found throughout the album, though here we will focus on the triad of songs "Gimme Shelter," "Midnight Rambler," and "Monkey Man." In different ways these songs represent the combination of the types of rhythm guitar that Richards had been pursuing since the beginning—bluesy, laid-back shuffles that are rhythmically complete without the drums, with soulful extensions that fill pockets of groove with subtle articulation and fullness, along with driving riffs and licks that are able to shift the band into rock and roll mode. These songs represent some of the most original guitar riffs that Richards would invent as he realizes his dream of translating the blues into a rock and roll style, much as his hero Chuck Berry had done for R & B. If on the *Beggars* material Richards found his guitaristic muse, on *Let It Bleed* he channeled and distilled it into a signature style.

So far in this book we have not discussed equipment and how it impacts the specificity of sound and timbre of a given song. Of course, every song is dependent on the recording context and the equipment used by the musicians, but as we move into the late 1960s and early 1970s there is less of a "plug-and-play" mentality and more attention granted to finding an ideal type of sound. As is well known, the Beatles were pioneers in expanding the sound palette for rock and popular music. Since their efforts, audiences started to demand that albums feature more technical experimentation and attention to sonic detail.

The topic of equipment is hard to avoid with songs such as "Gimme Shelter," what is often seen as their most ideal mix. Throughout the 1960s the music-products industry had undergone a veritable renaissance, led first by the needs of the Beatles and the Stones, among others, who demanded louder and clearer sound reinforcement for their live concerts that had also grown exponentially in size. But more choices became available also in the special effects and instrumental categories. This provided a boon to creating with new palettes of sound in the studio environment. Furthermore, though Gibson and Fender would continue to produce the most recognizable and in-demand guitars for virtuosos and professionals, after a decade of the guitar's dominance, there were ever-increasing numbers of boutique and custom guitar choices available.

From 1964 on, when he got his first of numerous Gibson Les Pauls, Richards seems most at home playing Gibson guitars, though his Epiphone Casino still figured into his setup (note that the Epiphone company had merged with Gibson in 1957). On the other hand, Jones played a variety of guitars, most famously his Vox Teardrop guitar, as well as a twelve-string Rickenbacker. But for "Gimme Shelter" and "Midnight Rambler," the two heaviest guitar tracks on the album, Richards turned to a rare guitar he never used before or would again, a Maton SE777. Made in Australia, the hollow-body electric guitar (similar to the Gibson ES line or his Epiphone Casino) was left behind in his apartment by a person who was staying with him.[8] Richards reports that the guitar's neck pickup fell off at the end of recording "Gimme Shelter."

Richards also used a different amp setup, a Triumph 100 that the band had acquired through Stewart.[9] A large and powerful amplifier, the Triumph relies on a solid-state system instead of the more common and warmer-sounding vacuum tubes for its power. Apparently there was a sweet spot on the Triumph amp where it reached its optimal tone, right before overheating. Furthermore, Richards developed a preference for the tremolo effect that was built into the amp.

Thus, playing the Maton guitar in E tuning, pushing the sound signal through the Triumph amplifier with the tremolo effect on, Richards achieves a guitar sound and texture in "Gimme Shelter" like no other Stones' song. He overdubs a laid-back bluesy lead over this (in standard tuning), while gentle vocalized "oos" float over the percussively varied texture. Miller adds to the rhythm section by incorporating worldbeat instruments like the güiro and then shakers, the former from Latin America and played with a scraper against its ridges. In the intro Watts plays syncopated accents, finally giving way to the pounding pulse of the song. Indeed, even before Jagger starts, the Stones have conjured one of their most menacing carpets of sound to date.

As we have already indicated, Richards's rhythmic playing in "Gimme Shelter" reads like a post–soul guitar manifesto. He has moved beyond his earlier appropriation of the style in "Mercy, Mercy," with its straightened treatment of the ornamented nature of the more finicky side of soul playing. The sound of his guitar is now shimmering in the warm glow of tremolo, with notes bouncing off one another because of the effect. Furthermore, and following in the path of the great soul players, he continually reaches for notes beyond the chords themselves. By adding little bits to the chords—mostly upward-reaching notes that he then suspends—each chord harmony feels like it is expanding, paradoxically moving while staying still. What makes this variety possible is the repetition involved in the chord progression. Indeed, the intro states the four-chord pattern in the space of four measures of common time that will provide the glue for the song. The four chords basically function as a riff.[10] These four chords also provide the backdrop for one of the most recognizable choruses in the Stones, on the line "War, children . . ." This is similar to songs from the 1950s that featured repeated four-chord patterns, such as the doo-wop progressions prevalent during the 1950s and early 1960s. For the verse, the tonic chord of C-sharp is held the entire time, similar to blues songs where often only a single chord or a riff rings through the whole song. Because of this simplicity of the chordal means, it is left to other elements—such as the discursive lead guitar, the vocals, the percussion, and the harmonica—to register the development and emotional journey of the song.

For his lead, Richards relies on his usual standby, the minor-pentatonic scale, at first shadowing the "oo" in the vocal part but then departing from it into his own voice. Joining the ranks of "Sympathy," it is one of the few songs he plays a single-note lead on. As we shall see, with the addition of Mick Taylor to the band, Richards was released from doing double duty as the lead and rhythm player of the band. His solo in "Gimme Shelter" picks up where the intro solo left off, starting in the middle register with well-placed bends before it pauses and then pursues the bend motif for the rest. Beyond his solo, Richards's lead also interacts with Jagger's harmonica and singing, as well as the female vocal part. In concert footage from at least the last twenty years, the song has become a showcase for Richards to stretch out and solo.

Clayton sings the female part that complements Jagger so well. Clayton was at this point in her career a session musician who had done vocal backups for Neil Young. Her part was added during the final mixing of the album at Sunset Sound in Los Angeles. Her voice intertwines with Jagger's until after the guitar solo, when she is given a solo pass on the chorus at what becomes the climax of the song. Hearing a black female voice sing the words "rape" and "murder" certainly speaks volumes about how far the Stones were willing to push the envelope politically, and in this way their art reaches beyond the aesthetic realm. With gender and race politics taking shape as parallel fronts in the antiwar movement, "Gimme Shelter" manages to encapsulate all three. After the third pass of "rape, murder," on the word "murder" her voice breaks and Jagger expresses his approval—Jagger's response can be heard on the released mix. The overdub in isolation is available on YouTube, and Jagger's enthusiastic approbation stands out.[11] Finally, a case can be made that this vocal insertion prefigures the depiction of slavery and its discontents on the next album's "Brown Sugar."

Continuing, "Midnight Rambler" also revisits the topic of violence against females from the perspective of male rape fantasy. For the 2012–2013 50 & Counting tour, the Stones brought back Mick Taylor and showcased his playing on this song (among a few others). Though many did not realize it at the time of the song's composition (including Wyman), the song takes up the subject of the Boston Strangler based on the confessions of Albert DeSalvo, who has claimed to be the Strangler, and his alleged murder of Beverly Samans.[12] After noting the shift in the lyrics to the first person, feminist critics have lambasted the song; Jane Caputi writes:

> The ritual of the song and performance invite millions of male listeners over the years to identify with the Strangler/Ripper via their hero, Mick Jagger, and millions of women to identify with the silenced victim.[13]

The song is one of the most performed in the Stones canon, with some early performances having Jagger act out parts of it onstage. Indeed probably the better-known version of the song is the "ritualized" live one from *'Get Yer Ya-Ya's Out!'* with Taylor on lead guitar. Caputi's line of attack recalls the one that Theodor Adorno unleashed in the mid-twentieth century against the primitivism of the ritual sacrifice of the girl in Stravinsky's *Rite of Spring*, where he writes:

> If the liquidation of the young girl is not simplistically enjoyed by the individual in the audience, he feels his way into the collective, thinking (as the potential victim of the collective) to participate thereby in collective power in a state of magic regression.[14]

For both critics, then, there is a real danger inherent in violent theatrical music in that it entices the listener to a collective identification with the regressive power of the rapist/murderer or the group over the victimized female.

Its theatricality has been called out by Richards, who retrospectively refers to "Midnight Rambler" as a "blues opera" that only they (i.e., the Jagger/Richards team) could have done. He sees the song as part of the long blues tradition of capitalizing on sensationalist news. We can here interpret the song as part of the murder ballad tradition, with songs based on actual news headlines like "Tom Dooley," "Frankie and Albert," or "Stagger Lee," songs among countless others that were passed down and well known to any folk or blues enthusiast. Richards writes that "you just happen to be looking at a newspaper, 'Midnight Rambler on the loose again.' Oh I'll have him."[15]

However, it is easy to see why a contemporary feminist critic like Caputi would jump on the Stones for such a song—this is the group, after all, that wrote "Under My Thumb," "Stupid Girl," and later

"Brown Sugar," and so on. But her criticism of "Midnight Rambler" takes aim not only at the lyrics, but in its ritualized performance. With a heightened awareness of the asymmetrical social conditions underlying what has been termed "rape culture," songs that deal with the alleged justification of rape (intended or not) will continue to invite controversy; this was seen most recently in the feminist criticism of Robin Thicke's "Blurred Lines" (2013) with its "I know you want it" line, thought to justify date rape.[16] Indeed, in today's hyper-politically correct college campus environment, "Midnight Rambler" would probably require a "trigger warning"—an alert that its content may cause some to experience negative thoughts—at many institutions of higher learning. Finally, this line of critique also recalls much of the negative reception of gangster rap, interpreted as yet another black genre steeped in violence, rape, and misogyny that encourages bad behavior.

We do not have space here to enter the full debate about trigger warnings and whether music or art can cause immoral actions. Yet in regard to the latter and in defense of the Stones, not only is there an extensive blues tradition that celebrates murder, it seems that in this period of the countercultural music aesthetic the Stones were also interested in pushing the boundaries of what a song could express. In contrast to Caputi's opinion, "Midnight Rambler" could also be interpreted as a critique of the repressed, violent society that continues to foster psychopathic behavior capable of committing such horrific crimes. Moreover, added to this is a racial component to the song. John Hellmann's perceptive article on the Stones makes a similar argument in terms of a historically specific black musical repertoire:

> In its cruel and bombastic language it is firmly in the traditions of the power-seeking sexual fantasies created by the oppressed but angry black composers of rhythm and blues, its knife-wielding fantasies being especially similar to such old blues songs as the one that promised an unfaithful woman that the singer would cut his initials into her intimate parts.[17]

He continues that "rambler" is an old trope for an "inveterate criminal, social misfit, or sexually promiscuous male." Thus through rhyme, Jagger transforms "rambler" into what become cognates, namely "gambler," "jangler," and "panther" (more on this rhyme below).

Furthermore, Jagger himself was also quite involved in acting at this time, and role-playing in concert performance has a long, storied past, especially if we view the song as part of a dramatic opera when it turns to and back from the first person. For example, as we sought to show in the previous chapter with "Sympathy," Jagger's identification with Lucifer, whether as real or acted out, is part of a reenactment of historical fiction. That is, these song containers told from a dramatic perspective are also operating under the classical aesthetic principle of distance dividing the viewer and the content, whether through the convention of the stage or the performative framing of the artwork.

After all, both "Midnight Rambler" and *Rite of Spring* occur as staged, artistic presentations of a shocking content (again, in the case of the *Rite*, the pagan sacrifice of a young girl) that is intentionally given as such. They offer imagined perspectives on gruesome violence within historically grounded contexts. For its full theatrical effect, there must remain a level of ambiguity as to whether either work condones what it shows. This latter conceit is perhaps what bothers some of the morally outraged critics. Thus, in this respect they can be seen as part of a theatrical tradition stretching back to Greek antiquity, where through the play's presentation of a tragic event such as the matricide in Euripides's *Orestes*, the audience experiences pity and compassion, leading to a purification (catharsis) of the emotions.[18]

Despite the strategy behind this riposte, the interpretation of violent artistic works, or works connected to fascism, will always be a problematic area for reception. Because of his appropriation by the Nazis and his own anti-Jewish writings, Wagner's music dramas continue to invite fierce debate, even if his music predates the Nazi movement. And with the direct power to elicit strong emotions in listeners, music, fairly or not, seems to be called out more often than not in such debates. Yet perceptions can change quickly based on real-time events. For example, interpreting "Midnight Rambler" with historical distance might be one thing, yet after another killing spree by a misogynist, it could give pause.[19]

In terms of Richards calling it a "blues opera," the song does exhibit many of the traits of the concept albums that were the rage in the late 1960s. As we have already seen, one expression of the concept album is to tell a complete story over a series of songs. The Who's *Tommy*, one of the best examples of this, had just come out in April 1969, and it does have a violent scene insinuating the rape of Tommy by his evil Uncle Ernie. But after *Their Satanic Majesties Request*, another attempt at a concept album would not be in keeping with the intended back-to-their-roots reboot started with *Beggars Banquet*. Yet in "Midnight Rambler" the Stones were able to unite the blues with a multi-part narrative, thereby participating in one of the significant musical trends of the time. With its speed-ups and slow-downs, the various sections of the song come off as more than a single song, almost as a mini-suite; the live version is usually stretched out to ten minutes or more, much longer than the album's version of close to seven minutes.

Similar to "Gimme Shelter," "Midnight Rambler" has a simple progression upon which layers of musical ideas coalesce. Not surprisingly, Richards recycles the "Sympathy" progression but in the key of B, which at this point is his go-to progression.[20] He plays it in the traditional blues shuffle pattern, with its back-and-forth swinging motion of an added upward tone that is largely responsible for the "roll" in rock and roll. The chords are B > A > E, but again, it is the voicing and timbre that stand out. With his amp slightly overdriven, Richards accents the second chord (A) to break up the urgency of the shuffle and voices it in a high range that helps to put emphasis on the chord. But then he very subtly shifts the progression halfway through the verse, from B > A > E to A > E > B (on the line "I'm sighin' down the wind so sadly"). Because it reconfigures the same chords, the difference is hardly noticeable on casual listening but its structural impact is enormous. This allows the music to land on the home key of B as they end the verse, which they vamp on with the harmonica after the verses. For the second verse, Richards overlays a slide guitar (tuned in open E) that shoots out a repetitive figure, both under the singing and then in a call-and-response doubled by harmonica. The slide lubricates the accompaniment, as it were, balancing the direct, unyielding quality of the rhythmic stew. (Note that Jones apparently added percussion to the song.)

After a brief instrumental interlude, verse three comes in truncated, with the line that marks the singer's self-awareness: "it's no rock 'n' roll show," also signaling the longer instrumental vamping section as the band ratchets up the terror by speeding up the tempo. This is the part where Jagger indicates the rape with his line "don't you do that" (first heard ca. 2:48). Here, at the heart of the climatic terror of the song, Richards pulls out all of the stops in his amalgamation of a snaking rhythmic part, where variations over the B chord meld seamlessly into one another, hardly noticeable, yet again showing his mastery of musical detail. Comparing this to the similar section vamp on the E chord in "Goin' Home," where Jagger sings "early in the morning," Richards's rhythm playing shows remarkable improvement in its sheer variety. In "Goin' Home," he often resorts to stock, idiomatic figures, and his guitar sounds thin compared to the fullness of his tone on "Midnight Rambler." There also is a bit of word painting going on, where the instrumental sounds try to mimic the violent action behind "don't you do that." Richards plays a descending glissando (3:10 and following), suggestive of some vile maneuver that is occurring.

Lastly, in a slow section that uses the typical blues gesture of stop-time, Jagger proclaims, "you heard about the Boston" very intentionally leaving the word "Strangler" out. Of course, the word "strangler" rhymes with "rambler" and "gambler," so we do hear the alluded-to proper name in the silence, even though he does not need to articulate it. But then the singer establishes ironic distancing from the Strangler, saying, "it's not one of those." This equivocal line presents a level of confusion in the song—if the "Midnight Rambler" is not the Boston Strangler, then who exactly is he? Or, does the "it" refer to the violent act, that this time it will be violence in excess of what the Strangler has carried out up to then, that is, the deaths by strangulation? Note that the murder of Beverly Samans noted above did depart from the other strangulations, as the murderer, the alleged Strangler, was apparently unable to kill her by strangulation and as such stuck a knife down her throat.

"Monkey Man" can be also be interpreted within the resistant literary figures of African American culture. The song contextualizes the irony of much of the Stones' approach to the blues. Brimming with food double entendres that ooze sex—Italian pizza, lemon squeezer, broken eggs—the song references the band, hoping they are not too "messianic" or "satanic" because when it is all said and done, they just "love to play the blues." Note that the early bluesman used food double entendres to avoid censorship and also as a source of empowerment over their oppressed, marginalized existence within the confines of institutionalized racism. Writing about the sexualized nature of what he calls the blues "argot," or slang, in the Stones, Hellmann analyzes "Monkey Man" to show how food metaphors give way to machine and animal imagery. He specifically cites Muddy Waters's "Tiger in Your Tank"; we could add Johnson's earlier interest in machine comparisons as in "Phonograph Blues" or "Terraplane Blues," or his "Dead Shrimp Blues" for bestiality. Hellmann mentions other animals found in the Stones' blues covers, songs like "King Bee" or "Little Red Rooster" or their original twelve-bar blues song, "The Spider and the Fly" (1965, B-side on a UK single but included on the U.S. version of *Out of Our Heads*) that probably takes its subject matter from the Mary Howitt poem of the same name. Hellmann concludes by summarizing the three layers of meaning piled onto the term "monkey man," all three of which come to bear on the meaning of the song, as in: 1) the black man versus the white baboon; 2) an effeminate male (Jagger was known for his androgynous stage appearance); and 3) a light-skinned West Indian Negro that was very attractive to American black women.[21]

The punchy, flirty style of Richards's guitar buttresses this last meaning of "monkey man." In the intro, he plays the typical descending blues line voiced over a C-sharp minor chord, and the minor chord gives this a funky, soulful twist, punctuated when he emphasizes the syncopated minor chord at the end of the phrase.[22] Note that he uses standard tuning without a capo, a rare move for him in this period for a song that relies so heavily on the guitar part. He first plays the stock figure almost as an accompaniment to the piano (Hopkins) and vibes (Wyman) that start the intro, but in his second pass (finally with the drums) he turns to an overdriven timbre as he assumes control of the texture. But the song is not a minor blues, as surprisingly the song turns to the key of E major for the verse.[23]

Still, there is only a fleeting sense of harmonic stability in what appears to be the tonic E, as the main riff of the song is on a C-sharp major chord ("that's not really true"). The riff's wandering evasiveness becomes the inviting seductive call affirming the monkeyness of the singer ("I'm a monkey"). Again, Richards's trademark riff vacillates between single-note bass notes and accented chords, coupled with upward non-chordal tones that build up the excitement. The verse slips around harmonically between these two chord areas (E and C-sharp), relying on hornlike lines drawing on a blue note from the minor pentatonic, the note E, that resolves back down to the C-sharp. The turnaround is also backward, rising up a whole step instead of descending as is usual (from A to B instead of B to A), but it resolves into the chord of the riff (C-sharp) instead of the home key (E) where it should resolve. (With this ambiguous resolution, "Monkey Man" can be conceptualized in C-sharp major, which is in fact the key of the song's fadeout.) Thus by playing with our harmonic expectations, Richards is able to map the upside-down world of the monkey man.

To summarize, in these three songs, Richards neatly shows the direction that his reformulated approach to the guitar will assume. Grounded in the funky, syncopated, and fill-centered idiom of recent soul playing, Richards adds a rock sensibility to the mix, switching into a rawer, forward-propelled attack. And the lyrics themselves vacillate between traditional blues topics and modern concerns, grafting the directness and frankness of the blues onto the era's mediated, moderated platform of commercial yet countercultural, pop/rock music. As the most identifiable aspect of each song, Richards's rhythm playing underlies the energy of each song, gluing the accompaniment to the lyrics and to the additive layers stacked above—the harmonica, slide or lead guitar, and so forth. Using simple chord shapes with suspensions and alterations, alternate tunings, a capo, and progressions that seem a part of the blues but are actually evolved from it, Richards encapsulates an inimitable sonic experience that underlies the challenging nature of Jagger's lyrics. The binding of the music and lyrics feels old and new at the same time, idiomatic yet encoded with a personal stamp.

ACOUSTIC GUITARSCAPE

For a player interested in the blues of Richards's generation, the folk and blues revival that climaxed in the mid-1960s clearly privileged the acoustic source of the blues, especially the Delta blues of Robert Johnson who was the guitar hero of many of the great British players, most notably Eric Clapton. And in the 1950s in England it was the skiffle craze that introduced numerous younger players to the acoustic guitar, including John Lennon and Jimmy Page, as they channeled the spirit of American folk songs. Finally, any analysis of the acoustic guitar in the 1960s must take into account the ubiquity of Dylan's songs, especially his influence on a plethora of bands taking up the acoustic idiom (though Dylan was interested at the same time in mimicking the electric idiom of the British), including the main rivals to the Stones, the Beatles.

But the acoustic did figure—sometimes prominently—in the early Stones; for example, Richards plays acoustic on "Not Fade Away" and blues covers like "I'm a King Bee" and "Little Red Rooster." For the former two songs, Richards plays his Harmony twelve-string acoustic. Recorded during the same session as "I'm a King Bee," the first Jagger/Richards single release, "Tell Me (You're Coming Back)," also features Richards playing his Harmony. Other early Stones' songs use the acoustic for color, where it often was subdued in the final mix or amalgamated with other instruments. An example of this is on their single "The Last Time" that finds Richards on acoustic; here, he is overshadowed by Jones's riff for the tune, which Jones played on his Vox Teardrop guitar. For a list of early period songs that utilize the acoustic guitar, see table 4.2.

Yet as we have seen, the *Beggars Banquet* material contains the major leap forward in terms of its use of the acoustic guitar. Perhaps their greatest original piece featuring the slide, "No Expectations" uses acoustic for both the rhythm and the slide parts. For the band's first released acoustic Delta blues, Richards plays it safe and renders "Prodigal Son" straight after Wilkins.[24] And "Factory Girl" has a wholly acoustic vibe with the guitar backing up the violin (Ric Grech) and mandolin (Dave Mason); unfortunately the band did not put enough time into developing the song. Significantly, what emerges from *Beggars* is a clarification in Richards's dual approach to the acoustic guitar. In most of the songs, the acoustic assumes its traditional role, similar to a folksong accompaniment as in the usual Dylan arrangement, the standard-bearer for 1960s acoustic music. But with "Jumpin' Jack Flash" and "Street Fighting Man," Richards attacks the acoustic in a way that makes it sound like an electric. Again, earlier songs like "The Last Time," with its integration of the acoustic into a primarily electric band situation, prefigures this latter tendency.

With respect to the acoustic guitar, *Let It Bleed* continues down the path of these dualistic roles for the instrument. On the one hand, "Love in Vain," "Country Honk," and "You Got the Silver" fall on the side of the expected, conventional use of the acoustic as a folk-blues instrument. On the other, "Let It Bleed" and "You Can't Always Get What You Want" place the acoustic as part of a full rock-band complement.

Table 4.2. Selected Songs with Acoustic Guitar (Up to *Beggars Banquet*)

Song	Year recorded	First release(s)
"Not Fade Away"	1964	single; *The Rolling Stones: England's Newest Hit Makers* (U.S.)
"Tell Me (You're Coming Back)"	1964	*The Rolling Stones*; also later as a single
"Little Red Rooster"	1964	single (UK); various compilations
"The Last Time"	1965	single; *Out of Our Heads* (U.S.)
"Play with Fire"	1965	B-side to "Last Time"; *Out of Our Heads* (U.S.)
"Mother's Little Helper"	1965	*Aftermath* (UK); U.S. single and *Flowers*
"Take It or Leave It"	1965	*Aftermath*
"Lady Jane"	1966	*Aftermath*; B-side to "Mother's Little Helper" (U.S.)
"Paint It Black"	1966	single; *Aftermath* (U.S.)
"High and Dry"	1966	*Aftermath*
"Back Street Girl"	1966	*Between the Buttons* (UK); *Flowers* (U.S.)
"Who's Been Sleeping Here?"	1966	*Between the Buttons*
"Have You Seen Your Mother, Baby, Standing in the Shadow?"	1966	single; various compilations
"Ruby Tuesday"	1966	single (UK); B-side to "Let's Spend"; *Between the Buttons* (U.S.)
"2000 Man"	1967	*Their Satanic Majesties Request*

Finally, Richards does not return to his technique of running the acoustic into a small tape recorder and so there is no song that repeats the aggressive acoustic strumming of a "Jumpin' Jack Flash" again.

In Richards's re-creation of Robert Johnson's "Love in Vain," Johnson's stark and pointillist style becomes smoothed out in a pretty-sounding arrangement that approximates the type of folk-song performance popular during the '60s. Richards also plays with a capo on the third fret, adding in an extra chord and some tastefully executed hammer-ons that serve as filler.[25] Although he keeps one of the song's main identifiers—adding a blue note to the tonic chord (in the Stones' version, heard right before "with a suitcase"), surprisingly he drops the descending melodic line in the middle range of the guitar and voice that is the signature of the song, at "all your love's in vain."[26] Note that this is the part of the song that Johnson lifted from Leroy Carr's "When the Sun Goes Down."[27] Ironically, "Love in Vain" is the only recorded song of Johnson's in open-G tuning.[28] But for the live, American touring version of the song in 1969 and as released on *'Get Yer Ya-Ya's Out!'*, Richards returns the song to the key of G, though keeping with standard tuning. The subsequent live unfolding of the song does provide different and interesting perspectives on the song, well worth exploring. For example, the Hyde Park concert in July 1969 has Richards playing it on electric guitar; here the same accompaniment (in G) essentially turns the song into a soul ballad. Finally, on the film of the sessions for the 1995 live studio album *Stripped*, Richards's mature and multivalent rendering of "Love in Vain" is fully exposed by the camera.[29]

The tender ballad "You Got the Silver" is notable for being the first Stones' song on which Richards sang the entire lead vocal, possibly an accident of circumstances as Jagger's vocal had appeared to be wiped.[30] And allegedly, because he was filming *Ned Kelly* in Australia, Jagger was unavailable to do another pass at it. Accordingly, the song begins with only the voice and guitar for the first verse, with Richards's overdubbed slide bursting in toward the end. The arrangement veers into country-rock territory, becoming more apparent as layers of the band enter. Nicky Hopkins plays piano and organ, and Jones strums the autoharp that echoes the sentimentality of the lyrics. Note that this is one of Jones's final contributions to a Stones' song. After an atmospheric, lush instrumental break, Richards returns to solo acoustic before another verse with the line "Hey baby, what's in your eyes?" begins a buildup. Director Michelangelo Antonioni used the middle part of the track for his cult-classic film *Zabriskie Point*, taking full advantage of these textural changes in the song. For example, with the second "Hey baby," he makes an effective cut to an airplane flying across a field.

Thus with the majority of its songs containing a noticeably present acoustic guitar grounded in the blues aesthetic, *Let It Bleed* reveals a hard-rock band tempering itself with softer acoustic strains. This dual combination of hard and soft will become a major stylistic language of the time. It allowed bands to plumb greater emotional depths while still being able to rock out and be rebellious. Other contemporaneous English bands exemplifying this tendency were the Beatles, Traffic, the Who, and Led Zeppelin. On the American side, the Grateful Dead were shepherding rock music down an acoustic path. Indeed, the acoustic guitar would shape some of the biggest hits and most iconic songs of the Stones and similar bands as the '60s became the early '70s, from "Wild Horses" and "Angie" to Zeppelin's "Stairway to Heaven."

FROM ACOUSTIC TO ELECTRIC: "COUNTRY HONK" AND "HONKY TONK WOMEN"

As we said above, "Honky Tonk Women" marks the Stones' final number-one hit in both the United Kingdom and the United States, and somewhat surprisingly their last number one in the United Kingdom. Jagger and Richards wrote this country-rock song while vacationing on a ranch in Brazil, adding it to the list of songs written while on vacation or away from home. For another "vacation" song from *Let It Bleed*, "Midnight Rambler" started out being called "Positano Grande," after the seaside village where they were staying in southern Italy. "Honky Tonk Women" has multiple versions of its lyrics, which can be heard on the three official releases recorded in 1969—the single, the album version, and the live one on *'Get Yer Ya-Ya's Out!'*

Back on the Brazilian ranch Richards conceived the song on acoustic guitar as a country song, imagining they were cowboys in Texas. This original acoustic version of the song was released as "Country Honk" on *Let It Bleed*, about five months after the much more well-known "Honky Tonk Women." The song as revealed in these two different renditions brings together two distinctive personal influences on Richards at the time, Gram Parsons and Ry Cooder. Parsons was in England in the summer of 1968 on tour with the Byrds. His band was on their way to South Africa for a concert tour. Parsons allegedly quit the Byrds in protest over South Africa's apartheid, which he apparently had only learned about in England. Parsons stayed with Richards at Redlands during the summer of 1968 and the two became fast friends sharing their similar musical tastes, with Parsons schooling Richards in country music—legends like Hank Williams and Jimmie Rodgers, and the newly fashionable proponents of the harder-edged Bakersfield school like Merle Haggard. Note that Parsons had led the Byrds in their turn toward developing country rock, an event cataloged on their album *Sweetheart of the Rodeo*. And as we have seen in the previous chapter, Cooder's contribution was the open-G tuning. He has stated that the

"Honky Tonk" riff was originally his own—that is, that Richards assimilated the riff and chord stylizations from Cooder's own playing.

Both conceptions of the song material are in the key of G with the same chord progression, but their guitarscapes and aesthetic effect could not be more different. "Country Honk" has an acoustic in standard tuning, playing an almost shuffle-style, lower-register riff. With the addition of the violin (Byron Berline, who later played in Parsons's Flying Burrito Brothers), it attempts to approximate the feel of a Hank Williams song. Indeed, many have pointed out that the title and lyrical conceit pay homage to Williams's own "Honky Tonk Blues," as alluded to in the Stones' lyrics.[31] But whereas most country songs and especially country-blues songs will only use the standard three chords, Richards distinguishes his by throwing in an extra chord, A, beginning on the word "summer" (in "Country Honk") during the first verse.[32] This is a similar move to the extra or fourth chord he inserts in "Love in Vain." For "Country Honk," Richards's main fill is also a country-blues riff (heard right before the entrance of the vocal and throughout the song), and this also acts as a response to the call of the fiddle. Note that the country blues use a different version of the blues scale from the standard minor pentatonic of African American blues.[33]

"Honky Tonk Women" has the distinction of being the first Stones' song as led by Richards in open-G tuning, the tuning that would come to define him and the band moving forward. Whether or not the licks were derived somehow from Cooder's playing or studio improvisations, Richards does depart from Cooder's slide, and he also hit upon the solution of removing the sixth string (though it is unclear if he had done so at this stage). Richards links the revived success of his songwriting and the band's performance to his discovery of this five-string, open-G tuning. He writes extensively on the personal significance of this new "primordial" system, which he links to the "tribesman of West Africa" and the American banjo. To explore this topic fully, the pages Richards devotes to the topic can be read in close detail; here we can only quickly highlight a couple of key points he makes:

> Five strings cleared out the clutter. It gave me the licks and laid on textures. You can almost play the melody through the chords, because of the notes you can throw in. . . . It was like scales falling from your eyes and from your ears at the same time. . . . With five strings you can be sparse; that's your frame, that's what you work on.[34]

In Stones' lore, this is the epiphany that would generate the band's legendary hits that were, again, so basic on the surface due to the simple chord progressions but so hard to imitate without knowledge of this tuning. Thus "Honky Tonk Women," with its sparse texture and guitar-echoed melody, riff, and droning at the same time, announces the turning point for the Stones, one that Richards says he is still exploring in his endless search for the perfect riff. As if to amplify this discovery, it seems symbolic that this was the song with which they broke in Mick Taylor as the new lead guitarist of the band.

Again, and often noted, it is the synergy locking together this new style of riffing with the recorded groove that gives "Honky Tonk Women" one of the most distinctive sonic footprints in rock music history. Miller's cowbell is at first out of sync with Watts's drum entrance; when Richard enters, everything straightens out. Rhythmically it is one of the hardest to fathom intros in rock history, which is probably why they kept it. The syncopated effect matches the sparseness that Richards was searching for at the time, with the guitar entering on the upbeat to the "one" and following with more syncopated accenting. Perhaps because of the impossibility of re-creating that opening, they begin the live version of the song with only Richards's part.[35]

For the final mix of the song, the band and their producers manage to keep the layered parts distinct. Instead, they achieve unity in the linear unfolding of the song. For example, Richards's rhythmic accompaniment part blends seamlessly into the fills, forming a quartet with the percussionists and Jagger's voice for the verses (without bass). Contrasting with the stark instrumentation of the verse is the richly scored chorus with the lead guitar and bass overdubs (Richards played bass on this track, too). This thickening buildup reaches its climax for the instrumental break, where for the first time on a Stones single there is a horn section. Unusually, there are no other verses after this break, perhaps to keep the energy building.

The song's topics of loose women, one-night stands, and perhaps prostitutes (some think that "honky tonk women" refers directly to prostitutes) again invite charges of sexism in the band's approach. And the objectification of women will only become more pronounced in the 1970s. But it is this openness toward sex that fed into the notoriety and appeal of the band and one Jagger would fully exploit in the coming years. If political rebellion was cast aside after *Let It Bleed*, the seedy, hedonistic side of the sexual revolution still offered more avenues for exploitation.

CONCLUSION

With its mélange of guitarscapes both electric and acoustic, *Let It Bleed* furthers the original blues mission of the Stones, while appropriating the strains of country and Delta blues for a rock soundscape. Again, and significantly, the album demarcates the first changing of the Stones' lineup, as it is the last one Jones would appear on, while being the first for Taylor. Although it had been a reality for years, with Jones finally gone it now became clear to the public that Jagger was the face of the band.

The album replicates the trajectory of *Beggars* while providing more tonal variety. But similarities abound. On both, the band punches out a first song meant to shock with its lyrical subject matter. After alterations of acoustic and electric blues-rock songs, both conclude with an anthem. "You Can't Always Get What You Want" is a generational singalong that references the demonstrations; as such it still retreats from progressive politics per se and advocates a squarely pragmatic point of view. With its use of classical music–inspired signifiers, as in a choir (the Bach Choir from London) and the French horn (Al Kooper, who suggested this instrument), the opening of the song seems more in line with the pomp and circumstance of Beatles records. And yet even at their most grandiose, the Stones keep the song simple—for most of it the band alternates on just two chords. The song is usually framed as the Stones' answer to the deflated dreams of '60s progressivism.

Finally, on the musical level, as Richards delved deeper into alternate tunings, he discovered the five-string (possibly), open-G tuning that would essentially determine the direction of their sound starting with *Sticky Fingers*. With Taylor bolstering lead and slide duties for the group and thereby relieving Richards of these facets, the guitar presence expanded accordingly on *Sticky Fingers*, an album to which we now turn. Jagger started contributing and writing on the guitar as well, and because of Taylor, Richards was now free to expand the texture and to continue his search for the symphonic possibilities for rhythm guitar.

5

1970S OVERTURE

Sticky Fingers (1971)

After successive and large fall tours of America (1969) and continental Europe (1970), the Stones finally gave a series of concerts in the United Kingdom for two weeks in March 1971. It was the band's first UK tour since 1966. As they re-established their live show in view of a rapidly expanding audience, they were riding their biggest wave of popularity yet. New songs kept them current, while old songs, from originals like "I'm Free" and covers such as "Carol," proved their staying power and provided a link to a more innocent era of rock and roll. Their brand surged as the concert exposure ignited album sales. It was during this period that they completely reorganized their business model. Still seen as societal rebels, their musical ideas remained fresh and vibrant. For their studio work, they had hit their stride in creating coherent, unified album statements in an era that valued the album above the single as the true repository of the artistic imagination. All of this the band combined on their best live album statement to date, *'Get Yer Ya-Ya's Out!'*, the title itself lifted from the Blind Boy Fuller ragtime-blues song.

This wave of popularity coincided against the backdrop of one of the most contentious moments in rock history. The public mourned the announcement of the official breakup of the Beatles in January 1970, even if expected. Coupled with the disaster at Altamont the previous year, the musical dreams and aspirations of the '60s for making the world a better place had swiftly been dealt a double blow. Further, the

Stones' 1971 UK tour, which should have been triumphant, was also billed bittersweetly as a farewell tour. With the reorganization of their business affairs came the realization that they owed an enormous tax bill, and thus they were forced to leave England for France (more on this in the next chapter). Though they were able to regroup in southern France, this financial catastrophe nearly sunk the Stones.

But with or without bands like the Beatles and the Stones in England, the rock and roll Party barely blinked. Things roared on with new artists like Led Zeppelin, David Bowie, and Elton John. Zeppelin's own brand of hedonistic rebellion came to symbolize the narcissism of the so-called "Me" Decade of the 1970s. Yet the similarities between their predecessors were obvious, as the Stones had paved the way for Zeppelin's success. Zeppelin guitarist Jimmy Page was a seasoned session guitarist who often crossed paths with the Stones; as the oldest member of Zeppelin he was also only a year younger than Jagger and Richards. He played on a 1964 demo of "Heart of Stone," released on *Metamorphosis* (an album of oddities and outtakes disowned and never approved of by the band), and worked as a producer with Oldham's orchestra. Thus under Page's leadership, Zeppelin honed in on the same roots musical tributaries as the Stones—Delta blues, Southern R & B, and folk—appropriating, and in some instances stealing from, past artists as they forged a very different and harder sound from previous bands.

Still, that the Stones were able to stay on top of their game in albums and tours through most of the 1970s is quite amazing, especially with the pivot toward other styles—singer-songwriter, glam, country, punk, disco, and more—in the fast-moving spectacle of popular music culture. But with Zeppelin leading the charge of hard, bluesy rock in the new decade, the Stones' blend of hard rock and blues (often acoustic or country blues) was not going out of fashion anytime soon. And again, the Stones were fortunate to maintain a privileged position in rock history, as their rivalry with the Beatles had played such an integral part in inventing the rock spectacle as something that mattered both culturally and politically in the first place. Finally, in a genre that privileged youth in all its passion and folly, the Stones managed to reinvigorate the relationship of rock to youth, as we shall see in these last chapters.

ON THE CHANGING MARKET DEMANDS OF THE ALBUM CATEGORY

When the Stones started in 1962 the album's function was to gather a group of songs together that represented the band's live show (for example). It was not an end in itself, but a grouping of material showcasing what the band was capable of. With the onslaught of Beatles' albums from *Rubber Soul* through *Sgt. Pepper's*, and American responses like the Beach Boys' *Pet Sounds*, the album became an autonomous artistic statement, analogous to the work concept in classical music. A piece of music became more than its technical execution and an immediate emotional response; audiences identified with the worldview of the album and its songs as a window granting perspective on their own lives. Serious bands were now expected to have a vision channeled into a central message within the album, nowadays considered under the rubric of the "concept album."[1]

In this era of the concept album, songwriters had to choose a narrative component running like a thread binding the songs together. Songs thereby formed a thematic matrix interlocking with other songs, generating cross-meanings and amplifying a message larger than the song itself, similar to movements in a classical suite or variations. Yet this posed a problem for the Stones. We have already seen that with *Their Satanic Majesties Request*, the concept album model did not fit in well with the Stones' self-identification as a blues band.

Although *Sticky Fingers* is not a concept album per se, like the previous two albums the ordering of the songs creates the impression of one.[2] If the self-contained nature of the blues did not lend itself naturally to this grander, sprawling thematic medium, the Stones were able to pull it off by carefully varying their musical textures and binding everything together through the tonalities and riffing we have to come expect from the band. That is, even if there was not a single theme per se, they did create a dynamic flow to the listening experience, with carefully balanced textural (timbral), aesthetic, and stylistic contrast in the track flow, and a dreamy denouement for the final song.

In a way, it could be argued that the Stones found a better solution to what an album should be. The problem with the concept album is that by its very investment in seriousness it contradicts the bare-bones simplicity of the rock genre (refer to the Bangs quotation in chapter 1), which had started as more than just a musical revolution, but also a fun social movement grounded in dance and rebellion against the boring, everyday routine of Western life and work. Indeed much of the era's serious or "progressive" rock was in danger of becoming music for listening, a pseudo-classical music, as it were, rather than music for unadulterated abandon. By sticking with a middle ground, the Stones synthesized the previous era's album as song collection with the concept album. The result was not only a satisfying hybrid with artistic integrity but also a listening experience that was not burdened by having to think too much about an extra-musical content.

This directed simplicity is evident in the flow of songs on *Sticky Fingers*. At once one of the catchiest pop tunes ever written, "Brown Sugar" starts the album off with one of the greatest guitar riffs of all time. Perhaps because of its immediately attractive melodic-rhythmic synergy, most people did not care to notice the outrageousness of the lyrics. Country-rock artist Gram Parsons inspires a burst of alternative roots Americana in the poignantly conceived "Wild Horses" on side one of the album and on the ironic country ballad "Dead Flowers" on the other. Again, these acoustic songs are offset with raunchier blues like "Can't You Hear Me Knocking." The Stones also reach deep into the roots record bin, this time with the plaintive African American spiritual-blues "You Gotta Move," based on Mississippi Fred McDowell's hypnotic chant with slide. Side two begins explosively with "Bitch," a sexualized rejoinder to "Brown Sugar." The album's closer, "Moonlight Mile," strives for the mystical plateau of drug-induced reveries of the Romantic poets, in one of the most evocative arrangements of any Stones song. Though they eschew the choral finale of the previous two albums, the string arrangement buttresses the emotional urgency of the song and provides a neat bookend to the album. It also continues the tradition of grand, epic endings to their albums, which started with *Beggars Banquet*.

ROLLING STONES RECORDS

Sticky Fingers is the Stones' first album on their newly formed label, Rolling Stones Records, ushering in a new and more independent financial phase for the band. Essentially a vanity label, this would be the band's label for the 1970s through the 1980s. Two factors prompted the band to form their own label—the need for both artistic independence and financial rebuilding. They had lost a bruising battle with Decca over their cover art for *Beggars* that resulted in a delay of the album's release, and in the process of extricating themselves from business manager Allen Klein (who had bought out Oldham) they learned that he had ownership rights to all their songs, up to 1971, the end of their contract with Decca. Later on, and in order to settle with him, they also had to concede "Angie" and "Wild Horses." Referring to their time with Klein as an "education," Richards diplomatically muses that he "made us and screwed us at the same time."[3]

The new label's first president was Marshall Chess, who was the go-between in working out a beneficial deal for the Rolling Stones label's distribution with Ahmet Ertegun at Atlantic Records. The Stones had great respect for both music executives, especially given their respective historical connections to the blues and R & B. Chess's father, Leonard, was the founder and owner of the incomparable Chicago blues label, Chess Records. Atlantic became legendary with its 1950s lineup led by Ray Charles and was now entering the '70s rock period with huge acts like Zeppelin, CSNY, and Yes on its roster.

The *Sticky Fingers* release date of April 1971 obscures the fact that many of the songs follow closely on the heels of the 1969 *Let It Bleed* sessions, and one of the songs even goes back to *Beggars*. Many of the songs were road-tested before the album's release, and one, "You Gotta Move," even before it was recorded. After years of Beatlesque studio withdrawal, the live performance bug had bitten the band, and many of their newly minted songs seemed tailor-made for the rock arena, as these quickly assumed their places as concert staples. While *Sticky Fingers* continues trends present from the last two albums; still, the guitar interplay has changed yet again, as Taylor adds longer and more fluid lead lines to the songs, freeing Richards to concentrate on his own melodically spiked rhythm playing. Furthermore, with a true lead guitarist now fully ensconced in the band, the musical conversation could develop with more jamming than on any previous Stones release. This new development fit in well with the tenor of the times, as bands like the Grateful Dead, Santana, Mothers of Invention, Allman Brothers, and Pink Floyd among others had already incorporated long jam sections into their concerts. Indeed, live audiences at this time were hungry for longer, more virtuosic solos as a sign of a band's musicianship.

As their inaugural post-Beatles album release, this is the first time the Stones did not have to worry about the inevitable comparison to their rivals. But the stakes were still high, and they were still competing in a crowded, competitive musical environment. Again, this was in part due to the rise of the concept album, where rock had taken on the trappings of a "serious" art form. If, indeed, "serious rock" could be construed as an oxymoron when the Stones had started, still the band forged ahead in this new era with a high-minded, carefully crafted approach that paradoxically rolled off effortlessly. In large part this was due to the open tunings, which offered a different spin on the same old chords. They also broke with their recent tendency to only write songs using major chords, and we will discuss their tonal excursion into the minor on *Sticky Fingers*.

LISTENING VIGNETTE: LISTENING TO *STICKY FINGERS* IN 1971

It is the end of the summer of 1971, and you are coming back to your third year at New York University. Hailing from a small rural community in upstate New York where you had played on the high school football team, you are thrilled with the vibrant music and cultural offerings of the city. The Vietnam War dominates the news cycle, and it seems that the country is more divided than ever because of it. Most of the students you know are anti-war. Plenty of young men from your hometown have and are serving in Vietnam, and you are aware of a few who have died. At NYU, your transformation from a jock to a hippie (at least on the weekends) did not take very long. Though some are attracted to the marijuana and LSD, it is actually the live music that drove you to the hippie scene. And yet the ingestion of drugs at a concert event certainly makes the music come alive in ways you never would have imagined. The revered folk scene of Greenwich Village is still happening, and there are loads of new venues where all the best bands can be heard. Your favorite is the Fillmore East. It has an intimate setting and the concerts there have the best sound. Earlier in the year you attended concerts at the Fillmore by the Grateful Dead, the Allman

Brothers, and Frank Zappa. The Zappa concert was especially memorable when John Lennon and Yoko Ono joined the band for an encore. But you were unable to get tickets for the closing of the Fillmore East in July, as it quickly sold out. You and some friends had thought about hitchhiking to the city to see if you could get in, but decided against going when your friend got busted for marijuana after being pulled over for speeding. Though the counterculture still seems to thrive, you are aware that it is still not accepted in places outside of the city, and that the older generation still wants to thwart the rise of the drug culture.

With great anticipation, you have finally purchased the newly released (April) *Sticky Fingers* album. You have never been to a Stones concert, but you have heard reports that they are the "greatest," especially from your older brother who was at the Madison Square Garden concerts in November 1969. Even without seeing their live show you are a huge Rolling Stones fan. Your favorite Stones albums are *Flowers* and *Let It Bleed*. "Brown Sugar" plays all the time over the radio and at parties for the last few months. The media hype around *Sticky Fingers* is huge, and with a cover by Andy Warhol—who some traditionalists decry for destroying "real" art—your expectations are quite high for their new sound, and especially to hear their new guitarist, whom many of your friends say is the next Eric Clapton.

You decide to listen to the whole album by yourself in the dorm room. High on marijuana, you feel fortunate to be witnessing what many are saying is a golden era for music, even with the Beatles gone. All the arts seem to relate to music in some way, and music is how your generation defines itself. Even an artist of the stature of Warhol wants to be part of the rock movement.

You are well aware that the Stones excel at both hard rock and the acoustic ballad, represented on this album respectively by "Bitch" and "Wild Horses," but there are some songs on this album that you do not know how to interpret as such. "Sway" is intriguing and ominous and seems to announce a more dirty direction for the band. You are especially drawn to the heavy guitar work and realize that this is a drastic change from the Brian Jones years. The outro solo (by Taylor) on "Sway," buttressed by strings and a pounding piano, brings the band into the present style of hard rock. By contrast, the forlorn "Wild Horses" is fantastic in its country rock way, though you don't really understand what the song is about—is it about drugs, as rumor has it?

The next song, "Can't You Hear Me Knocking," seems so utterly original. Without proper words to describe, in your mind you imagine the opening guitar riff like a bolt of lightning from Zeus, devastating yet somehow enlightening in its godlike origin. You are not aware of the Delta roots of the blues piece "You Gotta Move," but you perceive the ancientness of the spooky chant. "Sister Morphine" also has an antiquated sound that transports you to another realm, with Jagger's ghostlike moaning buttressed by the ringing acoustic. But "Moonlight Mile" becomes the song you obsess over for the next few months. Reminding you of Elton John, whose first album you own, it is the lush, cavernous sound and mystical, zen-like lyrics that draw you in. Is it the best Stones album to date? You know that only time will tell, but it may very well be.

MORE ON THE STONES' USE OF MINOR KEYS

As we noted with "Mother's Little Helper" and "Paint It Black" in chapter 2, minor keys are not so common in rock songs. Part of the reason for this is that for Western audiences, the minor tonality has long-standing associations with melancholy and sadness. These are emotions not commonly referenced in the celebratory space of rock music. The minor key also possesses less finality and more of a sense of openness. For the musical conveying of dark topics, such as in the two aforementioned songs, the minor key helps impart the necessary emotional weight and seriousness. Further, because of its open, equivocal quality, the minor often found its way into the psychedelic and space music of the '60s. For example, in the summer of 1967 during the *Satanic* sessions and while facing jail time, Jagger/Richards wrote "We Love You," a psychedelic song with an ambiguous key center, but that does have a minor-key intro and outro and verses and a bridge that swirl with major-minor exchanges.[4]

As the sentiment of much rock and pop music of this era expanded to embrace the complete variety of human experience, the minor chord found its way into the music as a widening of the simple three-chord formula of early rock and roll. For example, as part of a progression in a major key, the minor chord as a substitution for a major one can add spice to the predictable sequence or chords, or harmonize a bass line to produce smooth transitions between chords.[5] Indeed, in their own pop songwriting on *Aftermath* and *Between the Buttons*, the Stones often sprinkle the progressions with minor chords. In this regard a couple of songs from each that would prove influential on their later folk-ballad style of the 1970s are "Lady Jane" and "Back Street Girl."[6] And like their traditionalist take on the blues, the Stones derive their minor-chord injections from the immediate precedents in vernacular and popular music. It is worth stepping back for a moment to look at the wider musical context that has bearing on the Stones' songwriting.

In the 1950s taking a cue from American popular song (in particular the Broadway tradition) and jazz, one of the most popular chord patterns, often called the doo-wop progression, employs a minor chord as part of its sequence. Thousands of songs follow this template, from the Penguins' "Earth Angel" to the Beatles' "Happiness Is a Warm Gun." (We will look at this type of progression below with "I Got the Blues," and later on with "Beast of Burden" from *Some Girls.*)

Next, the folk ballad and its formulaic progressions in minor modality had already made significant inroads into '60s pop. This was also the time of the folk revival, and numerous English ballads were in minor keys; many of these old ballads had survived in the coveted Appalachian repertoire prized by folk purists. But besides the revivalists, folk-rock groups like the British group Fairport Convention also turned to this repertoire in the minor mode; for example, they released renditions of the possible medieval song, "Nottamun Town," and the seventeenth-century ballad, "Mattie Groves," in 1969.[7] In the 1960s Dylan did not often sing in the minor, but on *John Wesley Harding* he had two original songs in the minor (perhaps for the first time), "As I Went Out One Morning" and "All Along the Watchtower," the latter immortalized in a transposed cover version by Hendrix. Finally, many of these folk songs in minor use a cyclically repeating progression; below we will look at a particular folk progression in the minor that influences "Sister Morphine."

Finally, there is the minor-key subgenre of modern urban blues. With numerous examples, here we will cite a few of the most well-known. Some iconic representations of this type of blues are Albert King's "Born under a Bad Sign" (C-sharp minor; furiously covered by Cream), B. B. King's "The Thrill Is Gone" (B minor), and Zeppelin's showstopper, "Since I've Been Loving You" (C minor); note that this genre continued as a major style for guitar exhibition in the 1970s.[8] Because these songs also grew out of a jazz context, they often provide an open door for extended soloing and jams. Although unreleased, in October 1969 the Stones did work up an amazing minor-key urban blues number that features Bobby Keys on saxophone and Taylor's lead (though at times in a duet with Richards) called "Hillside Blues" or "I Don't Know the Reason Why" (F minor).[9]

For their last two albums, the Stones had avoided having any songs in a minor key and barely inserted any minor chords in their songs. In fact the only places are the bridge about the "faceless crowd" (sung by Jagger) in "Salt of the Earth," the intro to "Monkey Man," and one quick minor chord in their arrangement of "Love in Vain." From this time there is also "Blood Red Wine." It is a folksy, morbid ballad with a strong E minor presence, but it remained an unrealized *Beggars* outtake, though with great potential.[10] This was perhaps due to the band's intent to establish a harder, earthier blues-rock content to the songs, as minor chords and keys are hard to find in traditional rural blues and again were a specialty within the urban blues.[11] But though major is the main tonality of *Sticky Fingers*, there are some still some striking occurrences of minor on the album—in five songs to be precise, taking us back to the more varied chordal arsenal of their pop-rock repertoire of *Aftermath* and *Between the Buttons*.

Because of the overall rarity of minor in the Stones generally, we will take the opportunity to explore one of their minor-key songs in particular, "Sister Morphine," as a statement of a folk sensibility in an otherwise blues-enforced major-keyed and chorded repertoire, and then instrumental solos in the minor key in "I Got the Blues" and "Can't You Hear Me Knocking" as a platform for song expansion. From there, we propose that the Stones' use of minor chords on *Sticky Fingers* can be divided into two different sources—on the one hand, the folk ballad, and on the other, jazz and the urban blues. For example, songs like "Wild Horses," "Sister Morphine," and "Moonlight Mile" relate to the folk ballad, while jams in "I Got the Blues" and "Can't You Hear Me Knocking'" come from the urban blues and jazz respectively.

Of these songs, "Sister Morphine" is the only one actually in a minor key, in this case A minor. And chronologically it is also the earliest song on *Sticky Fingers*, with a somewhat convoluted recording history that could have seen it placed on either *Beggars* or *Let It Bleed*. Jagger allegedly wrote the "riff" to the song while on holiday in Rome in 1968, with later input on the lyrics by his then girlfriend, Marianne Faithfull, who received a credit many years later for her contribution of a couple of key lines (though the credit is not found on the original album jacket to *Sticky Fingers*).[12] In fact, Faithfull contends that she wrote more than a couple of key lines and that she brought the story idea to Jagger. She also recorded and released the first version of the song (as a B-side) in February 1969, arranged by Jack Nitzsche with members of the Stones and Cooder backing her. Faithfull's record company, Decca, promptly pulled the song because of the taboo subject matter of drug addiction.

According to Stones researcher Martin Elliott, the Stones (and session players associated with the band, probably with Cooder on slide and Nitzsche on organ) recorded a version of "Sister Morphine" during the *Beggars* sessions in May 1968 (available on bootleg versions only). But the take released on *Sticky Fingers* is from the *Let It Bleed* sessions. Being essentially a Jagger original with input from Faithfull, it is quite a singular song in the Stones repertoire, especially with the addition of Cooder's jabbing slide playing, his only credited guitar playing with the Stones. In this respect, too, it can be compared to another song that originates from late 1968 with Cooder playing, Jagger's "Memo from Turner." This latter song is in the key of A and has a chorus where the minor chords begin and are quite exposed.[13]

The minor key fits the subject matter of the song, inspired by the French Romantic poet Charles Baudelaire (according to Faithfull), who himself had abused drugs and died young, and once again the Velvet Underground's grungy "Heroin." The song's central motive presents the plea of a dying man, barely surviving from a car crash and lying in a hospital bed begging for morphine to ease his pain and soothe his last moment; in inserting us into this nightmarish scene, we can add that the story recalls the macabre stories of Edgar Allan Poe.[14] The song is alleged to have taken on personal connections as well, in particular to Anita Pallenberg who was recovering from a car crash near Redlands with Richards.

Richards lightly strums an A minor chord on his acoustic guitar (a Gibson Hummingbird) to get "Sister Morphine" going. But to make the chord interesting, he adds an extra note to the chord on the highest string (E). This changes the quality of the chord significantly, making for a more complex sound.[15] These added notes as harmonic-rhythmic devices become more prominent in the Stones' music as we shall see, and we will look at them in particular below with "Brown Sugar." Here, though, the point of the added note is melodic, as the descending alternation of the note (G) with the open string E forms a universally recognizable interval that is immediately familiar to most listeners.[16]

Told from the first-person narrative, the musical setting in the simple verse format (i.e., no chorus) attempts to replicate the dying man's foggy consciousness and fading grasp on reality. The song possesses a classic textural buildup where instruments are piled on as the verses intensify the story and we learn more about what is happening. The narrator addresses morphine, personified as "sister." At first, we think that this is a poetic touch. In verse two he is "trying to score," and then in verse three, when he calls out for "sweet, cousin cocaine," we realize that the dying man has experience with drugs and is probably a heavy user. While addressing "sister morphine" and "cousin cocaine," they use another minor chord (Dm), which is closely related to the Am.

The musical setting relies on an asymmetrical measure count for the verses, which might be the only time a Stones song has this rare feature (as far as I can determine). That is, for verse one, there are sixteen measures, a typical count. For verse two ("The scream of the ambulance . . ."), there are twenty-three measures (approximately); this is to accommodate the two extra lines of text.

Now, where it gets interesting is how the chord progression changes to map these extra measures. Everything in the second verse is the same as the first until the line "Why does the doctor . . ." Here, they play an E7 chord (the dominant-seventh chord in the key of A minor) for the first time in the song. Locally, with regard to the chords around it, the inclusion of this chord forms part of what is known as the "Andalusian cadence" (perhaps a misnomer on two counts—it is better described as a progression, and is probably not from the Spanish province). This is a very old descending bass line, with chordal realization going back to the Renaissance, that was utilized during the folk revival (sometimes it is called the "folk progression"); again, to my knowledge, this appears to mark the only time the Stones use it.[17] The E7 chord should resolve the tension into the A-minor tonic or home key, but here to extend the progression with the extra lines of text, they instead pivot back to an F chord (on the word "face"; F is a substitute chord for A minor, as they both share two common notes). But using the F chord out of the E7 only locks in the "Spanishness" of this passage, as this is a common modal move in flamenco music called "Phrygian," not so common in rock.[18]

At this point the flamencoesque affinity behind another iconic song of the era can be noted: Zeppelin's "Babe I'm Gonna Leave You," which also relies on both a version of the Andalusian cadence in A minor, and the E–F flamenco flourish.[19] We can only speculate as to whether Jagger had heard this cover of the song that had come out in January 1969, but he might have known "Babe I'm Gonna Leave You" as recorded by the Los Angeles–based folk-rock group the Association, from 1965, which uses the same progression for the verse as Zeppelin.[20] Or perhaps these types of changes, common for folk musicians, were in the air, as it were, and it is mere coincidence that the songs share such a similar chord patterning. But what does seem evident is that Jagger derived his chords and progression for "Sister Morphine" from these folk-flamenco types of guitaristic folk stylings, though it is not clear how conscious he was of distinct precedents.

The other verses (three and four) return to the shorter measure count (seventeen and sixteen, respectively), but, in keeping with the asymmetrical spirit of the song's verse measure count, offer similar though different chord progressions than the first two. Again, this is extremely rare in pop or rock songs and in songs by the Stones. Because they use the same basket of chords already heard, it is hard to pick up on unless one pays close attention. But as a musical effect, the variation helps lend the song its disorientedness—as the narrator relates, "things are not what they seem."

While "Sister Morphine" exhibits one of the more complex musical progressions of the Stones' repertoire, "I Got the Blues" is on the simpler side. The nostalgia of the musical style matches the realness of the lament of the singer's loss in love. Indeed, the song is understood as Jagger's other sendoff, along with "Wild Horses," for his relationship with Faithfull. It uses a variant of the doo-wop progression, and as such, the song sounds like it could have been written when the band started in the early 1960s. This repeated progression (G–D–Em–C) for the verse recalls a not-too-distant musical past of '60s soul, although Jagger and the band treat it with the same reverence in which they play their

Delta blues covers. In this respect, we will need to qualify the notion of "nostalgia" as it applies to the Stones.

And in fact, "I Got the Blues" updates an earlier song in the Stones' repertoire, "If You Need Me" (written by Wilson Pickett, though his recording was quickly supplanted by Solomon Burke's), which is in the same key and uses a similar progression.[21] For the guitar accompaniment, Richards plays arpeggiated chords, established in the intro with an overlaid guitar (probably Taylor's). Again, this technique recalls the early gospel-soul guitar found prominently in Stax and early soul records, for example, Otis Redding's "I've Been Loving You Too Long," but already would have sounded old-fashioned by the early 1970s. Further, the slow tempo of these soul songs is realized via an undulating time signature of 6/8 (**1**, 2, 3, **4**, 5, 6, where the bold numbers receive more emphasis, the one beat a little more than the four). And with the addition of the horns, the song's homage to Stax becomes complete.

Even as the Stones set their sights on an early 1960s idiom, they paradoxically manage to keep the song relevant to the times. That they could pull this off was demonstrated already in their rural blues covers, from "Prodigal Son" to "Love in Vain." Namely, they play these older songs not as nostalgia for the past, but with an emotional intensity, urgency, and sincerity as if they were conceived contemporaneously. They seemingly obliterate the distance of the past in a postmodern pastiche of blues revivalist aesthetics (i.e., that a song is "authentic" vis-à-vis the past) with the commercial demands of the capitalist music industry (i.e., that a song is "new"). This reflects one strategy for how an old band stays relevant to youth culture (for example, their 1995 album career retrospective, *Stripped*), but the Stones seemed to have found the solution quite early in their career through this postmodern collapse of history. Here the past and present function as temporal equals in an "imaginary museum" where nostalgia no longer functions as such, but rather becomes taken up in a hermeneutic space where old and new styles coexist side by side, while sublimating the concept of evolutionary development.

As if to demonstrate how nostalgia functions in a postmodern pop soundscape, we can turn to Billy Preston's organ solo in "I Got the Blues." Preston was a teenage session musician from Los Angeles when he played gospel-tinged organ on Sam Cooke's 1963 album, *Night Beat*, which also contained "Little Red Rooster" in which he was featured.

After stints in bands leading up to Ray Charles, he was invited by the Beatles to play with them, which he did on "Get Back" where he appears as a credited musician. This song marks a similar point in the Beatles' career, as they too were looking back on their roots after wandering far from their origins, but in a way where they could still claim originality. Preston's electric keyboard solo on "Get Back" certainly helped to boost the Beatles back to the top of the charts. As a follow-up to his Beatles debut, the Stones tapped Preston for "I Got the Blues," on which makes his first of many appearances with the Stones both in the studio and live.

Preston's organ solo, as it were, appears seemingly out of nowhere, and so does the turn to an unprepared C-minor chord. It is a very different solo from his bouncy, light bluesy jaunt on "Get Back." On "I Got the Blues," his playing is more soulful and heartrending, as befitting the song at hand. However in this era of jamming, where longer solos were becoming de rigueur, the small amount of time allotted (eight measures) for Preston seems, once again, to harken back to the early '60s. Coincidentally, his solo on "Get Back" is also eight measures, though at a faster clip in 4/4 time.

Despite Preston's solo, in critiques of the Stones the song does not fare well, perhaps due to uneasiness with the unexpected return to the chordal figurations of the end of the doo-wop musical era. Going back to the rural blues or old folk songs was in vogue at this time, and Stax-inspired soul music with some funk thrown in certainly continues in this era with the likes of Al Green and Curtis Mayfield among others, but once again the soul of the early to mid-1960s Burke-Redding-Soul Clan era had already been supplanted. Some critics have felt the song is undeveloped, although its sparseness seems befitting of its genre.

But as Andy Warhol's art attempts to reframe our relationship with recently passed pop celebrities and mass objects of consumer culture, a case could be made that the Stones do a similar thing in the 1970s to the 1980s and beyond with the '60s soul that they started with. Warhol's was a strategy about the theory of art, a challenging of what constituted a work; the Stones start by paying homage to their musical heroes, but end up with a viable path for ensuring their contemporaneity. That is, by continually raiding the past but creating new music, it becomes more difficult for younger listeners to distinguish the old from the new, as Warhol's *Brillo Boxes* were impossible to distinguish from their original.

Jagger ends "I Got the Blues" touchingly with a mention of three in the morning, here an hour of crisis and pain in a relationship, perhaps a neat homage to and twist on Redding's celebration of the hour (quarter to three, to be exact) in his "Cigarettes and Coffee." Finally, coming full circle, just as Redding recognized the soulful content of "Satisfaction," Solomon Burke, one of the fathers of soul music, pays tribute to the Stones in his 2002 recording of "I Got the Blues," complete with an organ solo. In contrast, when Al Green recorded "Get Back," he left out the keyboard part.

ON THE PRIMARY ROLE OF THE GUITAR

The Stones' music has always been about the guitar, an aspect they share with their British Invasion brethren. The vast majority of their music was conceived on the guitar, and the instrument determines the riff-driven focus. With Richards at the helm of the musical side of the songwriting, he also leads Watts and thereby the band's tempo in the studio and in live performance. Usually the tempo is something determined by the drummer's count off. The textural centrality of the guitar was challenged when Jones started to introduce other colors, as in when he experimented with other instruments for various timbre effects. But with the addition of Taylor and his replacement, Ronnie Wood, the guitar returns as the primal force determining the band's intricately layered or woven approach to texture, never to leave. And these guitarists would help the Stones immensely to remain on top of their game during arguably the most guitar-centric decade in popular music history, the 1970s, from soft, acoustic singer-songwriter ballads to hard and punk rock.

As pop music since the 1980s has, in fits and starts, generally moved away from the guitar and toward electronic music making through beats, samples, and synthesizers (techno, or now the enormously popular DJs of dance music or EDM), this has led to the marginalization of the Stones' style of rock.[22] If they are out of step with the zeitgeist of contemporary popular music making, their guitar-centered music still has no problem selling out arenas and stadiums worldwide at a time when only a few acts probably could do so. In this way, the Stones' métier will always offer a return to a time when the guitar ruled the music for the masses.

Sticky Fingers marks an incredible turning point in the imaginative possibilities for the emotional range of the guitar's voice. And unlike other late '60s Stones' efforts in which the guitar parts are basically all by Richards, even with some cameo spots by Jones, Taylor, and Cooder, *Sticky Fingers* witnesses a broadening of other band members besides Richards providing guitar direction and writing. Jagger had been learning the guitar for the past few years, coming up with the basic riff and music for "Brown Sugar" while doing the filming for *Ned Kelly* in the fall of 1969 in Australia. Richards also claims to have contributed to it—he says in *Life*, without elaborating, that he "did tidy it [the riff] up a bit."[23] But this is quite an achievement on Jagger's part, considering that he managed to have a role in one of the big three riffs of the Stones, the others being "Satisfaction" and "Jumpin' Jack Flash," in a band most identified with their command of the riff. Jagger also wrote the music for two other songs with a prominent role for the guitar, "Sway" and "Moonlight Mile," both of which might not even have Richards playing on them.

Taylor's solos and playing on *Sticky Fingers* also redefined the collective sound the early 1970s Stones would take on. No longer reliant on Richards as the sole input for guitar textures, the music takes on surprising twists and turns. Taylor possessed a fluid sense of melodic line and approached the songs as a lead guitarist. Furthermore, the weaving that had originally fascinated Richards could commence once again (though in different and unexpected ways). Coming up through John Mayall's Bluesbreakers with recording experience as well, Taylor was still spectacularly young at only twenty years old to be thrust into the limelight with the much more seasoned and already established Stones. Richards writes on their immediate rapport around the guitar:

> And we did the most brilliant stuff together, some of the most brilliant stuff the Stones ever did. Everything was there in his playing—the melodic touch, a beautiful sustain and a way of reading a song. . . . He'd get where I was going even before I did.[24]

Richards knew from his previous work with Taylor on "Love in Vain" and "Honky Tonk Women" that they needed to create artistic space for Taylor on the new album.

The most vivid example of Taylor stretching out is on "Can't You Hear Me Knocking," where the second half of the song turns into an impromptu, extended jam led by him and Bobby Keys on saxophone. As noted by Richards, they really had two songs that they melded into one—the second jam part being a live studio improvisation that was an unplanned section, fortunately captured because the engineers kept the tape rolling. Symbolically, the song presents the two signature guitar worlds of the Stones: the Dionysian, knife-like attack of Richards's rhythmic-melodic riff at the onset, and the Apollonian, mellifluous, and longer-line, single-note phrasing of Taylor for the jam. Finally, it is one of the rare Stones songs where Jagger's voice does not reappear triumphantly after an instrumental section. Apparently Miller had to convince Jagger to keep this jam extension of the song on the final release. But the melodic substance of this outro jam more than compensates—this is not a garden-variety, wandering psychedelic space jam. Adding to the melodic direction is the groove element, with the return of Dijon's congas to the worldbeat rhythm section and Preston's organ buttressing the song's Afro feel.

As we mentioned above, the outro jam turns to the parallel minor key of D minor; the song itself is in D major.[25] For the latter part of the saxophone solo (after 3:24), another minor chord is snuck in there as an appendage to the D minor, so by 3:51 the two-chord phrasing (D and E minor) can be distinctly heard. The jazz-rock texture departs from anything the band had previously done and shows a band willing to add a new stylistic element to its arsenal, and moreover one that was a natural expansion of the minor blues.

Taylor's extension to the song begins at 4:41, and Richards fixes the accompanimental groove into a repeating pattern on a single D minor chord. Though the band claims to not have been thinking along these lines, the comparisons to what the band Santana was doing with minor-key, jazz-rock jams of this era seem unavoidable. The rhythm-section instrumentation alone seems like textbook Santana, with congas and organ filling out the thick middle. Note that as a neat historical tie-in, Santana pays tribute to "Can't You Hear Me Knocking'" in brilliant fashion on his 2010 album *Guitar Heaven.* Taylor plays on a Gibson ES-345 from a family of guitars often used in the minor blues repertoire (B. B. King for one), whose dark, reedy timbre will become more significant for Richards and the band going forward.

If the Santanaesque, jazzier texture is new to the Stones, so is Taylor's classical procedure for building his solo. He does not fill space, as it were, with meandering and clever licks, but rather constructs a longer narrative with a beginning, middle, and end. He starts off with shorter statements that have ample space around them, deftly taking motives he discovers and then repeating those. These cellular repetitions effectively build tension, which he releases in long bends. Taylor holds his virtuosity in check, and instead of issuing a fast flurry of notes at the end, he opts for a riff that the players holding the groove respond to (starting at ca. 6:00). Rather subtly, he hands the open space back to the saxophone (6:35), as the riff becomes accompaniment. As these types of open-ended, minor-key jams can be difficult to wind down and get out of, Taylor pops in a concluding riff (6:58) that he repeats four times. This final riff takes the song out of the minor key and back to the major of the song's opening, and he outlines a rising D-dominant seventh chord that is one of the best outro riff conclusions in the Stones' vast repertoire.

LISTENING VIGNETTE: "DEAD FLOWERS"

If there were an anomalous song on the album, it would be the pleasing country-rocker "Dead Flowers." The song also carries distinction of being the first song the Stones recorded after Altamont, in an Olympic recording session December 15, 1969. As conceived by Jagger, its lyrical conceit bears much similarity to an old blues tune from Blind Willie McTell, "Lay Some Flowers on My Grave."[26] With its heroin reference, the song sets up "Moonlight Mile," another drug song and the album's conclusion.

But even as the only country song on *Sticky Fingers*, if viewed within the larger context, the Stones were strategically placing a country song on each of their albums from this period. These songs share an ironic delivery by Jagger, who has maintained that Richards's voice was more suited to country music than his. In "Dead Flowers," a satirical take on country music, it harkens back to "Dear Doctor" from *Beggars*, to a lesser extent "Country Honk" on *Let It Bleed*, and looks forward to "Sweet Virginia" on *Exile on Main Street*. Also note that at a time of open tunings, all of these respective country songs are in standard tuning, though "Sweet Virginia" is capoed up at the second fret. Furthermore, each of these songs contains a reference to an American location, echoed by Jagger's attempts to accommodate a Southern drawl. It is clear that all of these features—irony, standard tuning, an American location, and a drawl—are the generalized markers for the performance practice of country music for the Stones and will figure into perhaps their last real attempt at a country song—"Far Away Eyes" from *Some Girls*. Finally, instead of the employing a fiddle as they did throughout "Country Honk," with Taylor they now could have instead a proper guitar lead in the Nashville style for "Dead Flowers."

For this "Dead Flowers" listening vignette we will analyze the song's placement in the last scene of the cult classic crime film *The Big Lebowski* (1998). For some general context, the cinematic association of the Stones with the criminal underworld already goes back to the 1960s. For example, there is Jagger's singing of "Memo from Turner" in *Performance*, where Jagger plays a gangster. But probably the filmmaker who did more to solidify this association is Martin Scorsese. As one of the pioneer directors in the insertion of pop and rock songs that function as an ersatz film score, Scorsese places Stones songs at key dramatic moments to achieve maximum effect in his mafia-gangster films—for example, *Mean Streets*, *Goodfellas*, *Casino*, and more recently, *The Departed.* The respective scenes, with mostly diegetic music, are ominous and foreboding, as the Stones' music supplies the emotional backdrop of invincibility for the transgressive, criminal behavior occurring or about to occur. Because of his close identification with the Stones' music and the historical depth it imparts to a scene, Scorsese even made a live concert film of the Stones, *Shine a Light* (2006).

Following Scorsese's musical lead, the Coen brothers' *Big Lebowski* also relies on a sequence of pop songs for its soundtrack and carefully culminates with "Dead Flowers" in the last scene. The song's alt-country, outlaw ethos perfectly fits the decadently laid-back but fiercely philosophical nature of the main character, the Dude. In the last scene, the Dude, a zen-like, hippie throwback to the '60s, is in a bowling alley preparing for a tournament. He has spent most of the film inadvertently caught up in a criminal scheme through a seemingly arbitrary chain of events started because of a mix-up over his name. The bowling alley plays "Dead Flowers," and the Dude goes to the bar for some beer, where he chats with a cowboy (the Stranger; also the narrator, played by

Sam Elliott). When asked about how things are going, the Dude responds with his characteristically hopeful albeit melancholy resignation, "strikes and gutters, ups and downs." His last line in the movie is one of the most famous, where he says self-reflectively, quasi-religiously, and equivocally: "the Dude abides."[27]

"Dead Flowers" continues to play as the Stranger wraps up his part of the narration. In this way, "Dead Flowers" serves as amplification to the Dude's worldview of accepting one's fate, of remaining, abiding, or waiting (seemingly passively), while also thematically framing the movie. The Coen brothers allow the song to continue while the final credits play, as we continue to reflect on what "the Dude abides" means.

Finally, deepening the matrix of cultural interconnections that the song triggers, the Coens do not use the Rolling Stones version, but a live cover by Townes Van Zandt, an eccentric Texan songwriter—known as Texas's answer to Bob Dylan—who sings with an authentic drawl. Van Zandt's real-life persona, especially his struggles with substance abuse and addiction that probably sabotaged his career, resonates with the Dude's passive, nonchalant approach to life. Later, Jeff Bridges, the actor who plays the Dude, re-created a tragic character similar to Van Zandt in the film *Crazy Heart* (2009). Van Zandt slows "Dead Flowers" down considerably and captures the pain of drug addiction from his personal experience. Finally, note that *Sticky Fingers* was one of Van Zandt's acknowledged favorite albums.

ON THE TEXTURE OF *STICKY FINGERS*: FIVE-STRING/ OPEN-G TUNING, ACOUSTIC GUITARS, HORNS, AND STRINGS

For a band focused on the gritty sound and purity of the early blues, *Sticky Fingers* shows a group willing to delve into richly arranged textures using a variety of means. And still the timbral additions do not in any way depart radically with what the band had already done. By this time many of their musical tendencies and preferences had solidified, as the Stones had substantial working relationships with many of the industry's best engineers on the production side, and a significant reliance on favorite session players. Some of these contributions by session players were quite substantial, as we have seen in the case of Nicky

Hopkins. Although Hopkins is on only one song on *Sticky Fingers*, he comes back to play a major role on *Exile*. But on *Sticky Fingers* there are now major musical contributions from the horns. Furthermore, and reserving something special for the last song on the album, a unique string arrangement appears on Jagger's epic "Moonlight Mile."

But we will start our discussion of the unique sound of *Sticky Fingers* by considering the rethought and imaginative interplay of the guitars. The album completes the transformation of Richards as an open-tuning guitarist. He will occasionally still play and write in standard tuning, but from this point on it is the open-G tuning that inspires and continues to intrigue him. For the songs in open G, furthermore, Richards removes the lowest string (E, which would be taken down to D in traditional Delta open-G tuning), effectively making the guitar a five-string instrument. He could now strike the strings with his characteristic aggressiveness, without having to worry about hitting any unwanted notes. And this did not require Taylor to play in open tuning, and in fact his guitar in standard tuning complements Richards's timbre, as for example his fills in "Brown Sugar."

It is thus the aesthetic soundscape derived from the open-tuned guitars that shapes the album. Side one uses all open tunings, mostly open G, while side two has only two songs in standard tuning (refer to table 5.1).

Both songs that Jagger wrote, "Brown Sugar" and "Moonlight Mile," are also in open G. For "You Gotta Move," Richards uses open C as he plays a rare slide (for him) on his National guitar, and for "Wild Horses," Taylor's part is in the so-called Nashville tuning (more below), which gives the song its shimmering quality.

The two most iconic songs on the album with open-G tuned riffs are "Brown Sugar" and "Can't You Hear Me Knocking." Both possess instantly recognizable riffs that are created from the simplest of chordal means, and yet both take such different approaches to their respective head motives. The "Brown Sugar" riffing is centered on suspended notes above the chord and is pretty simple to handle for the intermediate guitarist.[28] In basic terms, the chords are barred with the first finger (as in any open tuning), and other fingers are added above to create the suspension. The suspension adds tension and excitement to the sound of the chord, providing a brief feeling of instability that is resolved back down into the stability of the fully barred chord (i.e., the main chord).

Table 5.1. Keys and Guitar Tunings of Songs on *Sticky Fingers* (Chronological Order)

Song	Key	Tuning
"Sister Morphine"	A minor	standard
"You Gotta Move"	C	open C
"Brown Sugar"	C	open G
"Wild Horses"	G	open G and Nashville
"Dead Flowers"	G	open G
"Moonlight Mile"	G	open G
"I Got the Blues"	G	standard
"Can't You Hear Me Knocking"	D	open G
"Bitch"	A	standard
"Sway"	G	open G

Listening to the first two chords at the very opening of "Brown Sugar," we hear a suspension give way to a full bar chord, which is the V or dominant chord (G). Then there is a chord change to the tonic chord (C), played twice, then two suspensions and finally the tonic chord again, alone. In addition to the suspensions, what makes this chordal riffing so compelling is that it is syncopated, with the basic accenting of the chord on the upbeats and weak beats, similar to the Bo Diddley beat and so much African American–derived music. The Stones had truly absorbed and learned from their sources.

Just as "Brown Sugar" does not play in the key of G but in C (this would be chord barred at the fifth fret), so "Can You Hear Me Knocking" also does not have its tonic on G, but is instead in D (barred at the seventh fret). Here Richards resorts to a twisty variation on his familiar rock shuffle style. The longer-line, downward glissandos heard at the very opening contend with the carved-out upward shuffle figures of the blues. The progression oscillates not between V–I as in "Brown Sugar," but between I–bVII (D and C), again the Mixolydian progression at the core of the Stones' music. For the verse, Richards leaves gaps and lots of space around the chords, in a style he feels is central to rock and roll going back to "Heartbreak Hotel."

Thus in the space of two songs, the open-G tuning manages to transform humble progressions at the basis of thousands, if not more, songs into symbolic containers of riffing energy that have come to define the musical 1970s. As both riffs are played as head motives, in this respect they are the heirs to the Stax horn-based approach to song creation. But the transfer of the timbre from a horn to a distorted guitar produces an entirely new sonic effect. The mellifluous legato of the horns on Stax records gives way to the percussive, edgy attack of the distorted signal of the guitar strings—the former offering a feeling of down-home comfort, the latter imparting thrown exposure to the raw grittiness of street life.

Adding to the variety of sound offered by alternate tunings, the acoustic guitar further anchors the album in the traditional category of the folk-blues genre, as it had done on *Beggars* and *Let It Bleed*. In short, *Sticky Fingers* poses an ideal balance between acoustic and electric guitars on a rock album. Even when using acoustic for the basic rhythm track, the Stones cannot seem to resist adding an electric guitar to the mix, which adds commentary through fills, similar in function to a pedal steel in country music.

Certainly the most exemplary acoustic playing on the album, and one of the finest songs in the Stones' giant catalog, is on "Wild Horses." Indeed, the song's chord progression, in the key of G major, became a staple for legions of amateur strummers and would-be rock stars by the end of the 1970s, similar in this regard to other play-along classics like "Angie," Led Zeppelin's "Stairway to Heaven," and Pink Floyd's "Wish You Were Here." For the chorus, Richards returns to his signature Mixolydian move—over the lines "Couldn't drag me away," the Mixolydian chord (or bVII, here F) is heard on the word "drag."

Even as the progression for "Wild Horses" is simple on the surface, the guitarists' interplay stuns with its clever intricacy, exemplifying a further evolution of the concept of weaving. There are three main guitar parts, without counting other possible overdubs buried in the track. The central guitar is a twelve-string of Richards, perhaps a Martin D12-20 acoustic that he played in concert at the time.[29] Richards got the idea to turn a twelve-string acoustic into a ten-string one by removing the lowest string as he did in his in open G, five-string tuning at this time; his guitar provides the backbone of the song's accompaniment and rhythm. Richards's playing offers a full, ringing sound, articulated with his trademark deliberate heavy pressure on the striking of the strings, though perhaps not quite as hard as his forceful strokes on "Jumpin' Jack Flash."

Overlaid on this and actually starting the song is Taylor's part, which was (according to him) played on one of Richards's Gibson acoustics.[30] This marks the second time (after "Jumpin' Jack Flash") that the Stones employ the Nashville tuning on one of their songs. Richards says he learned about the tuning from a guitarist in George Jones's band while the band was on tour in 1964. Strictly speaking, Nashville does not qualify as an alternative tuning, but its sonic difference from standard tuning may as well be. Though "Jumpin' Jack Flash" has this tuning, it is somewhat buried in the mix. On "Wild Horses" the Nashville tuning reaches the forefront of the texture, as Taylor strums the evocative intro. For this tuning, the bottom four strings of the guitar—E, A, D, G—are tuned an octave higher. In effect, it is like a twelve-string guitar without the lower string of the pair, thus, the higher range partials are heard in full clarity and detail without interference by the bassier, lower strings. A couple of other '70s classic rock songs that followed "Wild Horses" and also relied on Nashville tuning are "Dust in the Wind" by Kansas and "Hey You" by Pink Floyd. The most noticeable feature of Taylor's part is his tasteful plucking of harmonics, where the note is fingered above the fret and lightly activated with the pick, creating a bell-like sound. These harmonics, or upper partial notes, add definition to the chord changes during the verses, and their percussive incisiveness invokes a piano part.

Lastly, the third guitar part on "Wild Horses" finds Richards with an electric (probably his '54 Telecaster) playing country-style licks mostly in the tonic major key. Indeed this is perhaps one of the few times that Richards does not play in the minor pentatonic for his solo. In addition to its filler role, the arrangement spotlights the electric guitar for the instrumental breaks. The first such interlude (starting ca. 3:06) takes off from the Mixolydian chord (F), and here Richards flirts with a bluesier sound for the first time in the song.[31] Still, he keeps the style in check before going off too far in the direction of the blues. For the second and more integrated instrumental break, the guitar solo (in G major) substitutes for the singer's melody, as the band plays the changes to the verse. This is the quietest part of the song (other than the opening), and its meditative focus sets up the triumphant final singing of the chorus.

Turning to the horns, saxophonist Bobby Keys had already played a solo with the Stones on *Let It Bleed*'s "Live with Me." He would provide much more support on *Sticky Fingers*, *Exile*, and later albums, and after tours in the early 1970s would play live with the band from 1982 on. Trumpeter Jim Price joins him on the album's rousing rocker, "Bitch," which is perhaps the first Stones song to feature a true Stax-style head motive played by a horn section. The horns bolster the swaggering lyrics and add punctuation for Taylor's extended lead for the outro with Jagger's vocal extemporizations. Still, it would be on their next album, *Exile*, where the band takes full advantage of the horn section of Keys and Price.

In addition to the horns, string/orchestral arrangements appear on two Jagger songs, "Sway" and "Moonlight Mile." The band brought on Paul Buckmaster for the task of arranging these extra parts. Buckmaster is a cellist who had recently done work with David Bowie and some arranging for Elton John. Unlike "Space Oddity" (Bowie) or "Your Song" (John), where the carpet of strings overtakes (arguably) the core of the rock combo, the strings in these two songs are an additive element to the mix, complementing the texture like an extra guitar or horn.

For the dream-like ballad "Moonlight Mile," with its ambient double-tracked vocal, the strings help the band expand beyond the simple formulas of the blues. The equivocal lyrics of the song have led to much speculation about the song's meaning, from being a portrait of Jagger's anxiety at the time to a drug (cocaine)-fueled fantasy. The world-music exoticism of the song picks up where earlier efforts like "Paint It Black" left off. Jagger conceived the song in a meditative "Orientalist" vein—the song was originally called "The Japanese Thing"—and his acoustic guitar intro in the major pentatonic has a vaguely Asian ring to it.[32] But when the Stones reference exotic music, it is actually as a vaguely situated "Other," and it seems more accurate to conceptualize it as something from the East. In a later interview Jagger called the song a dreamy, semi–Middle Eastern piece.[33] But the purported Asianness or exotic Easternness of the song reaches full potential in the string writing of Buckmaster, with its glissandos and sharply defined rhythmic edges.

SONG CHRONOLOGY AND THE UNIQUE RECORDING CIRCUMSTANCES

The Stones recorded "Moonlight Mile" in March 1970 at Jagger's recently purchased mansion outside of London, Stargroves. This is one of the first recordings to use their newly purchased truck that they outfitted as a music studio, dubbed Rolling Stones Mobile Studio, or, according to Richards, "The Mighty Mobile." At Stargroves, the band relied on the great hall for their sessions, setting up camp in the nearly empty house. The creative freedom of working in a historical, architecturally rich environment would be followed by other bands of the era. Taking their cue from the Stones, Led Zeppelin, Deep Purple, and the Who, among others, also took advantage of the "Mighty Mobile" at various British countryside retreats, with some sessions even done at Stargroves.

The Stones recorded half of the songs on *Sticky Fingers* at Stargroves, but more importantly, with the mobile studio they discovered that they could record nearly anywhere, an exciting possibility that would be crucial for the creation of their next album, *Exile*. The Stargroves tracks from March and October 1970 were the last songs recorded (see table 5.2).

In terms of the sound, with good speakers or headphones on playback, the Stargroves songs seem to have more ambient depth to them than the other tracks on the album. This is perhaps because the natural sound of a very warm room comes through, with its richer overtones and a deeper bass presence.

The other main venue for *Sticky Fingers* was at the Muscle Shoals Sound Studio, where three of the songs were recorded in three days, right before they played at Altamont. As Richards says, "The setup had a legendary ring because some of the great soul records had been coming out of there for several years—Wilson Pickett, Aretha Franklin, Percy Sledge's 'When a Man Loves a Woman.'"[34] Located in northern Alabama, the Muscle Shoals vicinity was part of the so-called Southern soul triangle for record production that included Memphis, Tennessee, and Macon, Georgia.[35] Stanley Booth, author of the band-authorized book, *The True Adventures of the Rolling Stones*, who also participated as a guest on the American tour of 1969, writes extensively about the behind-the-scenes aspect to these sessions that produced the three

Table 5.2. Recording Venues and First Sessions for *Sticky Fingers*

Song	Primary Venue	First Sessions
"Sister Morphine"	Olympic Sound Studios (London)	May–June 1968
"You Gotta Move"	Muscle Shoals Sound Studio (Sheffield, AL)	early December 1969
"Brown Sugar"	Muscle Shoals	early December 1969
"Wild Horses"	Muscle Shoals	early December 1969
"Dead Flowers"	Olympic	mid-December 1969
"Moonlight Mile"	Stargroves (Rolling Stones Mobile, East Woodhay, England)	March–May 1970
"I Got the Blues"	Stargroves	March–May 1970
"Can't You Hear Me Knocking"	Stargroves	March–May 1970
"Bitch"	Stargroves	October–November 1970
"Sway"	Stargroves	October–November 1970

songs.[36] With his Southerner background and connections, Booth was also important in securing the venue in the first place. Jim Dickinson, a session piano player, also helped with the logistics for the recording session. Dickinson joined the Stones on "Wild Horses," taking full advantage of the tack piano that was available in the studio. Dickinson says about the collaboration that the song marries two opposing sentiments: On the one hand, Richards had conceived the song about missing his newborn son, Marlon, while on the other Jagger had rewritten the lyrics to describe his recent split from Faithfull.[37]

CONCLUSION

With material and sessions spanning from 1968 to fall 1970, the Stones' *Sticky Fingers* brought together the tendencies of the previous albums while showing that the Stones were still capable of leading the counterculture into the 1970s. The album participated in music-industry trends of the time, from soft acoustic, singer-songwriter style balladry, to screaming rock buttressed by horns, to one-chord jams backed by Latin-Afro grooves. Mobile recording techniques opened up new avenues for their layered approach to sound and, more importantly, would provide the practical solution to the recording of their next album. The album's visual packaging, with its provocative zipper as conceived by Warhol, reinforced the perception of the Stones' decadent disregard for societal norms. *Sticky Fingers* also included for the first time what is now one of the most recognized branding images in the world, the Rolling Stones' tongue-and-lip logo.

6

ELEGANTLY WASTED

Exile on Main Street (1972)

The *Exile on Main Street* sessions of the summer of 1971 at Nellcôte on the French Riviera have become the most romanticized in Rolling Stones lore. The circumstances make for one of the most alluring spectacles in rock history. Its reception provides a context in which the mythology of the band runs the deepest; that is, where art/imagination becomes life/reality and vice versa. Situated against a dramatic political backdrop, with *Exile* the Stones created rock and roll in order to continue as a band. And again, at a moment when music fulfilled not only the emotional but also the existential needs of young people, the promise of new music by the "world's greatest rock band" made for a life-changing event in itself.

Exile is also, as we shall see, a contested area of Stones criticism, with lingering disagreement as to whether it represents the "best" Stones album—that is, their masterwork. Further, with songs ranging from 1969 to 1972, it is not clear if it is accurately viewed as a coherent album/work or just another collection of songs, a topic we will take up below. This long gestation, with later substantial mixing and parts added in Los Angeles after the fact, at the very least complicates the notion that the Nellcôte period, the decadent/hedonistic celebratory centerpiece of Stones mythology, constitutes the core of the double album.

But, in fact, the story leading up to the album's genesis has less to do with artistic direction than with a more mundane matter. Seeking financial independence, the group broke from Klein when they learned that they owed a considerable sum of money in back taxes that they had thought their managers were paying on their behalves. Their new financial advisor, Prince Rupert Loewenstein, advised them to leave England and while abroad to earn enough money to pay the back tax owed.[1] Following his advice, they became the first tax exiles in rock history, though certainly not the last.[2]

The most obvious way for a popular rock band to generate income was to make an album, and in turn tour off of it. Only one logistical problem stood in their way—since *Aftermath*, they had made England their recording base. Because of whom they were and their hot streak of recent albums, expectations were set high for any album with the Rolling Stones name on it. On the flip side, they were now independent artists and thus could sidestep some of the usual record-industry pressure. That is, because they were now on their own label, they were no longer beholden to music industry executives driven solely by record sales (though Ahmet Ertegun, their distributor, remained influential). But they were essentially entering unchartered territory for a rock band. With no road map for what they were doing, they were on their own for guiding the album's production and publicity and later for generating sufficient buzz to sell out a tour.

In popular music, selling records and arena seats involves much more than just producing songs and an album; it includes the cultivation, promotion, and managing of image. After years of living in the intensity of the media spotlight as societal rebels, the Stones had learned the importance of controlling their brand and how they were represented to the general public via the mass media. Yet by this point they had become more than just musicians. They had been transformed from pop stars to cultural icons during the late 1960s. In particular, they emerged from the drug busts in 1967–1968 stronger than ever, empowered, and in many ways the equals of the establishment that sought to diminish them. As Marianne Faithfull writes:

> Before Redlands [i.e., prior to the drug busts], the Stones weren't perceived all that differently from a number of other groups—the Who, the Yardbirds, the Kinks—but subsequently they were on another level entirely. The other group in this category was the Beatles.[3]

Indeed, their fragile tax situation seemed a repeat of the drug charges, except that their freedom of movement was imperiled in another insidious way, as continued residency in their home country became impossible. And similar to the aftermath of the drug busts, once again they faced a potential public-relations nightmare. Though the outlaw status could enhance their rebellious reputations, still, fleeing from the tax charges might permanently affect fan perceptions of the band in England. They could not appear angry, and instead had to maintain an impervious attitude while using their status within rock and roll to change the topic of conversation to their advantage. In effect it became the Stones against the Establishment, part two. Given the unique and unprecedented context surrounding the making of *Exile*, the stakes of their work were clear: ascend to rock god status or wallow in a career-ending debacle.

In fact, the clever acceptance of their exile status was brilliant. The notion of exile usually implies a downward spiral, from a better to worse place, but not for the Stones, playing off the '60s romantic celebration of difference. The countercultural '60s notion of exile combined isolation, bohemianism, work, and a spirit of adventure. And the exile status offered not only the practical financial move to put off paying the taxes, but also a multivalent and fascinating solution to what could have been a public-relations nightmare. In embracing France, they were immediately empowered. The glamorous, wealthy, and decadent coast of southern France had long been a refuge for artists, aristocrats, and the wickedly rich seeking thrills. With its own mystery, inspiration, and matrix of deep artistic-historical interconnections, it was perfect fit to the Stones at this pivotal juncture of their careers. Despite its cultural renaissance and artistic status in the progressive '60s, London with its foggy, wet, and dark weather was still primarily a place for doing business, a capital of global finance spawned from its deep colonial and industrial roots. In contrast, southern France, though not quite on the level of Morocco, presented a romantic, exciting, exotic locale for artistic endeavor. And with the Stargroves recording experience behind them, they settled on a similar, unorthodox setting for their sessions: Richards's rented waterfront mansion, Nellcôte, located in an idyllic commune on the Mediterranean Sea, Villefranche-sur-Mer. As we shall quickly see, the mystique of the album is based on this spectacular setting and the strangeness of a bizarre (and perhaps for some unsettling) discovery once they moved in. Finding Nazi paraphernalia there, Richards maintains that Nellcôte was used as a Gestapo headquarters during World War II.

Thus they quickly channeled their exiled, pariah status into a heightened state of creativity to convince and show the world that even as exiles, they remained at the top of their musical game. And the romantic imagery was powerful: a drug-fueled, partying, raucous group of rock stars with family and friends convening for all-night recording sessions in a glorious mansion overlooking the Mediterranean. As fans have always projected their personal fantasies onto rock stars and other pop culture heroes, the Stones took this fantasy to a new level, as they exhibited a dream-like, aristocratic, hedonistic existence, living up to the popular cliché of "sex, drugs, and rock and roll." From nonstop parties attended by celebrity musicians and guests, daily feasts created by a personal chef who also was a drug connection, to daily boating excursions on the Mediterranean, they cultivated a lifestyle of excess, where pleasure was pushed to the limit. They joined the ranks of the privileged few, doing things on their own terms above, beyond, and outside of the law. In this way, they transformed their original image as societal rebels to become rock royalty, or even rock gods—indeed one Stones commentator, Bill Janovitz, goes so far as to say "they were creating *the* template for '70s rock stars."[4]

Of course, underneath this exciting but opaque surface was a much more complicated, messy situation. After a car accident left him with a morphine addiction, Richards, along with Pallenberg, both sunk into a serious heroin one. Richards was also a young father, trying in his own way to help raise his son Marlon. Simply getting the band together was difficult logistically as other band members were spread out in other towns across the south of France. On top of this, both Wyman and Watts did not want to be there. The introverted Taylor was homesick for London and had started down the destructive path of drug dependency and alcohol abuse, which he today blames on his time spent as a member of the Stones. Jagger had recently married the supermodel Bianca upon arriving in France, and she was expecting their child. The couple was staying down the road in St. Tropez, as Bianca wanted distance from the circus-like scene at Nellcôte. His marriage to Bianca had strained Jagger's friendship with Richards, as Richards considered her a "bimbo." And with an entire entourage of people assisting in the recording, some with families along, there were numerous mundane, daily things to manage.

Yet whatever the reality of the situation was, the Stones' myth-making machine triumphed from the start.[5] Today, the members of the band seem to have placed any bad feelings of the era well behind them and look back with nostalgia on those free-spirited days. Even Jagger, who has expressed reservations with the album, especially its deplorable recording and working conditions and the fact that they were not writing hit songs, has come around to celebrating the album for its polystylistic approach. Furthermore, there is the reception of *Exile* itself, recently reissued (2009) in a remastered version with its outtakes, which for many current Stones' critics constitute their best recorded effort. Note that this is quite a turnaround from its original reception. Though it charted initially at number one, the album received mixed reviews at first—it was, as we shall see, a sprawling and difficult work to comprehend.

Finally, propping up the myth is the testimony of others involved in the project, as well as the stunning photography and film footage taken at the time. Some of this material has been gathered into a laudatory documentary called *Stones in Exile* (2010), directed by Stephen Kijak. One of the persons interviewed in the film is Dominique Tarlé. Tarlé was a young French photographer and fan invited by Richards to live at Nellcôte. The guitarist was well aware that the Stones were making history and that a photographic record would be needed and necessary. Tarlé remains very positive on the era and the scene, maintaining that it was "rock and roll heaven," and emphasizes the softer side in contrast to the decadent drug atmosphere usually portrayed. His rosy perspective comes through in his pictures of the summer at Nellcôte, which are also some of the most beautifully conceived canvases of any rock group ever taken. Tarlé chose to show the band in the best possible way, and if anything has helped to contribute to the idea of the Stones as rock gods, his pictures surely have. Yet despite this, in another interview Tarlé talks about the myth making that the Stones were engaged in. They were fully aware that the "sex, drugs, and rock and roll" story was what the public wanted, not the one about the Stones having a family life or searching for British tea while in France.[6] Tarlé claims that Richards was quite a devoted father at the time, but that they needed the endless party stories to keep up their rebellious reputation and sell records. He also says that beyond family life the main atmosphere was directed at working, revolving around Richards's schedule of doing the bulk of the recording at night.

AMERICAN BACKDROP FOR THE ALBUM'S COMPLETION

With the basic song takes completed by October, in November the band had mostly left France for Los Angeles. The plan was to mix the album at Sunset Studio in Hollywood. Many of the songs still lacked coherent vocal parts and many still needed lyrics. Though Richards participated in the mixing, a lot of the detailed finish work fell to Jagger, who shepherded the songs to completion. But before they could even get to the writing/mixing/overdubbing stage, as Jagger says in Kijak's documentary, they had the difficult task of choosing which takes and even which songs to include on the album. The process would extend until May, as lead vocals, instrumental overdubs, and backing vocals were added to many of the tracks.

Although the Stones did record most of the songs at Nellcôte, many of these predate their sojourn to France, and some of the recordings were begun at Olympic and even Stargroves. Refer to table 6.1 for a list of songs begun before the *Exile* proper sessions at Nellcôte.

This somewhat contradicts the neat narrative that *Exile on Main Street* captures the exiled experience of recording at Nellcôte, in that some of the songs go back to at least the *Let It Bleed* and *Sticky Fingers* sessions. Yet by this point this was, in fact, a typical way for a Stones

Table 6.1. Songs on *Exile* Predating the Nellcôte Sessions

Song (Earlier Title)	Venue	First Sessions
"Loving Cup" (aka "Give Me a Drink")	Olympic; Hyde Park, London	May, June–July 1969; played live July 5, 1969
"Stop Breaking Down"	Olympic	June, October 1970
"Sweet Virginia"	Olympic	June, July–October 1970
"Shine a Light"	Olympic	July 1970
"Sweet Black Angel" (aka "Bent Green Needles")	Stargroves	October–November 1970
"Tumbling Dice" (aka "Good Time Women")	Stargroves	March–May 1970

album to be produced, for, as we have seen, those earlier albums also had songs going back to previous album sessions.

Perhaps because it is a double album with an abundance of material, *Exile* feels more like a culmination of something, more so than anything else the Stones have done before or since. Exactly what it gathers depends on one's perspective and agenda, but there are some common themes picked out on the album that we will look at in specific songs. Lastly, even if some of the songs' genesis extends further back, it appears that they were all mixed and completed in Los Angeles.

In general, the album's main artistic overture reveals itself in the title, with the bold reference to Main Street as a stand-in for America. Once again, the Stones were taking control of their forced leave-taking by embracing their new artistic orientation, shoving it back, as it were, at the British authorities. Note that on another, more specific level, "Main Street" could also have been a reference to the location of the album's completion in Los Angeles. The title itself is daring in what seems at first like an intentional oxymoronic formulation, in that there is a strong cognitive dissonance generated between "exile" and "Main Street." On the surface, we do not locate "Main Street" as a place of exile or banishment, with its nostalgia, charm, and quaintness grounded in small-town, local shopkeeper, and other idyllic associations. But as we said above, if the Stones were going to reimagine the concept of exile, they seemed to have also done the same with the concept of Main Street itself. For Jagger, "Main Street" no longer referred to this idyllic small-town locale, but instead had become grafted onto the "real inner city," where "you can see pimps, knives flashing."[7] "Main Street" had become the street itself, a place populated by drug dealers and prostitutes. And with this darkened and heightened sense of realism, we will see below how the Stones took the album's artwork and packaging as an opportunity to capitalize on the idea that as foreigners, they were most at ease making American music that could resonate on the mean streets of their adopted home.

And a lot was riding on a given record's artwork in this resplendent age of the album. Janovitz points out that *Exile*'s artwork powerfully informs the listener about how to feel concerning the music it contains.[8] Put differently, the wrapping artwork visually packages the way the artist intends the music to sound. In another sense it is the first and most vital advertisement for the music itself.[9] And with Warhol's brilliant pop art direction in *Sticky Fingers* upping the ante for a Stones' album release considerably, the band intuitively knew they would need to bring in people from the contemporary art scene if they were to equal Warhol's packaging.

They found their answer in the work of Robert Frank, a Swiss photographer whose 1950s Beat photographs were juxtaposed with new shots of the band. His outsider status is an essential ingredient in his depictions of Americans—Frank found himself the target of anti-Semitism by the police during his trip to the South. Apparently Jagger and Watts had discovered photographer Frank's *The Americans* while gathering ideas for the album cover in Los Angeles bookstores. It was an excellent choice. The grafting of a Beat perspective and aesthetic provides a perfect fit for the kind of music the album contains. Note that Jack Kerouac wrote the introduction for *The Americans*, which begins with his evocative and oft-quoted sentence that manages to not only describe Frank's work but also the Beat generation's desire to celebrate a weird America, one that diverges massively from the sanitized one of television and the movies. It is worth dwelling on this sentence as an orientation for the setting of *Exile*:

> That crazy feeling in America when the sun is hot on the streets and the music comes out of the jukebox or from a nearby funeral, that's what Robert Frank has captured in tremendous photographs taken as he traveled on the road around practically forty-eight states in an old used car (on Guggenheim Fellowship) and with the agility, mystery, genius, sadness, and strange secrecy of a shadow photographed scenes that have never been seen before on film.[10]

And since the Stones first toured America in 1964 and thereafter, the pictures resonated with the band's own direct memory of contact with this edgy, shadowy, other America. In this respect Janovitz writes that in *Exile* the Stones set out to reproduce Kerouac and Frank's vision of the "wide-open spaces and shadowy corners of America itself via the nation's music."[11]

Like many creative types of their generation, the Stones are huge fans of 1950s Beat culture; in the halcyon days of Swinging London, the Stones had hung out with the original stars of the Beat generation, including writers and poets like Allen Ginsberg ("Howl") and William S. Burroughs (*Naked Lunch*). Once they settled on using Frank and his images, the photographer suggested shooting in Super 8 film to capture the seedy, gritty, punk side to life they wished to convey. To put the whole package together using Frank's photographic content, including the front cover's collage of his images, they hired artist/designer John Van Hamersveld, who was famous in rock circles for his artwork that included the poster for *The Endless Summer*, the Beatles' *Hard Day's Night*, and Jefferson Airplane's *Crown of Creation*. Whether fairly or not, the idea for a collage album brings up yet another comparison to the Beatles, this time to the collage of faces on *Sgt. Pepper's*. Finally, the original, gate-folded album included twelve postcards of pictures of the band taken by Norman Seeff (the artistic director for the album), which were executed by Van Hamersveld at Richards's suggestion.

Musically, there is a tribute to the Beats on the song "Casino Boogie." With its shuffle in the key of A, the two-chord song ties in to "Shake Your Hips," the preceding song on the album. With its retro approach, "Casino Boogie" sounds as if it was a product of the Chicago Southside scene of the '50s or early '60s. Richards colors the song using some classic descending blues riffs, probably inspired by Robert Johnson's "32-20 Blues," heard in the intro and then in a variation at 2:12. Note that there is a bootleg recording of the Stones doing "32-20 Blues" from around the time of the album.[12] In "Casino Boogie," Richards strikes at the heart of the style with a simple, direct approach grounded in blues tradition that manages to say something new. This perhaps had an impact on ZZ Top, whose "La Grange" single (1973) from their first album also takes the riff.

Apparently out of lyrical ideas, it seems that Richards came up with the idea to try William Burroughs and Brion Gysin's "cut-up" technique for "Casino Boogie." Random lines were thrown into a hat and band members picked them out. They put together the lyrics based on the order that the lines were chosen. The finished product has no determinate meaning, but even so, a lot could be read into the juxtaposition of some of the tropes. The phrase "got no time on hand" does recur three times in the course of the song and ends the song. This suggests that the band did not follow the technique strictly but had used it as a unifying device.

EXILE AND THE RECEPTION AND COVERAGE OF THE SUPPORTING S.T.P. TOUR

Exile's mythological residue culminates in the Stones' 1972 North American tour in support of the album (and *Sticky Fingers*, to a certain degree). The mass media saturated the event as the Stones' touring circus progressed. Gauging the historical moment or its sensationalist potential, it was also well documented by famous photographers and illustrious writers. Dubbed "S.t.p." for the "Stones touring party," the tour marks a distinct moment where the communal, Dionysian rock events of the 1960s merged with the fame and ego-driven identity of the super-wealthy and untouchable modern rock star.

Fresh off of his photographic collaboration with the band, Frank was present shooting cinéma vérité, with an extra supply of Super 8 cameras available for anyone to use. He gathered his and the participant film data to produce his controversial documentary, the widely bootlegged but never officially released *Cocksucker Blues*, named after a song that Jagger sent to Decca as a sendoff when the band broke off with the label. At the end of the film Frank includes the Jagger song. With scenes of decadence and debauchery in full view, including a notorious plane scene of a near-rape by the roadies, to which Jagger, Richards, and others play a demonic percussion, the Stones went to court to try to block the release of the film for fear that they might be banned from America. They effectively won the case—the film can only be shown four times per year, and only in the presence of the photographer. Frank did film the band live in concert, and these scenes are well worth seeing. They are in color, vividly contrasting with the black-and-white of his documentary making.

The band also sanctioned a more traditional film, *Ladies & Gentlemen: The Rolling Stones!*, which contains live footage of concerts in Texas, scenes of which can be viewed on YouTube. The film was finally rereleased in theaters and on DVD/Blu-Ray in 2010. It is also perhaps one of the first films to be shown in theaters with quadrophonic sound, an audiophile process invented around 1970 that never caught on.

Life magazine hired Jim Marshall to photograph the Stones working in the studio, and he was allowed unlimited access to the tour for one week. Marshall is one of the best music and rock photographers of that time, with jazz, blues, and rock legends to his credit; one of his photos from Monterey is a glorious one of a glowing Brian Jones with Jimi Hendrix; he later shot Hendrix burning his guitar. These photographs do matter in the buildup, hype, and selling of the music in that they allow fans to connect the abstract art of music directly to its visual source in its creators and performers. To commemorate the Stones' fiftieth anniversary, a book of Marshall's photographs of the Stones from 1972 was published. Joel Selvin, former longtime music critic for the *San Francisco Chronicle*, writes about the tour in his introduction to Marshall's book:

> The Rolling Stones' cocaine- and tequila sunset–fueled 1972 tour would be rock's most glittering moment, with its four-million-dollar box office bigger than any before, and hangers-on the likes of best-selling author Truman Capote and Princess Lee Radziwell [née Caroline Lee Bouvier].[13]

In this era of classic rock and roll at its zenith, or of "British rock stars at their peak," Selvin suggests that Marshall's photographs show an era that was "over before we really knew it was an era." In this Selvin follows Terry Southern, another writer (known for his screenplays) also on the tour as a journalist. Southern wrote a mostly celebratory article for *The Saturday Review* about the elixir-like role of the tequila sunrise drink on the tour.

Truman Capote attended portions of the tour to write an article for *Rolling Stone*, which he notoriously never did. Yet as we shall see, Capote's observations certainly contradict the easygoing, nostalgic, fan-fueled praise of Selvin. Though he enjoyed the party, the scene around the Stones turned off Capote, in particular how everyone was imagining they were a member of the band—he mentions, in particular, his disdain for Marshall Chess "pumping his hips nymphomaniacally."[14] Capote toured as a member of the press, commissioned by Jann Wenner to write a feature article for *Rolling Stone* on the band and tour. Unable to write the article, he gave a taped interview with Andy Warhol, a transcript of which was published in the April 1973 issue of the magazine. An astute, quirky, and brutally honest observer, he was bored with the show until they played "Midnight Rambler," where he feels the audience finally came alive. That this song resonated with him is not surprising, coming from the author of *In Cold Blood*, a book about the brutal murder of a family in rural Kansas that rivals the Boston Strangler for its gripping and horrific effect on the nation's psyche.

Yet Capote goes on to remark that the idea of spontaneity was an illusion at the shows—"it's the most choreographed note-by-note thing that I've ever known in my life. There wasn't an ounce of spontaneity."[15] Capote feels genuinely bad for the kids attending the concert, feeling that they were manipulated and humiliated by the band and its mechanical approach to a live show. The fans spend months in anticipation for the concert, in awe of the band and the music, and are left desperately cheering for an encore while the Stones' plane takes off for the next show.[16] Ironically, seeing the kids in this light was the only "moving" element that Capote recognized in the event (he is not entirely clear whether the kids would have recognized their alleged rejection by the band). He categorizes the Stones primarily as businessmen and entertainers, duping their audience with the glamor of it all, bored with their own success.

Today it is hard to imagine a public intellectual and writer of Capote's stature going out of his or her way to criticize a popular band like the Stones. Though Capote admits to being a fan of the Stones—he does prefer the records to their performances—his indictment of the band goes to the heart of the problem of contemporary popular culture criticism. Are critics honest when they confront a pop culture phenomenon that by definition has wide audience approval? Capote refused to write his article on the band because he judged the presentation of their music performance to be predictable and formulaic. Put differently, he could not write on the Stones because what they were doing was too "obvious," leaving nothing unanswered to his imagination. The biggest problem with the Stones' live set, one that continues to this day, is that it changes very little from night to night. Often they will have only one or two spots where they will play an alternate song. In any case, because of what he deemed an imaginative shortcoming of the band, the musical performance lacked mystery, which for Capote is the prerequisite for art and writing about it. Without spontaneity, or the experience of the unpredictable, there can be no mystery.[17] For Capote, mystery invites us into the artwork, setting up a problem for the receiver to ponder and try to solve.

In defense of the Stones, whether or not a concert performance lacks mystery, an ineffable quality in itself as it were, does seem to be on the subjective side, and the Stones' live recorded work certainly grants the experience of it along with spontaneity. Furthermore, fans and critics would disagree with Capote's assessment of the band's live shows, especially from this era. Indeed, bootlegs of shows from 1972–1973 testify to a band at the top of its performance power. For example, the official bootleg of their early and late shows in Brussels from October 17, 1973, reveals the band at one of their live peaks.[18]

ON THE *EXILE* THEME: A UNITY, OR COLLECTION OF DISPARATE MATERIAL?

As we propose, the exile theme occupies a central place in the reception history of the Stones. In terms of its status as artwork, *Exile* presents either a concept album centered on the notion of exile as outsider, or an era-spanning collection of songs in the mold of the earlier Stones records. Thus we can reasonably ask: Is the idea of exile underpinning the album a real content, or a conceptual marketing tool dressed up as an external metaphor? At this point in time, over forty years later, it is to some extent both, as there are good reasons for each perspective. Finally, how does the notion of exile help us to understand the Stones phenomenon?

For most fans and critics alike, the idea of exile binds the album's songs together, thereby conforming to the model of the concept album in the early progressive rock era. Understood as such, the album's packaging, with it playful semantics of outsider, works its magic to create the framework that has since informed the reception of the Stones' music. Differently put, exile as a mode of existence becomes another of the master signifiers for understanding the evolving place of the Rolling Stones in rock music during the early 1970s. Furthermore, that they found a conceptual way to resonate with the baby boomer generation's youngest members allowed the Stones to buy at least a couple more years as a viable countercultural band and thereby avoid middle-age stasis. Jagger celebrated his twenty-ninth birthday at the end of the 1972 tour, and Watts and Wyman were much older than he and Richards. And from the beginning, the counterculture configured itself as an alternative to straight society, using drugs to mark their exit from straightness. Thus the Stones' embrace of the exile is neither shocking nor at odds with the post-hippie era, but rather a confirmation of how these refugees from the Party of the '60s probably already felt.

The Stones infuse the production of the album with rough borders and edges, qualities that were not yet so common in this progressive rock era of professional studio production. This unfettered recording process maps the concept of exile itself, for a component of the state of exile can be the experience of a raw reality, as the exile must cope with an unmediated, naked exposure to the vicissitudes of the world. Further, the rough edges indicate what rock critics mean when they link the Stones—along with similar bands like the Kinks, the Velvet Underground, the Stooges, and David Bowie—to the burgeoning punk rock movement in the mid-1970s. But, upon closer inspection, this alleged relationship with punk is fraught with difficulty. Although there is often a punkish style of abandonment and insincere attitude in the way the Stones pull off the final product, still, their music belies the professional perfectionism of Jagger and Richards that is at once at odds with a punk aesthetic, and especially the latter's lifelong striving to become a blues guitarist of the highest order.

But returning to the concept of exile, the fact that many of the songs predate the Nellcôte sessions might seem to undermine, at first, the notion that the concept permeates the album. And many of the songs from Nellcôte, seemingly detached from the notion, also reinforce this. Since then Jagger has clarified that *Exile* was a really a collection of disparate elements and that opportunistic business decisions were involved in its compiling:

> *Exile* is really a mixture of bits and pieces left over from the previous album recorded at Olympic Studios and which, after we got out of the contract with Allen Klein, we didn't want to give him: tracks like "Shine a Light," and "Sweet Virginia." Those were mixed up with a few slightly more grungy things done in the South of France. It's seen as one album all recorded there and it really wasn't. We just chucked everything in.[19]

Unfortunately for the Stones, they still ended up having to give Klein a piece of those tracks cited in the quotation above and "Loving Cup," among others. In a *New York Times* interview about the remastering of the album by Don Was in 2010, Jagger has said that Nellcôte was a good story, and that in the end, "it's just a sort of myth."[20] Yet on the other hand, mitigating the fact that so many of the key songs were started at Olympic, such as "Shine a Light," "Loving Cup," and "Sweet Virginia," there seems to have been some work done on them (except for "Loving Cup") at Nellcôte. Indeed, at least according to Elliott's *Complete Recording Sessions*, the Stones added something to the recording of each song at Nellcôte—whether a complete take or backing track, a horn section, a guitar part, or vocal idea is not entirely clear and would have to be determined on a song-by-song basis. In fact, it is probably impossible to know at this point what was done where, as Jagger himself has admitted.

Still, with the remastering of the album, the unity of the album came up as an especially thorny issue, with public disagreement between Jagger and Richards. In the same *New York Times* article, Richards takes issue with Jagger's view of the album as an incoherent work: "All of the bone and the muscle of the record was done down in that basement [at Nellcôte]." He considers the rest of the overdubs or work done outside of Nellcôte as "fairy dust."[21] Adding another layer of complication and seemingly at odds with Richards's view are the mixing and overdub sessions completed at Sunset Studio in Los Angeles, where it does seem to be known what was added to the track—some tracks, such as "Loving Cup" and "Torn and Frayed" were completely rerecorded there. As an historical aside, and not as well known, the band also worked at Wally Heider's studio while in Los Angeles, apparently to avoid being shut down by the musician's union, which demanded a 1 percent cut of proceeds for foreign musicians to work in the city.[22]

But in the end, Richards's view of the Nellcôte core of the album will always win out. In other words, the album's reception as a single work overrides the reality that the album is an unconnected potpourri of songs. Like all artistic myths, the Nellcôte core provides a powerful engine for decoding the enigma of the work. From this perspective, exile is the experience through which the album derives its intent, and again, when coupled with the vision of a decaying Main Street, this ideology dictates the album's reception as a complete work as such, whether or not it actually is. Finally, this collection of songs mirrors Frank's collage for the album cover, with its bizarre collection of odd and strange-looking people (especially notable is the man with three balls in his mouth), who function as exiles from normal society.

Just as the Frank's collage was intentional, so the album ordering of the songs follows a distinctive plan. Jagger intended that each of the album's four sides forms a cohesive listening experience. In terms of the songs that predate *Exile*, these were spread out throughout the album. Thus for the album's aesthetic effect, style helped to obscure chronology.

EXILE'S SONGS WITH ORIGINS PREDATING THE NELLCÔTE SESSIONS

With so many songs begun before the album's main sessions, what then is the *Exile* sound, as distinct from *Sticky Fingers* or *Let It Bleed*? There is no simple way to answer this, especially given that so many of the songs were started prior to the *Exile* sessions, but the most obvious place to start is with the instrumentation and performance practice. Perhaps the most direct instance of a signature *Exile* sound would be the group of songs with five-string, open-G tuned riffs of Richards that we will discuss in the next section. And many of these songs have musical ideas that go well back into the past. For example, "Tumbling Dice" was originally recorded at Stargroves as "Good Time Women." "All Down the Line" had an acoustic version going back to 1969. The other aspect of the *Exile* sound is the significant role of the session players, something we have seen on the previous albums but here becoming more pronounced. Many of these players were quite seasoned with the band already, especially the horn players (Price and Keys) and the pianist (Hopkins).

Turning now to the songs that predate *Exile*, note that roughly half of the album material could have ended up on earlier albums. The withholding of some of the songs was in part due to the battle over song copyright with Klein. Still, it increasingly became part of how the band worked, sitting on material for long time spans. This would become something of a habit, as some of their best later songs—"Start Me Up" is a case in point—actually were conceived much earlier.

Despite this, there remains, again, a magnetic pull around something like an *Exile* aura and soundscape that is worth pursuing. Some of the most cherished moments on the album that significantly predate the album—"Shine a Light" and "Loving Cup" would have to rank up there—perhaps owe their power to this elapsed time, this chronological distance that allowed the band to inject something extra in their interpretation. The Stones do their best when they allow things to "marinate," as it were, a word that Richards uses to describe how he would work out a particular riff.

Among the holdovers from the *Sticky* sessions at Olympic are a couple of blues covers, Slim Harpo's "Shake Your Hips" and Robert Johnson's "Stop Breakin' Down Blues." Harpo's tune finds itself near the beginning of the album, on side one, and Johnson's toward the end, on side four. Instead of the acoustic textures they had been using on other Delta blues covers, for the Johnson cover they return to the urban blues. Junior Wells had recently put out a version of Johnson's "Stop Breaking Down" using horns that come off as borderline soul instead of blues. On the Stones version, led by Jagger (Richards does not appear to play on the song), the group follows the formula used by other British bands since Cream when covering a twelve-bar Delta blues—fast, hard, and edgy, with slightly distorted guitar. Jagger plays the rhythm guitar and harp (Sonny Boy Williamson adds a harp to his 1940s version) with open-G tuning adding to the resonance (the song is in A, so there is a capo on second fret), while Taylor handles slide, more than making up for Richards's absence.

"Shake Your Hips" is a competent approximation of Harpo's original, a tribute in the way that their decade-earlier rendition of Harpo's "I'm a King Bee" was. Though it sounds like it could have written in the 1950s, Harpo's 1966 song about a hip shake dance presents a sped-up boogie in the style of John Lee Hooker's "Boogie Chillen."[23] The "shake" theme in the Delta blues goes back to at least Bukka White's standard, "Shake 'Em on Down" (1939); even Irving Berlin had a popular song about using dance to lose the blues, "Shaking the Blues Away" (1927). The Stones slow Harpo's song back down a bit, and like "Stop Breaking Down" it is in the key of A, with Richards now using open-G tuning (again, capo on the second fret) for the hypnotic groove-shuffle. They add horns to play the head motive from Harpo's. In a filmed outtake of a rehearsal from May 1972 in Switzerland, Richards plays lead on the song on his Telecaster, with a call-and-response with Jagger who is somewhat buried in the mix. This gritty version without the horns is perhaps deeper felt than the one on the album.[24]

We can interpret the inclusion of the blues covers in a couple of different ways. On the one hand, they are simply filler on the album, and betray an earlier mentality of gathering favorite cover songs into a collection. On the other, the songs also reveal what the Stones were trying for in their original music: a bare-bones, immediate access to the music's rhythmic dimension as a simple hypnotic groove, experienced as a synchronization process of brain waves and beats sometimes called "entrainment." Recall that *Exile* was not well understood and thus received when it first came out, taking some critics years to recognize what the Stones achieved on the album. The blues songs point directly to the privileging of the rhythmic parameter guiding the Stones' originals. As in African American dance music, the melodic instruments serve the groove through a process of additive textural thickening. Though there is some soloing on the album, the music is not about the opening of an abstract jamming space, but rather gathers around the inward concentration of a rhythmic plexus of the various instruments. This helps in understanding the riff-centered music dominating the album, in that the riffs direct our attention to the mesmerizing rhythmic structure of the groove. Finally, and in this way, in addition to setting up an aesthetic framework, these two blues covers powerfully contribute to *Exile*'s continuity with the band's previous work.

Moving on with other songs predating the *Exile* sessions at Nellcôte, the album's penultimate song, "Shine a Light," is another song on which Richards, Watts, and Wyman, for that matter, do not appear. As the track following "Stop Breaking Down," the transition brings out one of the best stylistic transitions on album, as Jagger takes an immediate turn out of the blues and dives into gospel. The song is probably the earliest conceived song on the album, perhaps dating back to 1968. Jagger had also recorded a version of the song with Leon Russell and perhaps Ringo Starr as "Get a Line on You."[25]

The intro is intentionally accidental, a recorded glimpse of the band waiting before they play. As we will see, they turn this into a structural part of the song. Within this space of what approximates dead air, an analog-echo effect issues from Taylor's guitar. The song proper begins with Hopkins's block piano chords, followed by Preston's organ and Miller's drumming, with Taylor's lead guitar not far behind. The uplifting chorus contrasts with the devastation of the verses, with the cautionary tale warning of the effects of drug abuse apparently written with

Brian Jones in mind. The phrase "shine a light" not only provides the gospel context, but also imparts to the song its status as the anthem of the album. Furthermore, the phrase resonates with the evangelical basis of a certain strain of American roots music. "Light" is the New Testament metaphor for conversion from the darkness of the absence of God, as in "I saw the light," immortalized in a song sung by Hank Williams among others. The redemptive theme actually harmonizes well with the exile theme, as the trope of exile functions in the Bible as a means for God to bring the sinner to repent and hence to come back home, for example in the great exilic episode of Jewish history called the Babylonian captivity. In this regard Jagger even mentions visiting black churches in the Los Angeles area with Preston for musical inspiration.

Like their previous anthem to end *Beggars*, "Salt of the Earth," the chord progression for "Shine a Light" relies on the standard three chords (I, IV, and V) for the chorus. The expected buildup uses black female backup singers, representing a church gospel choir as it were, while Jagger's preacher-like exhortations alternate with Taylor's soloing. The song also uses a minor chord in its verse progression—again minor chords are kept to a minimum for the album—that is in turn used as the opening chord for the guitar solo.[26] There is a slight speeding up throughout the song, as well as a pause for quiet reflection after the guitar solo at around the three-minute mark where the song comes nearly to a standstill, also a return to the emotional space of the opening. At this pause we realize that the opening is quite intentional, and, now with Preston spurring the others onward, the chorus reaches its full glory. The guitar outro rehashes the solo. The song ends with the reflective space of the opening.

Another very early song on the album is "Loving Cup," first recorded during the *Let It Bleed* Olympic sessions, for which an outtake exists. The song was also played at the Hyde Park event in 1969 as "Give Me a Drink." The outtake is with Hopkins and is one of the first times Taylor played with the group; it was released on the remastered *Exile* bonus CD. In his review, *New York Times* critic Ben Ratliff waxes poetical on this outtake. He says that it represents *Exile* in its "idealized form," namely, "a dark, dense, loosely played, semiconscious tour through American blues, gospel and country music, recorded in a basement in France."[27] Here Ratliff gets to the heart of the album's interpretation, that the myths surrounding *Exile* overpower the actual circumstance of individual songs. The outtake is much slower than the released one, and has Richards playing an overdriven lead guitar but in a country-blues style with idiomatic double-stop Nashville bends as befits the countrified flavor of the song. Indeed Richards's part drives the song and provides its color; it is unfortunate that he did not develop his lead playing more in this direction for the released version.

Ironically, the outtake that Ratliff extols as the idealized type of *Exile* song, knowing that the song was recorded at Olympic and thereby endorsing the opinion of Jagger that *Exile* instead denotes an era, also shows the creative hand of producer Don Was. Jagger has encouraged the creative input of Was in the remastering of the outtakes, while Richards seems to have taken a more cautionary, purist position, saying that we should not "interfere with the Bible."[28] Problematically, from the perspective of hearing a take of the song in its original state, Was edited the song, boosting levels, and, most inauthentically, seems to have spliced it with various versions.[29] In a sense, this "outtake"—along with others he remastered—is in essence a new, modern creation, compounding the already problematic attempt to hear the genesis of the album. Obviously this was done to make a more commercial product, but it does destroy the surviving historical record and adds more confusion to the issue of what exactly constitutes *Exile*. We touch on this issue again in chapter 7, where we look at one of the songs with new vocal tracks sung by Jagger for the bonus CD.

Returning to *Exile,* the album's more up-tempo version of "Loving Cup" forms the focal point of the album. Hopkins improves on his piano introduction, giving one of his best performances for the Stones. Substituting for the overdriven guitar, Richards instead plays his acoustic Hummingbird, with a capo on the fifth fret; Taylor is absent from the track. Richards's acoustic actually complements the piano timbre better, and the interplay between the two instruments keeps a tight focus to the song. For the contrast of the bridge ("I feel so humble"), the band slows down, and the horns provide a needed change of timbral direction buttressed by a chord change to the only minor chord of the song (E minor; the song is in key of G). The outro (ca. 3:20) also features the horns in an ostinato, this time with an added trombone and some extra Caribbean-sounding drums. Indeed the outro is a bit incongruous with what came before in terms of the mood, as they become exuberant, almost celebratory. Here it pays to compare the released version with the original conception of the outtake, which has them continuing in the dirt-infused country spirit of the song.

The last songs we will consider with origins that predate Nellcôte are "Sweet Virginia" and "Sweet Black Angel." These are the first and third songs of side two of the album respectively, a side devoted to acoustic-country songs. Written at around the same time as "Wild Horses," once again these and other Stones country songs owe much to Richards's friendship with Gram Parsons. Note as an aside that Parsons's band at the time, the Flying Burrito Brothers, even released their version of "Wild Horses" before the Stones' own, in April 1971.

As a genre, country is a natural fit for the Stones' obsession with American music. Richards writes about what he absorbed from Parsons, especially the harder Bakersfield sound of country from the likes of Buck Owens and Merle Haggard.[30] At Nellcôte, Parsons and Richards would play songs from country to the Everly Brothers for hours, often with Jagger joining in. Furthermore, and at least according to Richards, there seems to have been some personal animosity between Jagger and Parsons—Richards maintains that Jagger was jealous of his friendship and tight bond with Parsons. And as we have already mentioned, Jagger was not always at ease when performing in a country style, often resorting to vocal parody.

"Sweet Virginia" relies on an unorthodox chord progression that harkens back to the turn-of-the-twentieth-century days of ragtime. In the key of A, the verse starts on a D chord, passing to a B before coming down to the tonic A chord. Normally, the B chord would be minor in order to fit into the key signature of A. Fingering these three chords in open position is not difficult; yet playing them this way (i.e., in open position) does not produce the idiomatic guitar sound achieved on the recording, which uses a capo on the second fret. I hypothesize here that Richards hit upon this unique progression in the Stones' catalog through the use of the capo. That is, fingering the chords with the capo on, the chordal shapes become the standard ones that a beginner learns upon starting, C, A, and G chords, respectively. In other words, with a capo on at the second fret, fingering a C chord will produce a D chord, the A chord shape will sound a B chord, and so forth. Listening closely, there are neat little bass fills that Richards adds in to connect the chords; these are much simpler to play if the capo is used. Thus this somewhat unorthodox progression really comes together from the performance practice of using the capo, in that Richards is playing something that uses all idiomatic chord shapes but in a harmonically unusual pattern that gives the song its identity.

"Sweet Black Angel" is also cast in a consciously old-fashion style—Janovitz proposes mento, an Afro-infused, proto-country genre from Jamaica that is the predecessor of reggae. With marimba (Amyl Nitrate) and güiro (Jimmy Miller) carving out rhythms beneath the guitar and drums, their syncopations evoke what today would be known as a world-music soundscape, something not really heard on a Stones' song since Dijon's congas set up the samba-like grooves of "Sympathy for the Devil" or "Can't You Hear Me Knocking."[31] In the key of G, Richards plays a simple bass riff with an upper G note ostinato for most of the song; the chord changes are smoothed out, like in "Sweet Virginia," by these bass-connector riffs in the acoustic guitar part. The chord changes introduce a couple of minor chords, only the second place on the album up to then that these occur, and follow the soul progressions that we saw in songs like "I Got the Blues" from *Sticky Fingers*.[32]

While at Stargroves, the Stones recorded an instrumental demo for "Sweet Black Angel" as "Bent Green Needles." Jagger wrote the lyrics to commemorate the case of the recently arrested radical black activist Angela Davis. Like "Street Fighting Man," the song represents one of the rare directly political moments for the band. Davis was a controversial professor of philosophy at UCLA and also a member of the Communist Party and the Black Panthers. She was on trial at the time for her involvement in purchasing firearms used in a crime. Many thought the charges were for purely political reasons, and she quickly became a cause célèbre, garnering the attention of rock stars like the Stones and their extended family, and John Lennon, among others.

Jagger shows off his literary talents, appropriating the title and conceit of Agatha Christie's "Ten Little Indians" for his lyrics—Davis being another "N*" (substituting for Indian) about to fall; it is shocking even today to hear a white person use the "N*" word in a song (ca. 1:08, he says "ten little N*"). To the Stones' credit, whether or not one embraces the politics of Davis, this shows a progressive side of the band and affirms that they had much more balance, depth, and insight to their music than the "cock-rock" critics would give them credit for.

GOSPEL, SOUL, AND COUNTRY CONTINUITY

As we have seen with "Shine a Light," the gospel-soul tendency exhibited on previous albums carries through to *Exile*. Perhaps the closest the Stones ever get to a pure gospel sentiment is on the song "I Just Want to See His Face," where the protagonist proclaims his desire for a direct connection with Jesus. At the beginning of the song Jagger extemporizes in his falsetto range, a vocal style he will explore later in his career and which at this point is virtually untapped. Set to a primal rhythmic groove with organ, the song comes off as truncated, and so in this respect seems to promise more than it gives.

A more extended performance and the follow-up track to "I Just Want to See His Face," "Let It Loose" revisits and complicates the topical terrain of an earlier cover of Marvin Gaye's "Can I Get a Witness," where the secular theme of relationship problems (referenced here as the "bedroom blues") interfaces with the gospel-inflected soul music that we have cited earlier, as in "If You Need Me" or "I Got the Blues." On "Let It Loose," the Stones hit upon their greatest example of this hybrid style. Although not in the 6/8 time signature as these previous tracks, Richards begins the song with the classic 1960s picked arpeggiated style that he favors for this genre. He also employs a thickened timbre as he did on these earlier songs, achieved by using a Fender Vibratone amplifier.[33] The Vibratone uses a Leslie rotating speaker to realize its incomparable sound. The altered timbre produced with this setup—an uneasy, unstable one that sounds like a hallucination—becomes in Richards's hands at once forlorn, nostalgic, and withdrawn, providing an appropriately moody emotional platform in the lyrics for the pain and attempts to release it.

Astonishingly for a song at over five minutes, Richards's initial chord progression, with a couple of slight alterations, runs essentially throughout the song. It is a simple progression using the most standard three chords in their most basic ordering, albeit with some Mixolydian touches thrown in for color.[34] And he alters the progression for a couple of its rounds during the verse, throwing in a minor chord substitute for one of the chords; another time he vamps on only two of the chords.[35] Despite this, and because the arpeggiated tonic chord at the top remains the same, always starting each round of the progression, it can be heard as if one continuous loop. Furthermore, by playing it with a capo on the third fret and using a descending bass pattern to link the chords with some extra notes, this most basic of chord progressions takes on some complexity. With the Leslie speaker, the progression leaves its soul roots for the realm of classic rock, not too dissimilar to David Gilmour's intro to Pink Floyd's "Us and Them" recorded a short time after also using a Leslie speaker for its effect.[36]

A veiled overture to gospel also closes the album in the energetic rocker "Soul Survivor." When sung, the title becomes a double entendre, as in "sole" or only survivor. Janovitz interprets this as a jab from Jagger at Richards, increasingly estranged from one another and with Richards's drug dependency worsening; for this astute commentator the song becomes a metaphor for the fate of the band. But the song also presents the topic of mistreatment in a relationship. Using nautical metaphors throughout, Jagger registers his resistance to his degradation, finally proclaiming that he will "mutiny," as otherwise the relationship will be the "death of me." He directly references "Bell Bottom Blues," another soulful blues by Clapton's Derek and the Dominos about the fallout from another painful relationship. Finally, like the other gospel-styled songs on *Exile*, "Soul Survivor" uses vamping and call-and-response to dramatize Jagger's emotionally charged extemporizations on the lyrical theme.

As we have already seen, *Exile* continues the country vein of recent Stones' offerings. Indeed "Torn and Frayed" is one of finest country-rock songs the Stones ever wrote, with its forlorn tale of a gigging guitar player who suffers from a drug addiction. If we try to judge him or his independent, free lifestyle, he thinks you are "mad." With his heroin addiction, it would seem obvious to be about Richards. According to Janovitz, though, the song seems to be more about Parsons than Richards, especially the line about his guitar playing that can "steal your heart away." Stylistically he hears echoes of the Allman Brothers' "Sweet Melissa."[37] This latter song also is about the lonely wandering life, in this case using the trope (whether real or metaphorical) of the Gypsy. But one big difference is that "Sweet Melissa" relies on pronounced minor chords in its progression, whereas "Torn and Frayed" uses only major ones.

For the progression in "Torn and Frayed," the Stones fall back on their preferred three-chord Mixolydian progression we saw back in chapter 3 with songs like "Sympathy for the Devil," this time in the key of A.[38] For variety they also throw in the dominant chord (E). Again, note the sheer versatility of the chameleon-like Mixolydian progression—from blues/rock ("Satisfaction") and harder rock with a samba twist ("Sympathy"), to now country rock. And like these other songs, it is another timbral twist that establishes the song's unique vibe, in this case the addition of pedal steel guitar played by Al Perkins (who had played with the Flying Burrito Brothers and then was in Stephen Stills's short-lived band Manassas).

ON THE RIFF: THE FIVE-STRING, OPEN-G SONGS OF *EXILE*

The core of *Exile* revolves around the open-G tuned/five-stringed songs of Richards. At the time the guitarist was well aware that this was becoming his trademark and legacy. Although he discovered this new technique prior to *Exile*, he writes that when it came to the work for the new album, the songs "were just dripping off my fingers. I was really starting to find all these other moves, and how to make minor chords and suspended chords. I discovered that the five-string becomes very interesting when you add a capo."[39] The songs dripping off of his fingers that he specifically references are "Rocks Off," "Happy," "Ventilator Blues," "Tumbling Dice," and "All Down the Line," all of which have characteristic riffs that identify each song immediately and effortlessly.

Here we approach the essence of a riff. As a short motive or sequence of notes, it is similar to a lyrical hook in that it is immediately recognizable and allows the listener to find a pattern to the song. It should be simple, and capable of repetition or looping without boring the listener or player. In pop and rock music, these qualities combine easily in single lines on the guitar's lower strings, which do account for many of the famous riffs—for example, the Beatles' "Day Tripper," the Stones' own "Satisfaction," Led Zeppelin's "Dazed and Confused," or Deep Purple's "Smoke on the Water," to name some of the iconic ones. As songs like these show, in this era of guitar-driven music a clever riff will not only sell records, but can come to define a band's sonic footprint. Other riff masters during the '70s include Black Sabbath's Tony Iommi, Ted Nugent, and Kiss's Ace Frehley.

Continuing, riffs can be created from chords or snippets of chords. The original shuffle riffs of Berry, R & B, and early rock and roll, as well as later songs referencing these, also rely on chords. Further, much folk and acoustic rock fashion riffs using chords. Throughout the 1970s hard-rock guitarists from Jimmy Page (Led Zeppelin) to Joe Perry (Aerosmith) and Angus Young (AC/DC) found ways of combining shuffle patterns, bass note melodies, and power chords to continue rock's privileging of the riff. However, many of the hard-rock riffs of the 1970s are extremely derivative of the pentatonic musical language of blues and early rock. Moving much beyond this language involves some risk that the riff will not sound idiomatic to the received rock language.

Hence, striking a balance between participating in the stream of tradition while inventing something new is the most difficult part of becoming a visionary rock guitarist. Although standard tuning on the guitar can provide a powerful platform for suggestive idioms and characteristic ideas to be expanded, at the same time it can hinder the creation of new ones. A guitarist can easily become caged in, as it were, such that it becomes increasingly difficult to carve out new space in the matrix of possible note combinations. There is a limited amount of chord shapes, and again it can be risky to move too far beyond these in the context of rock. This is because a defining criterion of the genre is that the guitar part must sound simple and relate to other riffs and, just as importantly, appear to be simple to play. Any guitarist who gives off the impression of struggle will not make it in the theater of rock.

With his five-string Telecaster tuned to open G, Richards had a wide-open sonic palette upon which to compose. His signature open-G playing combines single notes with chords in an expanded notion of what a riff could be. This hybrid approach to riffing blends melody with accompaniment, making the song distinctive, memorable, and at the same time, simple to play. The tuning also gives a new twist to familiar, time-tested chord progressions, especially with the ornaments and suspended notes that Richards likes to hang on a chord. And he could still rely on the same basic chord progressions the band had been using since they started writing, at once fulfilling audience expectations of what a Rolling Stones' song should sound like. At the same time, the five strings "cleared out the clutter," as we already noted, meaning Richards was able to concentrate on chords as in their melodic implications, without worrying about the bass or accidentally hitting an unsympathetic note on the lowest string. Finally, as we have seen with the addition of the capo, Richards could freely explore other sonorities of the guitar's range; note that he often resorts to the capo in both his open- and standard-tuned songs and especially in his live reworkings of a given song—the best example of this latter that we have already cited would be in "Jumpin' Jack Flash," which he plays in the key of B but in open G with a capo on the fourth fret.

Let us start our treatment of specific riffs by looking at "Rocks Off," the first song on *Exile*, which begins with a stabbing, staccato chordal head motive. Lurking within the motive is what appears to be a dissonance rarely heard in a Stones' song. This occurs on the second chord, voiced in a low tessitura (i.e., on the three lowest strings), which resolves by pulling upward to the third chord. This dissonant chord connects the two most basic chords of any progression, the tonic and dominant. Blues songs often contain dissonant harmonies as passing notes or connector chords, that is, on weak or at least unaccented beats in between the more stable chords. Usually, these dissonances resolve downward. But here Richards uses a syncopated, accented chord to proclaim the dissonance. In so doing, the gesture at once establishes the album as an exegesis in the progressive blues. That is, most of the musical substance, for example the chord progressions and riffs, conform to our expectations of what a blues song is, yet with enough twists and turns that we hear it as a step removed from the tradition.

This dissonant chord, what we can call the "Rocks Off" chord in that it identifies the song, can be analyzed as a variation on the power chord. A power chord mimics the attraction of the tonic-dominant (I–V) couple at the local level in that it only has two pitches, the first and fifth notes of the diatonic scale. This sonority, in music theory the perfect fifth, has an empty, hollow ring to it, the result of the ratio of vibrations of the notes in the overtone series.[40] It is the most consonant harmony with two different pitches that is possible. In effect, the power chord functions as a drone. Lots of blues are essentially drone songs, one of the most primal techniques of musical expression with ancient roots throughout the world and especially in Africa.

By contrast, the "Rocks Off" chord twists the power chord into a dissonance. It does this by placing the bottom note a little below the perfect fifth, which creates the dissonant interval.[41] The upper note of the chord is actually a note that is a member of the next chord, the dominant. Thus by moving only one note, Richards indicates the guitaristic direction for the album, one that will take risks yet move within a well-honed grammar of the blues.

In addition, the "Rocks Off" chord that signals the opening gesture is also a foreshadowing for the bridge harmony. For this bridge (starting at "feel so hypnotized"), the first chord Richards plays is built from the same two notes of the "Rocks Off" chord, with a third note added making it a complete chord. With this third note added, the dissonance vanishes, as the chord is related now to the one it follows, which turns out to be a minor chord that is closely linked to the tonic E chord.[42] Thus, upon repeated listening it becomes possible to hear the intro's "Rocks Off" chord as the first chord in the bridge. Again, this chord initially seemed like an isolated, unique, and local event, but upon closer view it is actually integrated into the song structure proper.

It is worth dwelling for a bit longer on this bridge. Note that bridges are not, strictly speaking, a part of the blues legacy, but instead come from professional (composed) American pop music, especially the Tin Pan Alley or Broadway traditions of songwriting.[43] In short, bridges became a convenient tool for a songwriter's ability to express more than one emotion in a song. Thus when the Stones do use a bridge—most of the time they do not—it does not have the spontaneous sense that the music came from jamming or fooling around in the studio, but rather that they crafted the song in a certain way for a given aesthetic effect.

On "Rocks Off," the bridge slows the song's energy down rapidly, and the band's entire timbre changes with the introduction of a swirling, phase-like effect, perhaps that of a Leslie speaker.[44] Since their psychedelic days, the band rarely tended to change timbre within a song, preferring to keep the same tone color throughout a song. At the same time and emphasizing this change, Jagger modulates his voice to imitate a hazy, drug-induced stupor (starting at "feel so hypnotized").

Whereas the bridge and arrangement of "Rocks Off" shows the Stones as craftsmen intentionally constructing a song, according to Richards "Happy" came quickly and did not need much conscious manipulation. He wrote and recorded it within four hours, and if true, this would certainly rank as one of the fastest creations from start to finish for the Stones. Although in a sense, "Happy" barely deserves to be called a Stones' song, since Richards is the only band member playing on it (although Jagger did overdub vocals), handling both guitar parts and bass, with drums by Miller and Keys on saxophone. This instrumentation was due more to the logistics of their living situation—he wrote the song during the day, and since Nellcôte recording sessions were at night, no one else was there to contribute.

In discussing the song Richards reveals his working method for riff/song creation. After he has the idea for the song, he tries it on the five-string guitar and determines if it is a good fit. In his zen-like approach to the songwriting process, Richards writes, "Great songs write themselves." He muses on the intuitive process for creation: "You're just being led by the nose, or the ears. The skill is not to interfere with it too much. Ignore intelligence, ignore everything; just follow it where it takes you."[45] "Happy" exemplifies this process in its utter simplicity and bare-bones approach to a riff, for here the riff is the song accompaniment and melody and vice versa—they are indistinguishable, wrapped into one, as it were.

Like all their Chuck Berry–style songs, the chordal language is streamlined and uses only two chords, a B (tonic) and E (subdominant). The key of B is not a natural one for rock guitar, but by placing the capo on the fourth fret, the open strings (again, tuned to a G chord) will sound a B chord without any fingers depressing the frets. The intro riffing is not on the tonic B but rather on the E, resolving back down to B. The second chord is recognizable because it is marked by the slide melody, an outline of an E chord that functions as a suspension above the B. Richards structures the song based on the two chords in the following way: For the verse, he uses a shuffle pattern in B, while for the chorus "I need a love," he does it over the E. But even working within this severely reduced harmonic arsenal, the song does not appear to be harmonically lacking in any way because of Richards's deft use of suspensions—that is, extra notes hanging over the main harmony—with two guitar parts dialed in with his characteristic chattering melodic commentaries that weave in and out. And again, there are countless blues songs that use only one or two chords, and here Richards shows how he has absorbed and managed to build on that tradition.

Though *Exile* is not associated with hit singles like other Rolling Stones albums, there was one song that received generous radio airplay during the Stones' summer of '72 North American tour (aka S.t.p., once again, for "Stones Touring Party"). "Tumbling Dice" utilizes the same Telecaster setup as "Happy"—again one with a five-string, open-G tuning and a capo on the fourth fret. Another song in the key of B, it is the twin sibling of "Happy," adding the third chord (it is more typical for a Berry-type or rock and roll song to have three chords), the dominant chord or F-sharp. Another song that predates Nellcôte, the Stones recorded an outtake of the song called "Good Time Women" a year earlier at Stargroves. Although the structure of "Tumbling Dice" is not too recognizable in this outtake, at the chorus turnaround "good time women/don't keep you waiting around," the similarities are most noticeable. A major difference between the early outtake and the final product emerges in the choice of key—the early version is in G, and as such is played without the capo.

Generally for their songwriting process, Jagger adds lyrics to the song once Richards has the music, with Richards usually indicating what the song is about in a line or two. But in the case of "Tumbling," the lyrics are a complete afterthought. That is, Jagger wrote the lyrics for it while they finished up the album in Los Angeles. After their time on the French Riviera, gambling perhaps presented itself as a natural subject. But Jagger was not the gambling kind and had to rely on a housecleaner for information on the topic. Thus "Tumbling Dice" is a good example of the arbitrary, detachable nature of song lyrics, and why it can be misleading to privilege the lyrics as the ultimate arbiter of what the music means.

Surprisingly, perhaps the most representative song of the Nellcôte experience on *Exile*, "Ventilator Blues," has received only one live performance to date, at the first concert of the '72 tour on June 3 in Vancouver.[46] According to Watts, the band had frequently rehearsed the song but had enough trouble with the rhythm that they have not performed it since.[47] The band finished the song in Los Angeles; to hear what it sounded like at Nellcôte, there is a widely circulated outtake that represents the song before it was cleaned up for the album.[48] Richards plays the main slide riff of the song and on this outtake his guitar is out of tune. His competent rendering of the riff does not yet have the snappy, sharp staccato punch of the album's version, though it is moving in that direction. In terms of his guitar being out of tune, this was the biggest complaint about the Nellcôte basement—namely, that it was so hot and humid that no guitar could stay in tune for long. Taylor adds a long lead at the beginning over the riff, exemplifying the kind of jamming the band did in studio rehearsing to find and eventually fix a groove.

Furthermore, for "Ventilator Blues" Taylor finally received a songwriting credit alongside Jagger/Richards, his only one on a Rolling Stones record. Well aware of the monetary value of royalties, Jagger/Richards guarded the publishing credits of any Rolling Stones branded song to such an extent that it became nearly impossible for anyone to receive their proper due on songs, despite whatever input they gave on musical particulars. And it does seem unfair in that so many of the songs dating back to their early days were composed in an open, collaborative manner with the creative sharing of ideas that can occur in such situations. We do not know what Taylor's contribution was to "Ventilator"—the riff or the chord progression during the chorus—but he seems fortunate to have received anything at all, given the prior history that we have seen in representative dealings with Wyman, Faithfull, and Cooder. From the Jagger/Richards perspective, however, they had made and sustained the Rolling Stones, and so they would be the sole beneficiaries of any original songs emanating from their creative mark.

Unlike "Tumbling Dice," the harsh and violent lyrics of "Ventilator" are more organic to the musical material, the direct result of the languid atmosphere of the frustrating recording conditions and the need for fresh air. On the live outtake, Jagger also struggles to stay in tune, but the lyrics and vocal phrasing are essentially intact. This is not the case on the album, where everything is in tune, perfectly straightened out. This perfectionism, once again, marks the main irony of an album whose reputation has thrived on the idea that the album represents direct, supposedly unaltered sound.

On the surface, the "Ventilator" slide riff using a classic G-minor pentatonic scale would not seem difficult for a drummer to accompany. Yet playing in such a common melodic language runs the risk that the music will sound derivative. As one way out of this dilemma, other parameters such as rhythm, phrasing, and articulation can be exploited to great effect. Here we focus on the rhythm and phrasing. Indeed, it turns out that the rhythm of the riff is quite peculiar. In 4/4 time, the riff's accents fall on the second and third beats, whereas in traditional blues, it would be on the second and fourth beats, the so-called backbeat. If you count the notes at the beginning of the song, the fourth and fifth notes of the riff underline the second and third beats; incidentally, the fifth note, which Richards slides up into, is also the highest point of the riff. Complicating the rhythm of the riff is that the second half of the measure (after beat three) is syncopated, which makes for a non-symmetrical distribution of the emphasis notes, while at the same situating the uniqueness of the riff.

As we saw with the Bo Diddley beat in chapter 1, to understand on a deeper level what makes this rhythm tick entails analyzing the accented beat patterns within the measure. As if to announce the singularity of the riff, Richards starts the song with two rounds of it played alone, with Watts entering by marking the time of the eighth-note pulse on his hi-hat for two more rounds, which can be counted off easily as 1 + 2 + 3 + 4 + (or 1, 2, 3, 4, 5, 6, 7, 8, counting the eighth notes) for each round. But these two-round (or more technically, two-measure) groupings of the riff help clarify the structure of the song, which is the hypermetric structure of the song. The term "hypermeasure" is used to describe a local musical event where any number of measures is grouped into a larger whole, or one larger measure, as it were. Once Jagger sings, Watts plays the hypermetric beat for the song that ingeniously provides one rhythmic solution to the riddle of Richards's oddly phrased riff. For the first measure, Watts accents with his snare drum on the second beat and fourth beat as usual, but adds a snap after the fourth beat, on the "and" (represented by a plus sign, +) of the beat. For the second measure, he takes out the accent on the fourth beat completely, yet leaves the marking accent on the "+" of this fourth beat. We can represent it as $1 + \underline{2} + 3 + \underline{4\ +}$, $1 + \underline{2} + 3 + 4\ \underline{+}$, where the underline indicates an accent. This is not an intuitive solution, but it works. From the same quotation cited above, it appears that Watts could not figure out what to play, and that Keys clapped out what he should do. Watts compares his odd rhythmic figure to the asymmetricality of "Take Five." Note once again that Watts had a history of struggling with certain rhythms, for example we mentioned his difficulties with "Sympathy" and "You Can't Always Get What You Want"—this latter song even played by Miller—or his notorious "wrong" entrance to "Honky Tonk Women."

"All Down the Line" is the final rocker from *Exile* we will consider. The song also began earlier as a *Sticky Fingers* demo, as an acoustic guitar song in a different key (capo on third fret, key of B-flat). The early version has a distinct world-music vibe to it, though by the time of *Exile*, Richards had reworked it into another Berryesque shuffle tune in the key of G, taking full advantage of the ringing of open strings. The riff to this three-chord rocker—actually a head motive that returns throughout the song—has become one of his great signature pieces in concert. When it comes back after the chorus, the horns first accent it, but the second time they play a counterpoint (ca. 3:00) that will become the outro melody ("Be my little baby . . .").

The return of the riff-motive is also lowered by a whole step and takes on an even bluesier mood when heard against the tonic G.[49] By lowering the riff, the character of the music takes on a carefree, improvisational feel, as if anything were possible. For this harmonic change, we can conjecture that Richards relied on idiomatic experimentation with the guitar. That is, at the beginning of the song, Richards plays the riff in fifth position; for the return he goes down to third position, altering one of the fingers to stay within the key. This illustrates, as many songs do, that much of the soundscape and harmonic relationships for rock comes not from knowledge of music theory per se, but from parallel positioning on the neck.

"All Down the Line" presents an imaginative summation of blues topics in a musical style that combines the generic influences of the Rolling Stones—blues, rock, and soul. And like many of their songs that thread different themes together, the song calls on time-tested signifiers drawn from the deep well of Americana: trains and travel, work of the common people, religion, and a plea for love. Pushing this idea of the song as a gathering point, on their 50 & Counting tour the Stones used the song as a tribute to the iconic figures of American music. Namely, while they performed the song, they showed a video montage of the many artists that served as the source material for the band (not the first time they had done so, incidentally), drawn from early rock, blues, R & B, gospel, folk, country, and soul. Note that most of the clips they used are readily available on YouTube. Those presented included an impressive array of American artists, to name just a few: Elvis Presley, Howlin' Wolf, James Brown, Otis Redding, Merle Haggard, Miles Davis, Bo Diddley, Bob Dylan, Muddy Waters, and Tina Turner. As the Stones are well past their days of prime cultural relevance, the montage seems to remind us that the "line" or the heritage that leads up to their music is now universally regarded, ironically, as on the verge of becoming a classic tradition in its own right. Finally, as the song itself becomes recontextualized as it accompanies this videographic presentation, at the same time it grants the validity of the Stones' own and now lifelong project of the appropriation of musical Americana. The Stones have become, as it were, a stop on the line.

CONCLUSION

With their opportunistic gathering of their music around the concept of exile, the Stones stay true to their twin artistic roots of rebellion and a riff-driven blues-rock. *Exile on Main Street* provides them with yet another generational statement, showing that under adverse political pressure the band could still create music that spoke to the alienation of youth.

Channeling the Beat's vision of an alternative, deviant America, the album as a whole delves deeper into the seedier, grungier, multivalent side of a marginalized, working-class ethos than anything they would ever do. The Stones also navigate into the religious territory of this down-and-out America with its embrace of an ecstatic experience of Jesus. Conceptually, "exile" neatly bridges the marginalized existence of the oppressed classes and the religious dimension of one of the primary experiences of the Jewish nation in the Bible. It does seem fitting that the figure of "America" situates the exiled status of the Stones, given America's historical role as a place that beckons and welcomes exiles. Finally, somehow this marginalization of the exile and its merging with the exotic aspects of the American landscape manage to interface perfectly with the hedonistic, indulgent, and decadent lifestyle of the '70s rock star.

And with Jagger and Richards both fast approaching thirty, they were entering into uncharted territory as leaders of a popular rock and roll band. If rock is about youth and rebellion, must its progenitors fit the part? The '60s ceaselessly challenged the status quo of the older generation, with the Who even proclaiming that it would be better to die than to get old. Yet ironically, the Stones, along with a host of '60s bands and performers from the British Invasion, have relentlessly and effectively challenged this coupling of "youth" and "rock star" since the '70s. Indeed, the oxymoronic title of "aging rocker" has entered the public lexicon, often inviting controversy as to whether this class of musicians with their endless "final tours" and reunions are simply cashing in. In the Stones' defense, however, the band has never made the claim of a final tour, maintaining that they will play until they are no longer able to.

Finally, *Exile* solidifies the blues origins and recent direction (since *Beggars Banquet*) of the Stones while assuming an original stance via its texture, instrumentation, and mixing. Indeed, there seem to be more session players found on this album than any other Stones effort. After experimenting with scordatura tuning for years, Richards settles on an open-G approach, dialing it in with a removed sixth string for added clarity. This allows him to achieve an unprecedented number of original riffs; again note that acoustic blues and folk artists usually employ alternative tunings, but this is not as common for electric rock guitar. Further, because of the simplicity of open-G tuning, the chord progressions on these songs assume a repetitive effortlessness. If earlier guitar shuffles by Richards had seemed indebted to Berry, with *Exile*, he had found his own voice.

7

TWILIGHT OF THE IDOLS

To *Some Girls* and Beyond

Exile on Main Street proved to be the apex for the Stones. Although the band still created sporadic great songs, as well as at least one more landmark album with *Some Girls*, the band lost its raison d'être post-*Exile* as beacons of rebelliousness and the counterculture. (Some would have *Tattoo You* as their last landmark album, which in terms of its reception might be true, although musically the album consists of a reworked potpourri of previous outtakes and material.) As Stones commentator Sean Egan succinctly puts it, the world changed and the Stones did not.[1] He explains that the "austere," rigid, disapproving society that the Stones grew up in was no more, thus negating the social purpose of their music. And now with punk rock on the rise, the Stones were targeted (rightly or wrongly) as the Establishment itself, something they acknowledged tongue-in-cheek in songs like "Respectable." Ironically, if the Stones and their music helped unleash the wave of openness and permissiveness toward sex, drugs, and living freely that swept Western societies in the late 1960s and beyond, the political repercussions of which are still felt today, the new openness meant that their (and other like-minded bands') music no longer posed the revolutionary danger it once had.

Rock and popular music still matter in everyday life, but arguably not to the extent they once did in the '60s, and certainly no longer as a vehicle for mass discontent or political resistance per se. The entertainment marketplace is increasingly crowded as people engage with various iterations of screens for diversion. Furthermore, the music industry has been on a steady decline since 1999; it was the first sector of the entertainment industry to get hit hard economically in the digital age.[2] And with everything so readily available with a click of a mouse, standing by in ready reserve as it were, we are bombarded on a daily basis with not only new entertainment means but with content and information generally; as one example, music now competes for the conscious attention of many people with social media platforms.

With most aspects of musical creation smothered by slick digital production techniques (Auto-Tune is perhaps the most notorious of these) intended to increase commercial viability, music assumes its place among other virtual items to promote consumerism in the globalized, postmodern world of e-commerce. Beyond its facile distribution, music's fragmented content and message—what it is "about"—is seemingly difficult to locate in a connected world awash in content. Finally, late capitalism has had the ability for some time now to appropriate the oppositional, anti-Establishment stance of any artistic milieu opposed to it. Great examples of this are the use of '60s anthems (starting in the '90s at least) to sell products such as cars, computers, or phones to the baby boomer and now millennial generations.

Despite all the social changes and charges of irrelevance, the Stones persist and continue to sell out large arenas, outlasting nearly every other band of their era. As of this writing (summer 2015) they are in the midst of yet another North American tour. Perhaps it is a sign of collective nostalgia for the '60s, but the Rolling Stones brand still fulfills a powerful niche on the world stage, attracting a young audience to the events alongside the expected baby boomers. Again, these concert events possess very little contemporary countercultural significance, but they do show society's collective reverence for the '60s and the potential for (or promise of) liberation it represents. Yet it is difficult to level the nostalgia charge against the Stones, given their ability to sell out such large venues—so many people have grown up with the Stones, they can hardly imagine a world without them. And even with superficial stylistic changes and deviations throughout the later years, the Stones have stayed mostly true to their initial championing of African American blues, rock, and R & B. And as we analyzed with "All Down the Line," this call and commitment has placed the band itself within this venerable heritage as they have become its most famous curators.

Of course, there is also one last seismic event in the band's biography. Mick Taylor quit the band in December 1974, potentially leaving a gaping hole in the band's guitar sound. According to Jagger, he never provided a reason at the time. A couple of possible explanations were his worsening drug dependency and his realization that he would never get the songwriting credit he craved with the Stones. He had expected to get a couple of credits on the album *It's Only Rock and Roll* and was upset to see that he did not.

Taylor's departure was met with a long, disciplined search to find a replacement. Many famous guitarists such as Jeff Beck and Rory Gallagher were auditioned—whether they knew it or not—before they settled on Ronnie Wood, the guitarist for the Faces. Wood agreed to tour with the band in 1975 and officially joined in 1976 when the Faces broke up. Wood knew the Stones' material intimately and had worked with Richards and Jagger in the past—most recently on his solo album, *I've Got My Own Album to Do* (1974). Though credited to Jagger/Richards, the album credits for the song "It's Only Rock and Roll (But I Like It)" state that the song's "inspiration" was Ronnie Wood.

Thus in this final chapter, we survey the Stones' output from the rest of the 1970s, the last decade perhaps that their music had a mass societal impact, and will point toward the basic tendencies of their approach as they continued onward. During the '80s the band—more precisely Jagger and Richards—were often fighting, and the quality of output started to diminish. Yet they continued to create new music in the '90s and beyond, and in their highly lucrative tours will incorporate one or two new token songs into their stage act. Perhaps their most revealing and excellent late work since the '90s is their retrospective and partly live album *Stripped*, which revisits their back catalog with a roots orientation.

GOATS HEAD SOUP AND *IT'S ONLY ROCK 'N ROLL*

After the emotionally raw and at times bitter energy of the experimental magnum opus *Exile*, *Goats Head Soup* covers more familiar territory from a song perspective. It is also the last album produced by Jimmy

Miller. As such, many commentators rightly view it as the end of an era. Most of the album was recorded in Jamaica, though the reggae influence per se does not yet materialize in a stylistically significant way. The sinister side of voodoo does appear in the album's chuggingly rocking opener, "Dancing with Mr. D," which harkens back to the demonic side of "Sympathy." However, the "D" reference is not to the Devil, but rather to "Death" personified, as in the medieval genre of the dance of death—that is, paintings, music, and poems that dealt with the plague.[3] Horror breaks through in a bloodcurdling female scream at 2:15 during the guitar solo, alleged to have been recorded during an actual voodoo ceremony.

"Angie" brings back the soft-rock acoustic ballad that forms another side of the Stones and at first glance seems derived from the same musical means as "Wild Horses." For the chord progression, the song instead revisits the constellation of chords around the A minor in "Sister Morphine" (refer to chapter 5). We can thus consider the similar guitar part of "Angie" that results as the evolutionary heir of this predecessor. Further, the guitar part has more subtlety and complexity than the essentially strummed one of "Sister Morphine," with Richards or perhaps Taylor picking more of the notes (starting in the solo introduction) and adding in suspensions (i.e., held notes that are not part of the chord proper, but placed above the correct note), recalling *Let It Bleed*'s "Love in Vain," which had remained in their live set lists at the time.[4]

One sharp difference is that in "Sister Morphine," the progression had slight but significant divergences in subsequent verses, giving the song a structurally asymmetrical quality but also a floating, ambiguous feel reminiscent of the fogginess induced by the drug. In "Angie," the song is essentially symmetrical, with two instrumental interludes (the second one shortened) and the traditional eight-measure bridge. One way of analyzing the form is to have the verse part starts on Am for the line beginning with "Angie," and the chorus starts on G for the line beginning "with no loving . . ." The second verse is the most devastating of the song, where the event of the breakup becomes clear yet undermined by the strong feelings the former lovers still obviously have for one another. The interludes present an instrumental break as a substitution for the voice, with strings arranged by Nick Harrison and a soulful piano part that juts through the texture played with the subtle touch of Hopkins.

And with another chordal gesture toward "Sister Morphine," the unexpected bridge ("But Angie, I still . . .") starts with vamp on two chords, D minor and A minor, the same two that started off "Sister Morphine" (though in reverse order). And yet, even if "Sister Morphine" seems to be strongly implied in "Angie," one major difference is the overall key itself. Despite the strong presence of A minor in "Angie," especially the fact that the song and the first part of the verse begins on it, the song is actually in the key of C major (A minor being the relative minor), whereas "Sister Morphine" is in A minor.[5]

With its '60s-styled folk leanings, grown-up lyrics, and sentimentality that was apropos of the time period, "Angie" easily rose on the U.S. *Billboard* charts to achieve number-one status. The follow-up to "Angie" and second single from *Goats Head Soup* was "Doo Doo Doo Doo Doo (Heartbreaker)," a potentially abrasive rocker that, along with the controversial "Star Star" (another single, with the original title of "Starfucker") exemplifies the Stones' '70s approach to the hard-rock genre. The lyrics strive for gritty contemporaneity and realism by portraying the toxic mixture of crime and drugs and their lethal effect on young people in New York City. Though we can conjecture that Jagger is talking about the impoverished, marginalized African Americans of the gang-infested streets of the Bronx, this type of information is kept intentionally vague. Too, the destructive line of the chorus, "I want to tear your world apart," refers to the system (the "world") that condones this inner-city tragedy and hints at the social revolution of "Street Fighting Man." Yet by this point in time, the possibility of revolution in Western societies had passed, and the critique itself was undermined by the song itself, namely, by juxtaposing this critique with wordplay that could fit into a love song—the "doos" and the song's subtitle, "Heartbreaker." In this way, what could be trenchant and angry social commentary gets sublimated in double entendre.

"Doo Doo Doo Doo Doo (Heartbreaker)" has a standard four-chord intro, using E major as the tonic with other chords that are related to the E-natural minor scale.[6] The resulting sound from this harmonic deviation is bold and aggressive. With the propelling timbral energy of Preston's keyboard and Taylor's wah pedal animating the chords, the chorus recycles this intro. Now, in an unusual twist for the Stones, the verse turns to the parallel minor key, E minor, played in a dark jazz-funk groove conversant with the era. Without going into the music theory behind this switch, the other chords of the introduction share common tones with the E minor of the verse and seem to prepare, as it were, the way for the modulation. Thus, what seems at first glance to be a colorful deployment of chords can actually be analyzed as a structural edifice that underscores the twin lyrical themes of social commentary (the verses in the minor) and love gone wrong (the chorus in the major).

On a trajectory for an album a year at this point, the next year's *It's Only Rock 'n Roll* has a back-to-basics, workmanlike air to it, with more input by Taylor. It is the first album produced by Jagger/Richards as the "Glimmer Twins." The Glimmer Twins would go on to produce every Rolling Stones album (alone or with co-credits) going forward. It seems prophetic that the title track and lead single, "It's Only Rock 'n Roll," connects to their future guitarist, Ronnie Wood, on the album that would be Taylor's final one with the Stones. Jagger recorded the song at Wood's home studio, and later Richards mostly took out Wood's guitar parts and overdubbed his own (there is a possibility that the twelve-string guitar is played by Wood). The song itself is intended as tongue-in-cheek, with Jagger musing about what the audience wants from him—would a spectacular, suicidal death finally satisfy the public's desire to devour him? As critics were starting to write off the Stones, their response takes the form of a rock anthem. That is, the song reflexively poses the questions: What is the purpose of rock, and how do we relate to its performers? Essentially dismissing the idea that rock had grown up to become more than an outlet for teenage lust, Jagger's reply is the song's hook, a marketable refrain that was an instant classic and that has since become a Rolling Stones concert staple.

"It's Only Rock 'n Roll" also announces their return to the uncluttered, simple days of rock and roll via Chuck Berry. The rhythm guitar plays a simple shuffle pattern that even in 1974 would have sounded like a throwback to an earlier time. Yet during the verse and lead parts respectively, Richards's distorted sound and offbeat chordal jabs help give the surface of the song an updated sheen. In the key of E, it trots out the Stones' privileged chord progression in this familiar key, similar to "Satisfaction" and "Sympathy." Again, the hallmark of this approach is the use of the Mixolydian or bVII chord, in this case D, in predictable conjunction with the IV (subdominant) chord of A. Richards's lead playing is similar to what he had done in "Sympathy," here though with more double stops (playing two notes at once) and double-stop bends (where the lower note is pushed or raised upward), both à la Berry.[7]

Taylor's favorite solo with the Stones is on "Time Waits for No One," one of the songs that he had also expected co-writing credit for. It is one of his most extended solo efforts since "Can't You Hear Me Knocking." Although the verse of the song is solidly in A minor, the chorus is in C major, the key of the song. Taylor's solos are in C, over the two oscillating chords of F and C.[8] As the F and A minor are closely related chords, the solo possesses a minor feel to it as the F can be heard as a substitute for the A minor. The main theme of the solo is an oft-repeated rising diatonic scale. Taylor stretches out in the second solo, in a manner reminiscent of the softer side of modal jazz-rock of the early to mid-1970s. Unlike "Can't You Hear Me Knocking," there is no closing theme that winds the solo down—instead, his solo is faded out, as the opening drum part is recycled to give some closure. The solo is a fitting bookend to Taylor's tenure with the Stones, and the song itself reveals another aspect of the melodic-lyrical tendency of Jagger and the Stones' songwriting.

A NEW GUITARIST AND *BLACK AND BLUE*

After an extensive search, the Stones settled on Ronnie Wood as their new lead guitarist. Wood was still a member of the Faces when he toured with the Stones in 1975, and he joined the band officially in February 1976. In many ways his joining the band seems preordained. His older brother, Art, had been a member of Alexis Korner's Blues Incorporated that included Watts for a time and was part of the blues scene at the Ealing Club at the same time when Jones, Jagger, and Richards got their start, even playing with them. Wood dreamed of being a Stone back in the '60s, and apparently Jagger even phoned him in 1969 when they were looking for a guitarist. Finally, he bore a striking resemblance to Richards. According to Wood, in the 1960s Muddy Waters even mixed up the two, insisting that Wood was in the Stones.[9]

Although they auditioned a couple of Americans, including Wayne Perkins (see below), Richards wanted to keep the band an exclusively English one, perhaps feeling it would affect the character of the music. In his *Ronnie: The Autobiography*, Wood considers himself a Gypsy, which if he does in fact have Romany roots would connect the latter-day Stones to the massively famous and world-renowned performance practice of Gypsy music. He states that he was the first member of his family born on dry land, coming from a clan of "water Gypsies."[10] According to Wood his family traces their English roots back to the 1700s, living uninterrupted on the canals in Paddington (near London). Although he signs the book "with Gypsy ink," and includes a drawing of himself in front of a traditional Gypsy/Traveller caravan site, it is still not entirely clear if his branch of so-called water Gypsies (or "bargees," those who live on the water barges) are in fact Roma, the tribes of nomadic people who swept into Italy starting in the fifteenth century and who also settled in England. Note that "Woods" is a name used by Roma, and his father and brothers were also musicians (a typical/stereotypical Gypsy occupation), and yet he does not mention anything else specifically that would identify his Gypsy heritage as such.

Although he is pictured on the backside of their next album, *Black and Blue*, Wood only appears on half of the songs, along with the other guitarists they were "auditioning" during this period. These auditions were the basis for much free session work for the album. Once again being stingy with their credit allocations, the album lists a couple of songs with the equivocal "inspiration by," where Wood gets the nod with "Hey Negrita" and Preston with "Melody."

"Hey Negrita" departs sharply from the Stones' songbook, as does the experimental and wholly underrated album *Black and Blue*. During his audition that turned out to be stealth sessions for the album, Wood suggested that they try the piece. Watts reports that he was already struck by Wood's brashness. Harmonically, Wood's riff alternates over two chords, a C and an F. The riff has a world-music character to it, in particular an African character with its sharp ostinato characteristic of Gambian griot music as played on the Koro, a plucked, harp-like instrument. Jagger wrote the lyrics, basing the song on his nickname for Bianca. It joins the pantheon of songs like "Brown Sugar" that have led to charges of racism and sexism. Jagger has defended the song, saying that "Negrita" is the word used to refer to girls in South America. But he goes on to say that the song is not on a particularly deep topic—it deals with a man trying to negotiate the price of a whore.

As indicated by the multivalent title, *Black and Blue* engages the Afro styles that have animated the Stones' project from the start. But the title also flirted with the violence that the group was known for inspiring. For example, a giant billboard on Sunset Boulevard for the album's promotion courted controversy by promoting this meaning of the title. The billboard depicted a bound and battered woman, who says that she is "black and blue from the Rolling Stones and I love it."[11] After a feminist group challenged the sexually provocative image with its alleged embrace of violence toward women, the Stones had the ad removed, but not without first gathering a fair amount of publicity.

But returning to the Afro dimension of the album, the record's sole cover is a reggae song, the slow and hypnotic shuffle of Eric Donaldson's "Cherry Oh Baby." Wood notes that they were all listening to reggae at this time. Though the song never reached any of the notoriety as Clapton's cover of Bob Marley's "I Shot the Sheriff" (1974), in many respects—especially the backing rhythm and Jagger's attempt at a Jamaican patois—"Cherry" has a more authentic ring to it than most attempts at the genre by white rock bands.

The lead single, "Fool to Cry," provides a '70s spin on the previous ballad and soul efforts of the band. The "fool" conceit squarely places the song within a venerable tradition of such songs, chronologically both before and after. Jagger manages to pull off his most affected vocalizing to date. His falsetto and emotionally charged delivery—sometimes bordering on camp—signals the band's embrace of popular trends in the '70s, especially black soul and disco, a vocal style to be followed up in other hit singles like "Miss You" and "Emotional Rescue." The confessional lyrics depict someone in the midst of what seems like a midlife crisis, torn between his familial responsibility and the attractions of a lover from the other side of town, perhaps a prostitute. Jagger exploits the ambiguity of the words "fool" and "daddy" as his tale bridges these two worlds, especially in the respective responses of the daughter and the lower-class lover to the narrator's blues or depression. With its overt class consciousness, the song continues down the path of many of their '60s songs dealing with socially awkward relationships that cross class lines like "The Spider and the Fly," "Back Street Girl," and "Factory Girl."

The band plays "Fool to Cry" at a lackadaisical pace with Jagger's speechlike phrasing. The song is basically a two-chord vamp in F overlaid with some jazzy harmonies. The repeating of the chorus's main line, "Daddy you're a fool to cry," presents an opportunity for some of the best background and call-and-response vocals in the entire Stones' catalog. Indeed, the chorus itself is construed as the response to the verse. Adding to the emotional urgency of the song is the way that Perkins handles the busy and tasteful lead guitar that runs throughout the song, augmenting the wah-altered guitar of Richards. Finally, the minor-key outro (ca. 3:52) makes the song into something at once more profound. Again, the band turns to D minor as the key for this vamping intensification of the material, the same chord used in the outro to "Can't You Hear Me Knocking" and in significant parts of "Angie" and "Sister Morphine" (see above).

Before Wood got the gig, Wayne Perkins was the Stones' choice for the lead guitar position. With a strong recommendation by Clapton and having toured with Leon Russell, Perkins had started out as a session guitarist, at one point working with the group of studio musicians known as the "Swampers" in Muscle Shoals. This part of his résumé must have carried much weight with the Stones, too, given their experience recording there in 1969 with songs such as "Brown Sugar" and "Wild Horses." Furthermore, Perkins also had a reggae connection, playing lead guitar on a couple of songs—including the hit songs "Concrete Jungle" and "Stir It Up"—on Bob Marley's breakout album on Island Records, *Catch a Fire* (1973).

Perkins's description of working on "Hand of Fate" is instructive about the informal way the Stones worked up a song in the studio and how fast everything came together once they recorded the final take:

> We started out cold on "Hand of Fate" one night. We were just kind of starting from scratch with something that Keith had a musical idea about. . . . I was playing a counter-guitar part to Keith, and I started doing this Motown lick that goes along to what he's playing. And so we're cooking along there, and Mick's walking around the room with a tambourine, and he'd go stand in the corner and shake that damn tambourine. And he's singing to himself, and he's off in his own world trying to figure out what's what. . . . It was like the worst garage band I'd ever heard in my life. Then the engineer turned on the red light [to begin recording] and it's like somebody reached out with a magic wand and went, "Bing!" And all of a sudden, it's the Stones! Damnedest thing I've ever seen.[12]

This process of trial-and-error studio creation can be witnessed on the rehearsal for "Sympathy for the Devil" on the Godard film.

"Hand of Fate" shows the ability of the band to keep the rock torch alive in this era of stylistic transition. It is one of the strongest tracks on *Black and Blue* and performed live makes for a great open-G, mostly two-chord rocker along the lines of their signature "Tumbling Dice." The song is a murder ballad, a popular folk genre that also accounts for numerous hits from the '50s on, from "Stagger Lee" to "Tom Dooley" and "El Paso," and of course the contemporaneous mega-hit "I Shot the Sheriff." Perkins's textbook guitar solo over the verse-chorus chords is well received among Stones critics and fans. With its liquidly flexibility and controlled bends, it conjures some Tayloresque touches, while the ending flourish (starting ca. 1:58) exhibits a more American—that is, less mannered—sensibility toward the blues. Finally, the song, in the Stones' preferred simple verse-chorus form, unexpectedly includes a funky, minor-pentatonic blues eight-bar interlude in G (ca. 2:38).

After *Black and Blue*, the next album would be a live one titled *Love You Live*, culled from tours in 1975–1977. Apparently it also marks the opening of yet another rift between Jagger and Richards; the latter reports "collaboration was giving way to struggle and disagreement."[13] Ironically, for a "live" album, much of the guitar and backing vocals ended up being overdubbed. Side three is intended as a tribute to the band's sources, a trip back to their early days in the small clubs of their native London. For this side they booked themselves under an assumed name at a club in Toronto, the El Mocambo Tavern.

The songs show the twin origins of the band—the blues that Jones obsessed over and the rock and roll cherished by Richards. Thus two of the four covers are classic urban blues—Muddy Waters's "Mannish Boy" and Howlin' Wolf's "Little Red Rooster"—while the other two straddle rock and roll—Bo Diddley's "Crackin' Up" and Chuck Berry's "Around and Around." Whereas Diddley plays "Crackin' Up" in a Latin-inflected style, the Stones' 1977 performance of it is infused with reggae. Further, with the exception of "Mannish Boy," side three revisits songs the band first covered back in 1964. Though the El Mocambo gig itself was beset with technical difficulties, it perhaps represents a turning point in bringing the Stones back to their origins, a pivoting to their roots that helped inspire *Some Girls*.

THE RENEWAL OF THE STONES: *SOME GIRLS*

Commentators and Jagger alike view their next studio album, *Some Girls*, as the Stones' response to punk and disco, the two main stylistic innovations of the mid- to late 1970s. But the album also marks a return of the Stones to their calling—Richards sees it as a "renewal," or another *Beggars Banquet* moment, as it were.[14] Much of the album's mystique is probably due to the way the album looks back to the band's origins while remaining firmly a child of its time, both of which were intentional. In interviews Richards has maintained that though the punks gave them a "kick up the ass," it was more the attitude that the Stones were going for rather than playing in a punk style per se. The date of the first punk verbal attacks on the Stones seems to be with the Sex Pistols in 1976.[15] And with regard to disco, Richards continues that there was no conscious decision to play disco (more on this below).

The album's contemporaneity owes much to Richards's guitar timbre, a sharp departure from his usual practice of very limited use of effects pedals. He cites the use of a green box for his sound, perhaps referring to a MXR reverb echo pedal, though the really noticeable effect is that of the MXR Phase 100 on songs like "Some Girls," "Beast of Burden," and "Shattered."[16] Ironically, for a guitarist who does not favor the altered signals of effect boxes, when he does use them (think of the fuzz-tone effect "Satisfaction") it is to great acclaim. And some of this sound was due to the amps, as the band switched from Ampeg to Mesa Boogie; note that the boutique Mesa amps have a much fuller, complex, and darker sound to them than their mass-produced counterparts.

Furthermore, there is the increased presence of Wood, who was there for his first full studio album with the band. Though he has some excellent lead breaks, his contribution lies also in his deft ability to participate in what Richards calls the art of weaving, something that had once shown great promise with Taylor. Because of Taylor's preference to play lead, his later work with the Stones has less weaving than when he had started. Wood is also a quite versatile guitarist and on this album reveals his wide-ranging talent. Following in the path of Jones and Taylor, he took over the slide duties with ease, and like Jones he demonstrates multi-instrumentalist, polystylistic tendencies. Wood's highlights on *Some Girls* include "Far Away Eyes," where he shows off his pedal steel, and "When the Whip Comes Down" and "Respectable," where he uses a Parsons-White B string Bender guitar.

Beyond equipment and personnel changes is a stylistic transformation of their studio approach. Recording at the Pathé Marconi Studios near Paris (more below), sound engineer (and perhaps co-producer) Chris Kimsey convinced the band to stick to a simpler approach, using a 16-track recorder instead of a 24 and to remain in the studio's small room with a less advanced recording desk (though a legendary, proprietary EMI one) instead of moving on to the bigger, more modern recording space with a Neve sound board (the industry leader).[17] He rejected the recent "clinical" sound of the Stones and wished to bring them back to their gutsy, rootsier tone. In this respect he succeeded. Note that Kimsey had recently recorded the acclaimed albums *Frampton Comes Alive* (1976) and Bad Company's *Burnin' Sky* (released in 1977). Further, he knew the Stones from Olympic Studios where he started in the late 1960s. On *Sticky Fingers* Kimsey had assisted Glyn Johns and had been the engineer for Bill Wyman's first solo album release, *Monkey Grip* (1974). He states unequivocally that he was not a big fan of rock and so was not intimidated about pushing them in the direction he felt they needed to go.

All things considered, the band required this cumulative sonic reorientation to stay potent. For, by the late 1970s and stylistically adrift post-*Exile*, the Stones were fighting for relevance in the crowded and generationally transitional space of the period. They knew that their reputation as the standard-bearers of rock was on the line. Yet with *Some Girls* they pulled off the feat of proving that their gutsy live-music aesthetic approach could still work in the new era. It was an extraordinarily redemptive moment in the band's career, essentially proving their critics wrong. With the album's lead song and single, "Miss You," they not only scored another number-one summertime hit, but also captured the essence of the era's dance/disco milieu.

While the concept album still remained an aesthetic goal for most bands, *Some Girls* overwhelmingly coalesces around the theme of sexual desire and fantasy, grounded in Jagger's personal experience of the grimy but glorious decadence of the New York City club scene in the 1970s. For example, the album's one cover song, "Just My Imagination (Running Away with Me)," the 1971 number-one hit by the Temptations, folds these themes together, as the narrator's ecstatic desire for a girl who is not aware of his existence leads to a desperate plea to the Lord. But the aspiring love song becomes something more than a mere nostalgic tribute to Motown. Jagger takes liberty with some of the song's lyrics, including specifying the location of the song in New York. His vocal delivery is influenced by punk (especially on the official live version), while the once-again busy, restless guitar-driven arrangement of the mostly two-chord vamp departs radically from the original Temptations' string and orchestral arrangement but gels perfectly with the straight-up arranging of *Some Girls*. Indeed, in the context of the album's idealization of runaway desire in New York and its discontents, the song's chorus is perfectly tailored to the album and comes off as if they wrote the song.

For an album fixated on New York, its recording location near Paris had a profound effect on their day-to-day work ethic and thus the album's outcome. Unlike the dramatic circumstances of *Exile,* the Stones were there for more practical reasons. Though they were now on their own label, they had distribution deals with other record companies. Thus having just signed a deal with EMI, they booked space at one of the company's studios in France. Their return to France for recording—this time on the outskirts of Paris, specifically the Pathé Marconi Studios in the commune of Boulogne-Billancourt (near the old Renault factory, according to Richards)— reignited the creative juices of Jagger, as he primarily drove the music and the sessions from this period.[18] Too, his amateur guitar playing helped the band to place its music within the burgeoning punk spectrum, in particular its "DIY" fixation. The studio space was on the smaller and more intimate side, and with its purposely chosen, out-of-the-way location it fostered a focused work environment without the comings-and-goings of a constant stream of visitors and other musicians. However, there is one story of Keith Moon, the drummer for the Who, showing up and helping to instigate an inspired night of music making (November 4, 1977).[19] But that seems to be exception, and Richards comments that the studio was in an area lacking any restaurants or bars. He also reveals that on the daily car ride there he would listen to Jackson Browne's new live album, *Running on Empty*, which could have had some influence on *Some Girls* (more below). Finally, unlike their other albums from the 1970s, there were no extra musicians involved except for overdubs after the main sessions and that in turn the band members were "more focused" and had to "work harder" because of this.[20]

Like *Exile*, *Some Girls* displays a thematic aesthetic unity that is also reflected in the tonality and musical arrangements (see table 7.1).

Most of the songs are in either A or E, the traditional keys of early rock and roll and blues. Following the punk movement's back-to-basics, garage-rock approach, with mostly verse-chorus formats and seemingly lacking in exposed virtuosity, the songs possess the direct, energized punch prized by early adherents of the punk style. That is, the Stones avoided both the musical excesses of hard and especially progressive rock and the sappiness of many of the singer-songwriter acts of the time, like Billy Joel. But was this approach really anything new for the Stones? Though they were targets of the punk rebels for representing the Establishment—a supreme irony given their role in the 1960s as societal agitators—if anything they could lay claim to being the spiritual proponents of the raw style advocated by the younger rockers. Their '50s style rocker, "Rip This Joint," can certainly be heard as a progenitor of the punk style. But the attacks bothered the Stones nonetheless, who fought back. Richards writes that the band became determined to "out-punk the punks."[21] In addition to this was the grim prospect that Richards could face extended jail time in Canada, again stemming from drug charges, and clearly echoing their problems with British authorities in the late '60s. As we shall see below, Richards channeled his frustration

Table 7.1. Keys of Songs on *Some Girls*

Song	Key
"Miss You"	A minor
"When the Whip Comes Down"	A Mixolydian
"Just My Imagination"	A
"Some Girls"	A
"Lies"	E Mixolydian
"Far Away Eyes"	F
"Respectable"	A
"Before They Make Me Run"	G Mixolydian
"Beast of Burden"	E
"Shattered"	E

with the Canadian authorities into one of his best songs and now concert staple, "Before They Make Me Run."

Before getting into the songs themselves, the reception of *Some Girls* has been complicated by its recent re-release. That is, following in the path of *Exile*'s recent re-mastering and re-release with bonus tracks (2010), *Some Girls* was also given a similar extravagant box-set treatment (2011). The bonus CD tracks also have mostly new vocals or parts added, a couple of exceptions being "Petrol Blues" and "Claudine" (this latter for at least the lead vocals).[22] And like *Exile*'s reworked songs, the idea of altering something that is part of the historical record problematizes the legacy of the Stones. But again, this is the musicologist or archivist's point of view. For the music/entertainment industry, the task is to keep the band and their music as commercially relevant as possible, whatever it might take. Jagger appears to want it both ways in that he is willing to release outtakes previously only available as bootlegs, but in an adulterated way that violates the authenticity of the original recording. Though there is precedent for this in the Stones' catalog, most famously with "Waiting on a Friend," the passing of decades would seem to preclude this kind of updating. Finally, there are some online commentators who have taken issue with the paucity of the Stones' re-releases given the large amount of archival material still available.[23]

A good example of a song with new vocals (and probably some instrumental overdubs) is "No Spare Parts," released as a single in 2011 with a music video directed by documentary filmmaker Max Whitecross. The song is a simple country-rock ballad; compared to the original outtake, Jagger reworked the lyrics to make a clearer story out of it. Though Jagger thinks his voice has not changed that much, the new one seems too professional or polished compared to the original. Of course the original was not a completed track, but Jagger's desperate drawl and pleas are preferable (at least in my opinion) to the shinier new one. The video, furthermore, takes us down the path of collective nostalgia, asking us to ponder where we were in 1978, and then mixing up footage from the *Some Girls* tour with a newsreel from the time that depicts violence in the Middle East and beyond. The intended point of the video is not clear, nor is the connection of *Some Girls* and its tour to the politics of what is going on in the world at the time. On one reading, this juxtaposition seems to depict the Stones and their audience as oblivious and insensitive to the tragedies around them, yet it would seem that the filmmaker's intent would be quite the opposite.

THE SONGS OF *SOME GIRLS*

Despite its musical unity, there are a couple of tracks on the album that are musically anomalous, "Miss You" being one of them. It was Jagger's idea to do a disco-inspired song, which they took to a new level—Bill Janovitz posits the song as primarily funk. Jagger's marriage to Bianca was falling apart, and he wrote the song to the Texas supermodel and his future wife, Jerry Hall, whom he had just met. The simple hook played by Wood—really a riff in the guitar's mid-range—is as recognizable to most classic rock fans as the one in "Satisfaction." The riff starts the song, and, given its use of four notes in the most common scale used in rock, the A-minor pentatonic, it is quite startling how refreshingly original the riff actually sounds. It has also held up well with time. The riff is doubled on the harmonica played by Sugar Blue, at the time a blues street musician who had played on a couple of prior blues albums. Blue phrases his riff to mesh with the guitar, and his timbre blends effortlessly into the final mix. The riff is also the main melodic hook of the song's chorus, sung in a high falsetto. The chorus builds throughout the song and becomes more emphatic as a call-and-response as the song unfolds.

As we have been tracing the use of minor in the Stones' catalog, this is also the only minor-key song on the album. And though minor keys are associated with sadness or melancholy, in this case the A-minor key has a triumphant quality to it. This is due to the group energy generated by the unique arranging for each instrument. Both the drum and bass parts were based on Billy Preston's ideas at the song's conception. Preston introduced the rhythmic basis of disco to Jagger at a rehearsal at the El Mocambo. And the song's most obvious dance motivator is the pounding beat of Watts, the so-called four-to-the-floor bass drum pattern where each beat of the 4/4 measures is accentuated with the bass drum. Commenting on this beat in an interview, Jagger says that at the time it was not just a disco beat but a dance beat that was popular in the clubs. As an instigator of the exuberant scene of the time, Jagger connects its lineage to big band music and jazz and notes how the dance dimension had always attracted both him and Watts. In the same way he commends Wyman's octave leaps in the bass line, which he thinks was one of the first bass lines to do so. Though Wyman was not the first to do so, octave leaps in the bass also have earlier roots going back to boogie-woogie piano lines and continue on through big-band jazz and R & B and then funk. At the time, though, this funky octave figure was quickly becoming a hallmark of disco.[24] Wyman's active, loud, and at times walking bass line adds spice to the potential monotony of the two alternating chords. Finally, thickening the spaces (though not too audible) is yet another keyboardist, Ian McLagan, who makes his first of two studio appearances on a Stones recording, the other being "Just My Imagination."[25]

And the guitar weaving in the song is at the highest level, with Wood playing a complementary lead underneath the vocal to Richards's jazz-like comping. The saxophone solo (played by King Crimson's Mel Collins) is followed up by a harmonica one, and their respective liquidly flowing timbres give the song a '60s retro R & B flavor. Part of the song's charm was also due to its rapid-fire spoken parts, seemingly improvised (though probably not), that are meant to approximate street dialogue.

Finally, note that "Miss You" was released in three versions at the time—two different singles, one of which is an extended (12") disco remix, and the album version. The song was originally quite long and had to be edited down to the shorter lengths. The extended remix provides the most satisfying experience of the song, with extra lyrics, instrumental parts, and generally great interplay among the musicians.

As seen in table 7.1, the next three songs—"When the Whip Comes Down," "Just My Imagination," and "Some Girls"—keep A as the tonic pitch and hold the changes to a simple vamp from the A to D chords (I to IV). "When the Whip Comes Down" takes on a controversial topic, the experience of a young homosexual, and the music assumes an appropriately aggressive stance. Jagger says he wrote it about a gay person coming to New York to become a garbage worker, but the "whip" in the title and chorus line would seem to refer to sex and imply that the narrator is working as a prostitute. Essentially played in their pounding new punk style, it has a tonally interesting guitar break of the A–D chordal exchange at 2:09, moving to G, the Mixolydian or bVII chord of the key of A. Again we see the continued importance of this quintessential '60s harmonic move in their '70s music. Second, what makes the tonal contrast so apropos here is the juxtaposition of the older Mixolydian sound with the driving punk attitude. That is, the Mixolydian recollection brings us back to a reassuring and comfortable sonic space from the past, a respite from the song's modern foray into punk.

Also exhibiting this type of tonal variety between tension and release is "Some Girls." In particular, a release is heard in the parallel minor at the chorus ("gimme all your money"), where the chords are A minor and E. The musical tension relaxes here, as the singer sarcastically agrees to give away half of his possessions. Interestingly, as they build up the song through subsequent verses, the A-minor chord is dropped in the final chorus (where the beach is specified as Zuma, a popular beach in Malibu).

The album's title track is also the first song in open-G tuning, though it is capoed up on the second fret to sound in A. The guitars employ the phase-box effect in a swirling manner, which works well in the numerous guitar interludes led by Wood. Sugar Blue's piercing harp playing punctuates the intro and the outro. Jagger notes that the song's lyrics could not have been written in the politically correct environment of today, but that in the '70s it was still possible. Jagger is still surprised that the song made it through the vetting of the record company. It is perhaps hard to fathom that no one would have flagged the line about black girls. Perhaps only the Stones could get away with such a statement. But it was the '70s after all, and record execs were not exactly immune to the party scene—Ertegun was as notorious as anyone in the debauched Studio 54 scene. And the line probably helped make the case for the Stones continuing as the bad boys of rock.

Despite their insouciant, punkish stance, the Stones also returned to country music. Not since *Exile*'s "Sweet Virginia" had the Stones delved into country, and "Far Away Eyes" is probably their most authentically sounding example in the genre and certainly their most humorous. Wood's pedal steel manages to strike an ideal balance between tradition and the Stones' own style. Yet at the same time, the lyrics mock the genre. Namely, Jagger employs stock elements from country—the narrator is a truck driver looking for a good time while the girl is a prostitute waiting for him at a truck stop.[26] The singer drenches his vocal delivery with his own imagined take on a country drawl, a style that is congruous with the song's setting in the California oil town of Bakersfield. The verses satirically depict the TV evangelicalism that preys on rural- and lower–working-class America, while the chorus kicks into a more traditional theme of finding a way out of loneliness through the comfort of a woman.

The Stones' renewed interest in country can also be gleaned from other contemporaneous songs released in the 2009 box set, including "No Spare Parts," discussed above, and also their cover of Hank Williams's "You Win Again." Furthermore, there is "Claudine," a shuffle-like rockabilly-styled outtake (especially the echo effect on the guitars) with country leanings. The song was strong enough that it was intended for release but held back due to legal issues. Another murder ballad like "Hand of Fate," "Claudine" differs from this earlier effort in that it is based on real events. It tells the story of the French actress and singer Claudine Longet, who was cheating on her boyfriend at the time, Olympic skier Vladimir "Spider" Sabich, and then fatally shot him in March 1976.

In *Life*, Richards relates the backstory to "Before They Make Me Run," his first solo vocal effort for an entire song since "Happy."[27] Summarizing, it was his "cry from the heart," a plea to the Canadians to dismiss his case concerning drug trafficking charges. As we have already seen, Richards likes to linger over material until it is really ready or "marinated"; he relates that it took five full days of studio time, after four of which he collapsed under the studio console. Like "Miss You," the song is a stylistic anomaly on the album, with a thicker, chunkier guitar part that looks back to his earlier sound. Some of the sonic differences might also be due to Richards's bass playing on the track (which does not seem all that unusual, unlike his bass line in "Sympathy") or that engineer Dave Jordan recorded the song (although apparently it was still mixed by Kimsey).

In his signature open G, it is also another Mixolydian song. After an intro in G that will become the progression for the chorus, the verse starts on the Mixolydian F chord. At the end of the line of verse it pops back into G ("draggin' around," then "Well, it's another good buzz"). This lift from the F to the G is what gives the song its unique character. Further, though the F is harmonically below the G by a whole step, in open-G tuning and as voiced by Richards on the tenth fret, it is played as a minor seventh above the G. This can be seen on the live performance video where Richards plays the open strings quite theatrically, matching his singing.[28] That in turns means that in context, the G rings with less tension on the strings than the F, another small detail that is significant for the song's musical impact. Finally, on an album having lots of loud guitar fills and interludes, the lead guitar parts are kept at bay and are subordinate to the rhythm playing (on the live version discussed above, even when given space for two guitar solos, Wood keeps it simple and is barely heard above the mix). And this is in keeping with the song's integrity as a personal manifesto, where even the outro licks seem perfunctory.

The second single and penultimate song on the album, "Beast of Burden," employs a much cleaner, pristine guitar sound than the Stones usually have. In its rhythmic phrasing it harkens back to the soul style of guitar of the mid-1960s that we have seen, for example, in songs like "Mercy, Mercy." It is also another prime example of the weaving that Richards and Wood are capable of together, and on the live, filmed version from 1978 Richards often adds in his own, mostly bluesy, lead-style licks.[29]

But a couple of other musical markers of "Beast of Burden" also relate back even further, particularly to pop music from the '50s—the variant of so-called doo-wop progression in the key of E and Jagger's falsetto.[30] Indeed, with the music coming from Richards, it connects—consciously or not—to the Jackson Browne album mentioned earlier. For that album's conclusion, Browne arranges and lyrically extends the doo-wop classic, "Stay" (1960), a number-one hit performed by Maurice Williams and the Zodiacs. The doo-wop progression has a mechanical aspect to its rigid repetition of the four-chord pattern over a couple of measures. It can run the risk of becoming monotonous if not properly handled. At the same time, again there is a positive trade-off with the use of the progression: with predictability comes security. Namely, by the 1970s the doo-wop chord sequence had become a nostalgic piece of musical material that could potentially transport the listener back to a comforting psychic space. In this zone there is the experience of what we can call harmonic entrainment. In this process, the listener becomes so attuned to the progression that it is internalized to the point of generating synchronous brainwaves.[31] And Richards is careful in his phrasing and voicing of the progression—he does not grant the same amount of time to each chord (the second chord, a B, is played for only a beat, almost as a passing chord), while having the latter three chords each enter on an upbeat. This chordal syncopation adds a soulful feeling to the phrase, and with the light, transparent voicing around the guitar's ninth fret coupled with a sparkling-clean guitar signal, the standard progression assumes its timeless quality.

For the final song, "Shattered," also released as a single, the band remains in E but the phase effect is put back on the guitars, one of which is tuned to open E. This is also the first time they would release three singles from the same album, albeit with a B-side of a song not on the album, the very strong track "Everything Is Turning to Gold."[32] Without Wyman again, Wood plays bass on "Shattered," with harder riff-style phrasing as is typical when a lead guitarist plays the instrument. The song sticks to the pat harmonic formulas of the album, with simple two-chord exchanges (E and B) for the verses that mock (somewhat tongue-in-cheek) the superficiality of Manhattan living. Simon Kirke, the drummer of Bad Company, plays congas on the song, and there are some partly credited hand clappers.[33] The guitar solo (by Richards) and instrumental break (with Wood on pedal steel) where the extra percussion comes in are also notable in switching to a new chord progression and in fact contain the most chord changes on the entire album. Richards utilizes pentatonic blues bends but mostly relies on his double and triple stops in his post-Berry way. Simultaneously mixed in the background are various overdubbed guitars that complicate the perception of his solo.

As the album closer and as a bookend to "Miss You," Jagger's expansion of his vocal style—from timbral effects including falsetto and his newly developed speech-song—reaches its apotheosis on "Shattered." In this regard, he even claims to have been influenced by early rap. It is possible, though rap was still underground (mostly confined to the South Bronx) and not in mainstream circulation in 1977. Perhaps while clubbing he managed to experience rap or early hip hop in a live setting, most likely in Manhattan (it is hard to fathom Jagger hanging at the clubs in the South Bronx), though the scenario does seem tenuous.

Finally, *Some Girls* marks not only the Stones' return to their proper form but also an compelling achievement in a fast-changing music environment. It blunted the writing off of the band by the new punk rebels of the younger generation. At the same time it captured the dance mania of the 1970s, appealing to a mainstream, disco audience at odds with punks. Though not the towering virtuoso of Taylor's ability, Wood proved himself to be a satisfying choice for a follow-up guitarist, with ample and wide-ranging guitaristic moments that help grant the album its status as a major entry into the Stones' canon.

LOOKING FOR DIRECTION: THE 1980S

In their provocation, the Sex Pistols did the Stones a great service. The Stones were among the first rock bands to demonstrate that an aging band whose landmark first hits were over a decade past could still make a groundbreaking album. Further, and probably even more difficult to pull off, the band managed to complete another album that culturally addressed the historical moment. Though there are many great songwriting efforts post–*Some Girls*, still, Stones albums as albums have been mediocre.[34] And without needing to prove anything, and their legacy ensured, the Stones' albums have been few and far between.

Thus the milieu or backdrop that defines the Stones' music remains tied to their prime songwriting years in the '60s and '70s. Placed in a larger context, with a career spanning over fifty years now, the Stones produced the significant bulk of their greatest hits repertoire in a thirteen-year or so time frame (1965–1978). For their tours since, the band draws their selections mostly from this back catalog, though they do sprinkle in songs from whatever new album they might be trying to promote along with some latter-day tunes like "Start Me Up." But there is no doubt that their mass audience comes for their classic hits, while at the same the hard-core fans long for the Stones to dig deep into their back catalog, which is why the band generated a lot of buzz in the spring of 2015 with rumors that they were going to play *Sticky Fingers* in its entirety.

Does this open up the band to the charge of being an oldies act, a weathered nostalgic trip down memory lane? Perhaps. But I would argue that as long as they keep improvising and interpreting, injecting the songs with something new—whether musical or emotional—they can plead not guilty to the nostalgia-act charge. Restated, there needs to be a level of musical risk taking when they play, otherwise they are reduced to mechanical entertainers going through the motions, no matter how refined the performance. And it seems they are well aware of these issues and that their performances are walking a fine line on these matters. But certainly as a player Richards has absorbed enough of the blues aesthetic to avoid redundancy; for example, their 1995 album *Stripped* sheds new light on many of their classic songs.

Of course, after 1978 there is still one great riff to come, in "Start Me Up." This riff is immediately recognizable to any classic rock fan. Another open-G song, the riff is very close to other songs in this tuning, and like these other ones they had to be careful not to be veering too close to "Brown Sugar." And although the song was released in 1981, its genesis dates back to the *Some Girls* sessions and further back, a reggae version of it called "Never Stop" having been recorded at the Munich sessions in 1975.[35] In fact it was Kimsey who suggested that they construct a new album around archived song artifacts, which explains the album on which "Start Me Up" appears, *Tattoo You*.

The chordal riff for "Start Me Up" has a similar upward extension as in "Brown Sugar," where over the straight barring the second and third fingers play notes on frets above the bar. There are two chords contained in this movement, though it gives the impression that it is one chord, the second one. Played at the fifth fret in the key of F (the second chord), it also recalls "Brown Sugar" by being in the same key. But after two measures of the F chord riff, Richards takes the bar down two frets to play a B-flat chord, to which he adds the traditional rock and roll shuffle pattern. In this way, the song's character seems both old and new at the same time, a surprisingly simple yet original twist on music material—a I–IV vamp—that must be seen as seemingly exhausted by the 1980s. Keeping with this simple harmonic language, the chorus ("You make a grown man cry") reduces to two chords, the C (V) and the F (I), barred at the fifth and tenth frets (note that this is a different voicing for the F chord), respectively.

Musically and structurally, the new songs would continue to follow the old templates, though often with up-to-date studio and production techniques, much to the chagrin of Richards. In a modern studio environment, engineers usually prefer to keep the individual instrumental tracks separated from one another so that there is minimal or no sonic bleeding, achieving the blend instead in the mixing and mastering stages. This can often achieve a cleaner, leaner, and more precise finished product. But the clarity comes at the expense of a thicker live sound, where instruments mesh with one another in more fluid, messy, complicated ways, and with less precise rhythm.

Another '80s song with roots that go back to the previous decade is "Waiting on a Friend." Janovitz writes that it is the "note-perfect passage into middle age," and one of their most beautiful songs.[36] He is referring to the lyrical demeanor of the song, penned by Jagger in 1980, which is a tribute to his bandmates, especially Richards. This is clearly depicted in the video to the song, filmed on the streets of the East Village and at St. Mark's Bar and Grill.[37] The song's conception goes back to 1971, and the backing tracks for the song were recorded in late 1972 during the *Goats Head Soup* sessions. The video is a landmark one for the Stones, generating early MTV exposure for the group and showing the members in a relaxed, conciliatory manner. It is also the penultimate video for them shot by Michael Lindsay-Hogg, whose work for the band stretches back to "She's a Rainbow" and continues in a whole series of videos throughout the 1970s to this time.

The syncopated guitar intro of "Waiting on a Friend" sets a laid-back vibe, with a gentle Caribbean feel that makes excellent use of an added chord tone that defines the song.[38] Furthermore, the added tone gives the song its lazy, jazzy atmosphere. The verse starts on an A-minor seventh chord, the sonority heard at the openings of "Sister Morphine" and "Angie," and its changes over four measures recall a variant of the doo-wop progression.[39] Sonny Rollins plays the overdubbed saxophone part. Having the legendary jazz saxophonist on the track certainly helps to legitimize the band as a serious musical institution. Rollins's mellifluous timbre and phrasing recall the populist origins of his sound going back to the 1950s hard bop style on songs like "St. Thomas."

If "Waiting on a Friend" fosters a nostalgic trip both lyrically and musically, "Undercover of the Night" embraces an abrasive '80s electronically manipulated sound. From the album of the same name, the sessions began at Pathé Marconi EMI Studios in Paris and were followed up by more sessions in the Bahamas (Compass Point, Nassau) and New York City. Even though *Tattoo You* was their first official '80s album of newly released material, most of the album dates back to the '70s. By contrast, *Undercover* represents the band's first foray into the pop-centric waters of the '80s. During this period Jagger steered the band toward the striated textures of the 1980s as he attempted to bring the band into line with current trends. In this process, layers of instruments seem pasted, as it were, on top of one another, and the album, despite some strength, does not capture the band at its textural best.

Richards has expressed his dismay at what they were doing during this period; indeed, according to Wood, Richards was largely absent while they worked up "Undercover of the Night," the album's first single and best track.[40] Richards himself writes about the sessions in the following passage: "A hostile, discordant atmosphere. We were barely talking or communicating, and if we were, we were bickering and sniping . . . Mick would come in from midday until five p.m. and I'd appear from midnight until five a.m."[41] He continues by stating that Jagger had an affliction by this time known as LVS, "lead vocalist syndrome," and that Jagger had got too caught up in the flattery known as show business. Indeed, in this section of his book, Richards is scathing in his criticism of what Jagger had become at this juncture of his career, "acting as if he was someone else."

But despite Jagger's chasing of the latest musical fashion, there are still some fascinating musical conservations that came out of the period. In this regard would be the band's further exploration of worldbeat music (a hybrid music combining world/folk with rock/pop). Jagger and Richards have acknowledged African and Jamaican percussive influences on the song and on the album itself, and accordingly they deployed outside percussionists. The legendary Jamaican reggae drummer Sly Dunbar plays drums, and there are also a couple of West Africans on there as well.[42] Placed in a wider percussion context going back to "Sympathy," the Stones' excursions into worldbeat climaxed in the 1980s with this song and album (see "Feel on Baby, " especially in its instrumental version, released as a B-side to the single of "Undercover of the Night") and "Continental Drift" (discussed below) on *Steel Wheels*. Another world-music influence is bassist Robbie Shakespeare, who appears to have substituted for Wyman on at least one version of the song.[43] Note that Shakespeare and Dunbar form one of the most prolific rhythm sections in reggae music, known especially for Black Uhuru and their backing up of numerous other reggae bands. Finally, another positive coming out of the work on the album is the integration into the band of Chuck Leavell, the Southern keyboardist formerly with the Allman Brothers who plays for the first time on a Stones studio recording. Brought into the band for live support by Ian Stewart, he would become the de facto Stones keyboardist, assuming the position to this day once Stewart passed in 1986 at age forty-seven due to heart failure.

After a percussive assault and the stabbing, punchy bass riff, the guitar roars into the mix of "Undercover" (starting ca. :14) in an adrenaline rush that also fades out with some delay. Solidifying the separation of the mix, the bass motive trades off for the first part of the verse in a call-and-response with the guitar. The timbre of both the drums and guitar is elusive and harsh, the result of a delay and heavy signal processing on the part of Kimsey (now credited as a co-producer), while the bass retains an edgy, pointed timbre to it. All things considered, it is one of those produced moments that seem possible only in the studio, something that the Stones had tried to avoid in their earlier music. Because of the simple nature of the music, the song is able to work live simply by adding in delay and phase-type effects.

In keeping with Jagger's embrace of both pop music and worldbeat, chords for "Undercover" are minimal, with a nice Mixolydian inflection for the main chordal riff (B-flat to a C chord). Wood's guitar break is a funky one that revisits the scalar minor pentatonicism of "Hey Negrita." The break becomes more urgent when Jagger doubles it after the second verse, and it also appears as the conclusion to the guitar solo, with Jagger again. Preceding the guitar solo is also the most dramatic part of the song (starting at 2:34), where the raucous opening idea is recapped.

And also like "Sympathy," Jagger reveals the literary source behind the lyrics, William S. Burroughs's *Cities of the Red Night*, with its tales of "sexual and political repression." The song is about the secret hit squads in South and Central America and the disappearance of young men (the missing or *disparus*) for going against the regimes. The video, directed by filmmaker Julien Temple, sets the story in San Salvador, and has Jagger as a journalist being taken out by Richards and his henchmen (the secret forces, or those who are the "undercover of the night"). The video spoofs the gangster and Spaghetti-Western film genres, culminating in a gunfight at a church scene that would be right at home in a Sergio Leone film. At the time the satirical nature of the video's violence was misunderstood, and it was originally banned by MTV and British television, though later it was shown in a censored format. Commenting on it, Wyman says, "It was really good, that track ["Undercover"], and they did that really good video for it which was banned by everyone."[44]

Coming off the heels of Jagger's first solo album, *She's the Boss* (1985), the Stones' next album, *Dirty Work* (1986), was not well received, as Jagger seemed to have lost interest in the band.[45] Richards is rightly critical of this juncture of the band's career, saying that with the solo album came the realization that Jagger was no longer making an impact, and thus "Mick had lost touch with reality."[46] Kimsey was not called in to help (or he chose not to), with Jagger bringing in Steve Lillywhite, whom Janovitz says was the "big-name producer du jour."[47] Often noted is the fact that the album's lead single release was not a Jagger/Richards song but a slick cover of Bob & Earl's "Harlem Shuffle" (1963). Were they losing confidence in their songwriting? The second single, "One Hit (to the Body"), tries to make up for it with a Jagger/Richards songwriting credit shared with Wood, and they even handed off a cameo guitar solo to Jimmy Page, who barely rises to the task. The now de rigueur video for "One Hit" speaks volumes, as Jagger and Richards fling themselves around the warehouse/stage backdrop as if they are still in their twenties. Symbolically or not, Jagger and Richards even come to blows at one point in the video. Though probably not intentional, it recalls an alleged episode the previous year where an enraged Watts punched Jagger in the face over a callous remark by Jagger asking where "his" drummer was.

With yet one more album to go in the 1980s, *Steel Wheels* (1989) was generally much better received than *Dirty Work.* Marketed as a comeback/reunion album, it also witnessed the return of Kimsey as co-producer and the final studio album with Wyman. The album contains one of the most intriguing songs the Stones did from an ethnomusicological perspective, the previously mentioned "Continental Drift." The song started with Jagger on a drum machine and synthesizer, aided by Matt Clifford (who got credit as a co-arranger), but they quickly realized it should have some live percussion to it.[48]

But if they were going to bring in outsiders, Jagger wanted some continuity with the Stones' past. As it turned out, Bachir Attar, a Moroccan musician whose father's band Jones had recorded on his "Pipes of Pan" record back in July 1968, contacted Jagger around the same time.[49] Attar suggested doing a concert with the Stones. Instead Jagger, Richards, and Wood flew to Tangier for recording sessions. Immediately realizing it would be impossible to record in the remote village of Jajouka located in the Ahl Serif mountains to the south, they had Attar's village musicians record over a three-day period at the sixteenth-century Palais Ben Abbou in the Casbah of Tangier. The three-day event in

June is captured on film and is also readily available on YouTube.[50] Beat novelist/composer Paul Bowles, a longtime resident of Tangier who first heard the Jajoukan musicians with Brion Gysin in 1950, was on hand and also provided a link to the band's first sojourn to the ancient city in 1967.

"Continental Drift" starts with the pipers and drummers, punctuated by Richards strumming a bicycle wheel; the studio version of the song also served as set opener on the 1989–1990 tour. The song's ancient soundscape collides quickly with a contemporaneous, '80s-style synthesized bass ostinato, which subdues the pipes for the entrance of Jagger's vocal. Indeed, in line with its worldbeat aesthetic, the song eschews chord changes for the recurring mantra of the ostinato or groove. When the pipes do return, they are used echo-like to answer Jagger's descending cry in a standard call-and-response. The electronically altered rhythm becomes trancelike and hypnotic, while the use of the natural minor mode (F minor) recalls the exoticism of "Paint It Black," especially in the stepwise chorus melody (listen especially at "open the door . . ."). The text describes the power of love, yet remains equivocal in whom it addresses and could be interpreted as secular or religious. Indeed, with the addition of the mystical pipes and drums that speak to both the profane and the sacred, the text seems intentionally vague in this respect, similar in this regard to a Sufi love poem.

After a bridge section ("It's as pure as silver") is a mostly instrumental section (starting at 2:43) that tries to re-create the ritual ecstasy of the Jajoukan Pan festival. The synthesizer starts and the drums build up in a slow accelerando, when a voice bounces from left to right on "cha." Jagger quotes lines from the bridge in a haunting, apparition-like fashion, approximating a hallucination, while the pipes creep subtly into the mix. Lasting well over a minute, this Jajoukan-led section is at once one of the densest sections of any Rolling Stones–released song. In its abandonment it shows a vast improvement over the generic demo tape made in Montserrat that does have the basic architecture of the song already mapped out.

In a sense, this Jajoukan-infused version of "Continental Drift" can also be read as the final appropriation of the legacy of Brian Jones. That is, after Jones planned the release of his *Pipes of Pan at Joujouka* album, he wanted to continue to play and experiment in what is now called world music, perhaps with a new band that incorporated what he had experienced in Jajouka.[51] As he had once led the way into the blues revolution of the 1960s, he perhaps thought he could do the same with an even more ancient, primal music. The Stones did release Jones's Jajouka album on their own label in 1971, but did not return to Jones's vision for a Moroccan-infused, polyrhythmic music until "Continental Drift." Jagger mentions in an interview from 1989 that Jones was also visionary in adding in phasing effects to the original field recordings he placed on the album.[52]

WINDING DOWN: 1990S ONWARD

When it was announced that Wyman was officially retiring from the band in January 1993, it would have been hard to imagine that the band would still be going twenty-plus years later as of this writing (2015). Often unnoticed behind the Jagger/Richards juggernaut, his contribution to the Stones has been acknowledged in recent years. For example, Janovitz waxes poetic over him, noting his foundation in American soul and R & B, the home territory of the band, whereas his replacement, Darryl Jones, has more of a jazz sensibility. Wood sums up this difference by saying that Darryl is more a precise, efficient, "contemporary" player. Though meant as a compliment, in a rock and roll context it is the lack or downplaying of these qualities that often makes for greatness. Wyman was known for playing slightly behind the beat, which gave the Stones tracks a uniqueness and free quality—when coupled with Watts, it gave the Stones their "roll." In other words, his bass prowess provided a certain hard-to-quantify ingredient to their sound, something that in its imperfection was perfect, that distinguished their music from the increasingly rigid, mechanical, and sterile quality of modern rock and pop.

For the last three studio albums, Don Was was brought on as co-producer. Winning a Grammy for producing Bonnie Raitt's *Nick of Time* (1989), the Detroit native encouraged the band to return to their rock origins (like Kimsey before him), which Jagger apparently had regretted subverting on their first post-Wyman album, *Voodoo Lounge* (1994). He has since assisted on all of their albums and helped with the *Exile* and *Some Girls* reissues. In the Was co-productions, the band's mixes have grown hotter (i.e., louder), probably achieved through more compression, EQ, and other mastering effects in the studio. This follows the general tendency of the music industry for ever-louder mixes, which also has the negative by-product of destroying the dynamic range and variability of a song. In the *Some Girls* remastered reissue, for example, the loudness was extremely pronounced.

One of their best rockers from the '90s onward is "Love Is Strong" on *Voodoo Lounge*. Another open-G tuned song written by Richards while in Ireland, on early versions he did the vocals.[53] In its overt appeal to the blues-rock vibe of "Midnight Rambler," Jagger brings back his harmonica, a timbre sorely missing in later Stones. Indeed, stylistically the song is a return to the classic values of the band in songs like "Start Me Up," especially after the pop attempts of the spotty '80s. The verse's bluesy progression's reliance on three chords (A–C–D) is transposed upward in the chorus ("what are you scared of . . ." over the chords D–F–G). Subtle guitar fills reverberate during the verse (Richards's descending one is particularly identifiable), while the chorus represents a powerful buildup accented with Wood's lead (a bend up to the note A) and "oohs" from the backup singing. Jagger sings in a growly, low tessitura unusual for him, but he really hits his vocal stride by letting his voice relax into his higher range for the last verse, especially after "heart" (ca. 2:44). Marring the song, unfortunately, is the '90s production value of a hot mix and too much separation therein. In terms of this latter element, the famous blending and depth of the Stones' analog recordings seems lost with the crispness and coldness of this newer approach to a mix. In any case, the blend does get stickier as the song progresses.

Jagger's "Saint of Me" from their next album, *Bridges to Babylon*, revisits the terrain of "Sympathy for the Devil" both musically and lyrically. Like an African American spiritual, Christian figures are trotted out to illustrate the power of conversion, in this case St. Paul, St. Augustine, and John the Baptist. For the chorus ("I said yeah"), Jagger uses the verse progression of "Sympathy," the Mixolydian downward move from E > D > A (though it sounds in F as there is a capo on the first fret). But the song seems barely to qualify as a Stones song, as Richards does not play on the song, and again its impact as a Stones' song is marred by its overproduction.

Critics lauded *A Bigger Bang* (2005) as once again a return to the blues roots of the Stones as they reverted to a stripped-down sound.

The album features the core players of the band, although Wood has a diminished role. The band released "Rough Justice," the opening track about an aging love affair, as a double A-side single with the retro ballad "Streets of Love." "Rough Justice" presents another shuffle-like rocker in open G (at least in the studio version), in about as simple a musical arrangement harmonically and riff-wise as even the Stones could manage, though with some added punch supplied by Wood's slide guitar. Once again it also references the Mixolydian. With its loose double entendres taking us back to the blues, namely the traditional barnyard references of "Little Red Rooster," it was quite absurd that the NFL silenced the song's use of "cock" for its 2005 Super Bowl performance. Apparently the NFL was playing it safe after the previous year's fiasco with Janet Jackson.

The last song we will analyze is "Plundered My Soul." The song was an unfinished outtake from *Exile* for which Jagger wrote new lyrics in 2010. By adding in new vocal parts, the song's identity becomes equivocal. Note that with the updates the band made to songs in the '80s like "Start Me Up" or "Waiting on a Friend," it was very difficult if not impossible to tell that the band was updating older material. But with "Plundered My Soul," the new vocal parts stick out—Jagger's voice had changed too much in nearly forty years—and completely muddles the era to which the song belongs. In addition to Jagger, Taylor added in guitar fills for the new recording, which, though they blend more seamlessly, on repeated listenings do indeed seem to be added after the fact. Yet the song was generally well received among Stones fans; writing in *Rolling Stone*, music critic Rob Sheffield cannot resist a countercultural/religious simile to describe the ecstatic experience of listening to an unreleased *Exile* track from the archive not previously available on bootlegs: It is like watching "video footage of Jesus skateboarding."[54]

"Plundered" can be reduced to the two-chord exchange of the verse, which goes from B minor to A major.[55] I would argue that both of these chords are significant in the song's reception among Stones' fans, especially its ability to trick the listener into believing that she is hearing an authentic *Exile* outtake. Namely, the B minor, a rare chord for the Stones, is the chord that gives "Wild Horses" its melancholy ring (it comes in right at the onset of the verse), while the A is not only the key of guitar-driven rock itself going back to Chuck Berry but is found all over the place in the Stones' hard-rock efforts. Thus the sweet melancholy of B minor combines to temper the hard, charging energy of the A chord, a "ying and yang" moment, as it were.[56]

In 2014–2015, the Stones have come off some large and successful world tours of the United States, Europe, China, and Australia. Their brand is as powerful as ever. At these concerts and in the Zip Code tour (current as of this writing), they are even playing a newly recorded 2012 single, "Doom and Gloom," from the *GRRR!* album, a greatest hits compilation. But there is no denying that we are also witnessing the final act of the band. In December 2014, within a day of one another, two Stones' sidemen passed away, saxophonist Bobby Keys (b. 1943) and keyboardist Ian McLagan (b. 1945). For the former, the Stones' official Facebook page mentions that they are "devastated" by the loss of Keys, who made a "unique musical contribution" to the band.

CONCLUSION

Throughout our journey of approximately fifty years of Rolling Stones recordings, we have endeavored to show the musical unity underpinning the Stones' oeuvre. For example, the band is able to get an amazing amount of mileage from a basic constellation of similar chord progressions. Too, their riffs will remain among the greatest in the rock genre, impeccable in their efficiency and directness. They have stuck with a basic roots-oriented sound, with a commitment to a sonic richness and layered depth, for the most part eschewing sonic effects and studio tricks. If there is a secret to the Rolling Stones' winning formula, we would venture that it lies in their overall commitment to the simplicity of the blues, rock, and R & B genres. Yet paradoxically they achieve this simplicity through constant reworking, reimagining, and honing of the basic musical parameters of a song. Furthermore, the simplicity to their sound can become maddeningly complex if one tries to replicate it. Perhaps theirs is an illusory simplicity.

As we have maintained, the Stones were fortunate—like the Beatles and other '60s bands—to have come along at the right time in history, as the baby boomers were coming of age into a time of economic prosperity. Starting from the blues and R & B, straight-up rock and roll, and soulful balladry, the Stones stylistically connect these great story lines of twentieth-century popular music, steeped in primarily African American roots.

The Stones are also central to cultural history of the 1960s and beyond. Their sheer longevity, rare in the popular music world, ties their musical endeavor to not only the aesthetic and artistic realms, but to the political sphere. The Stones' music challenged the status quo, and helped unleash a powerfully potent youth movement whose effects are still felt today. Their rebelliousness has become mainstream: public morality has loosened its grip in Western society, and the appreciation for the artistic achievements of the marginalized, as well as multiculturalism in general, have gone mainstream.

And this story is not over. Despite many recent deaths in the Rolling Stones family, most prominently saxophonist Bobby Keys, the saga of the Rolling Stones continues. As of this writing (June 2015), the band is on yet another North American summer tour, which is nearly sold out. Instead of supporting an album, the Zip Code tour is partly a celebration of *Sticky Fingers*. Following the path of deluxe versions of *Exile* and *Some Girls*, *Sticky Fingers* was reissued in a multitude of formats in June 2015, along with previously unreleased material. And Richards has stated that after the tour he wants to bring the band back to the studio for another album. The guitarist also has a new solo album that is finished and will be released upon the completion of the tour.[57]

Even if a guitar band that does not rely on sonic effects and musical trickery seems hopelessly old-fashioned in today's digitized musical world, it has not diminished the public's fascination for and love of the Rolling Stones' music. Though we have been critical of the latter-day Stones' ability to strike gold on the songwriting level, it always remains possible that another great riff à la "Satisfaction" or "Jumpin' Jack Flash" lurks on the horizon.

NOTES

TIMELINE UP TO *EXILE* (1972)

1. The set list appears on the Rolling Stones website, "12th July 1962," http://www.rollingstones.com/release/12th-july-1962.

2. Jagger claims that Howlin' Wolf told him that Son House did "Little Red Rooster" first.

3. Richards states that Jones had stopped contributing in the studio around this time and that he had to take up the slack.

4. Jagger reports that "Yesterday's Papers" was the first Rolling Stones song he completely wrote.

INTRODUCTION

1. Written by Bobby Troup, the King Cole Trio released the song as a single titled "(Get Your Kicks on) Route 66." It was retitled "Route 66" on the Chuck Berry album, *New Juke Box Hits* (1961).

2. "Mona" appeared in the United States on *The Rolling Stones, Now!*, released in February 1965.

3. Using music recognition technology and Billboard charts, a recent academic study has generated sensational interest in the mainstream media by proposing that hip hop is the most "important development in pop music" since 1960, and that the evolutionary years for pop are 1964, 1983, and 1991. We do not have space here to refute the study's conclusions, but briefly, its methodology seems flawed: 1) Billboard popularity is only one indicator among many for a song's significance; 2) an algorithm run through a computer repre-

sents one interpretation of a song, a surface one at best, but cannot take into account differences between songs in the same style. For a summary of the study see Jethro Mullen, "Is Rap the Most Important Music Since 1960? Scientists Say They Have Proof," CNN.com, May 6, 2015, http://www.cnn.com/2015/05/06/tech/pop-music-study-hip-hop-the-beatles/.

4. See "Bob Dylan, 'Like a Rolling Stone,'" in the "500 Greatest Songs of All Time," *Rolling Stone*, April 7, 2011, http://www.rollingstones.com/music/lists/the-500-greatest-songs-of-all-time-20110407/bob-dylan-like-a-rolling-stone-20110516.

5. See "The Rolling Stones, '(I Can't Get No) Satisfaction,'" in the "500 Greatest Songs of All Time," *Rolling Stone*, April 7, 2011, http://www.rollingstone.com/music/lists/the-500-greatest-songs-of-all-time-20110407/the-rolling-stones-i-cant-get-no-satisfaction-20110516.

1. THE EARLY STONES

1. Bill Wyman in *Stone Alone* (76) writes: "Through his vision of music and his lifestyle, Brian was the inventor and inspiration of the Rolling Stones. The band would not have existed without him. He never received that proper credit during his life and I intend to ensure he gets it now."

2. Quoted in Trynka, *Brian Jones*, 95.

3. Egan, *The Mammoth Book of the Rolling Stones*, 12.

4. Ibid., 10.

5. Richards, *Life*, 87.

6. Dalton, *Rolling Stones*, 26.

7. Bangs, *Psychotic Reactions*, 65.

8. For more on the payola scandal, see Kevin Dettmar, *Think Rock*, where he describes how many record execs testified to Congress: "Payola was the only reason that rock & roll was popular" (43). Dettmar also describes how establishment figures despised the new genre.

9. Richards, *Life*, 139.

10. As of this writing, this historic venue is in serious danger of being torn down. See Camilla Horrox, "Historic Music Site Where the Rolling Stones Formed Could Be Torn Down by Developers," Getwestlondon, February 20, 2015, http://www.getwestlondon.co.uk/news/west-london-news/historic-music-site-rolling-stones-8681388.

11. Matthew Goody, "Thames Valley Cotton Pickers: Race and Youth in London Blues Culture," 38–39.

12. See Richards, 77–79, for a recently unearthed letter Richards wrote to his aunt in April 1962 recounting this fateful meeting.

13. Wyman, *Stone Alone*, 76.

14. This is inherent in the subtitle of Trynka's book: *Brian Jones: The Making of the Rolling Stones.*

15. Trynka, *Brian Jones*, 56.

16. Ibid., 62.

17. Ibid., 67.

18. Stewart's testimony is in Wyman, *Stone Alone*, 100.

19. Baldry appears as a vocalist on Korner's debut album, *R&B from the Marquee*, recorded in June 1962 but released in November of that year on Decca.

20. Cross harp is a technique that facilitates the playing of blue notes.

21. Richards, *Life*, 94.

22. Trynka, *Brian Jones*, 227. For a full account of this episode beginning with the drug bust, see especially 213–28.

23. "Clave" is the Spanish word for pattern or code.

24. Here the "-" indicates a rest, and the ":" a bar line. Note that this rhythm can also be written using one measure, which may be more likely given the tempo; however, I think it is easier to conceptualize and represent, at first approach, in two measures.

25. An interesting connection between "It's My Party" and the Stones is in the person of Phil Spector, who helped the Stones while making their first album. As a producer he had shown interest in "It's My Party" for his group the Crystals.

26. Norman Meade is a pseudonym for Jerry Ragovoy. Original pressings of the Stones' single also credit Jimmy Norman, who added lyrics to Meade's song for Irma Thomas's version. The first version of "Time Is on My Side" by the Stones was recorded in June 1964 at Chess Studios with an organ introduction; this appears on their second American album, *12 X 5*. The band rerecorded the song at their November 8, 1964, Chess session with the lead guitar introduction, and this is the version released on *The Rolling Stones No. 2*, their second UK album.

27. Richards, *Life*, 105.

28. Many Internet sources mistakenly say that "Little Red Rooster" was recorded in November in Chicago. This might stem from a still unreleased bootleg album that contains music from the Chess recording sessions called *2120 South Michigan Avenue: The Unreleased 1964 Blues Album*, itself a confusing subtitle since one of the sessions is from 1965. Willie Dixon states that it was recorded again at Chess on November 8; however, the version does not appear to exist, if it ever did.

29. According to Trynka, the recording of "Little Red Rooster" marks another harsh episode in the band's treatment of Jones. Jones thought he was

recording the song with the band, and when he arrived at the studio to find the band not present, he was "frantic." *Brian Jones*, 131.

30. Guralnick, *Sweet Soul Music*, 21.

31. Also known as "Have Mercy," the song was co-written by Don Covay and Ronald Alonzo Miller. It first appeared as "Mercy, Mercy" on the Rosemart label in 1964. Members of the Soul Clan were Wilson Pickett, Otis Redding, Covay, Arthur Conley, and Ben E. King, all associated with Atlantic Records in some way (Guralnick, *Sweet Soul Music*, 272).

32. The pentatonic or five-note scale is the basis for much African American music.

2. TOWARD AN ORIGINAL DIRECTION

1. Trynka, *Brian Jones*, 109.

2. There is the creation myth around "As Tears Go By" that Oldham locked Jagger and Richards in a kitchen together to write a song. Richards confirms the episode in his autobiography, *Life* (142).

3. Ibid.

4. For more on this topic, see Earcandy, "A Degree of Murder—The 'Lost' Brian Jones Solo Album? [Ronnie]" http://earcandy_mag.tripod.com/rrcase-brianjones.htm. Thanks to Rob Weiner for pointing out this source on the existence of early Jones compositions.

5. Martin Elliott, *The Rolling Stones Complete Recording Sessions*, says that the "song was written almost exclusively by Keith and Brian Jones," 85.

6. As we have already noted in the introduction, this revelation is especially ironic, and possibly hypocritical in light of the fact that the band (actually Allen Klein's ABKCO, which owns rights to the song) sued the Verve over their sampling of "The Last Time" (albeit in the Andrew Loog Oldham Orchestra version) for their huge hit "Bitter Sweet Symphony" (1997), for which Jagger/Richards have been added as the songwriters.

7. Brill Building songwriters Barry Mann and Cynthia Weil composed "We Gotta Get out of This Place."

8. Hale, *Nation of Outsiders*, 59.

9. Elliott, *Complete Recording Sessions*, maintains that Jones used a sitar on "Mother's Little Helper" (69), but other sources do not appear to agree—for example, Babiuk and Provost, *Rolling Stones Gear*, 205.

10. Richards, *Life*, 174.

11. Friedan, *Feminine Mystique*, 20.

12. Graham Gouldman wrote "Heart Full of Soul" as the follow-up to his first successful song, "For Your Love," also recorded by the Yardbirds. Note

that the Yardbirds' "For Your Love" also used a timbral novelty for the time, the harpsichord. Furthermore, there is also an earlier version of "Heart Full of Soul" using the sitar. Kinks front man Ray Davies wrote "See My Friends" after visiting India. In his essay "Indian Resonances in the British Invasion," Jonathan Bellman has argued that the Kinks' song is the first Raga Rock song.

13. With its open strings serving as drones, the guitar is presumably tuned down a half step to E-flat.

14. The song can be analyzed as a modal hybrid, combining chords drawn from both E Phrygian (E–F–G–A–B–C–D) and E Aeolian (E–F#–G–A–B–C–D). The F chord appears as after the E minor, moving through D major to get to G major, and thus serves a dual function as the Mixolydian seventh (b7) of G. The D chord uses the F#, but more importantly, the F# appears melodically as the first note of the guitar riff (the "re") that is then replicated in the vocal melody.

15. Richards, his emphasis, *Life*, 182.

16. There is a dispute over the originality of the jam for "Goin' Home." The band Love, led by Arthur Lee, claim that Jagger and Richards heard them perform their song "Revelation" live (released on the album *Da Capo*, in late 1966 after *Aftermath*) and stole the jam idea from it. It is interesting that "Revelation" was also recorded at RCA Studios with Dave Hassinger as engineer. Still, the idea to get a long-form song on vinyl was in the air at the time; on *Blonde on Blonde* (May 1966 release), Dylan released his extended and rambling eleven-minute "Sad-Eyed Lady of the Lowlands."

17. Decca originally released the song with a comma insertion, as "Paint It, Black," and it is still referred to in this way in some sources.

18. That is, it is in E minor when they play it live now. The original recording sounds almost in F minor; perhaps the tuning discrepancy is due to a faster tape speed to match Jones's sitar. When they currently play it live in E minor, Richards uses a capo on the second fret, so in standard tuning the chord fingerings are in D minor. In the past they have played it in D minor (that is, without the capo), which is too low for Jagger's vocal range. For an example of a D-minor version before they settled on E minor, see "The Rolling Stones—Paint It Black—Live 1990" on YouTube, https://www.youtube.com/watch?v=QCgwCJt5NQI.

19. Here the Dorian mode (E-F#-G–A–B–C#–D) is combined with the minor scale with a raised seventh (D#). Whereas "Mother's Little Helper" turns on the second scale degree, the seminal note here is the seventh degree.

20. From a 2003 interview, Jagger's quotation is taken from the website Time Is on Our Side, "Paint It Black," http://www.timeisonourside.com/SOPaintIt.html.

21. Originally the studio had a different location in London, which is where the Stones had recorded their first single, "Come On."

22. Elliott, *Complete Recording Sessions*, 80.

23. Wilson still mentions the song specifically in recent interviews as one of his favorites from this period; see his interview with Marc Myers, "Still Picking up Good Vibrations," *Wall Street Journal*, October 7, 2011, http://online.wsj.com/news/articles/SB10001424052970204524604576609000066845070.

24. Richards, *Life*, 184.

25. This episode is the subject of a recent Hendrix biopic, *Jimi: All Is by My Side* (2013), which features André Benjamin from Outkast as Hendrix.

26. Hopkins does play on one track on *Between the Buttons*, the humorous "Something Happened to Me Yesterday." In the tradition of British dance hall music, according to Elliott, the song was directed at their "Carnaby Street" fans (*Complete Recording Sessions*, 80). The track also features contributions by Brian Jones on trombone and other stringed instruments. Jones is also the one whistling in the song, which ends with another insider joke, as Jagger thanks everyone in a voice imitating a British TV personality.

27. Specifically, the instrument used on "Good Vibrations" was the Electro-Theremin, a variant of the theremin, and was played by Paul Tanner who helped invent the instrument.

3. SUPERNATURALLY CHARGED BLUES

1. Richards, *Life*, 240.

2. See Wyman, *Stone Alone*, 482. Wyman then repeats the claim in *Rolling with the Stones*, 300. Martin Elliott seems to accommodate both viewpoints by maintaining that Wyman came up with the chord changes.

3. *Rolling Stone*, "100 Greatest Rolling Stones Songs: [no.] 7 'Jumpin' Jack Flash,'" October 15, 2013, http://www.rollingstone.com/music/lists/100-greatest-rolling-stones-songs-20131015/jumpin-jack-flash-aa968-19691231.

4. Landau's *Rolling Stone* review (1969) of the album is reprinted in Dalton, *Rolling Stones*, 328–31.

5. Richards, *Life*, 237.

6. The December 11, 1997, cover has Jagger and Richards on it with a subtly altered magazine title to "Rolling Stones." Thanks to Rob Weiner for calling this cover to my attention.

7. Wyman, *Stone Alone*, 487.

8. To attract an audience given the Stones' huge following, the producer changed Godard's own title of *One Plus One* to the more marketable *Sympathy for the Devil.*

9. Richards, *Life*, 252.

10. The novel was completed in 1940 but not published until 1966 and appeared in an English translation in 1967. So when Jagger read it, it was essentially a new work of literature for the English-speaking world. This literary background for the song closely parallels the occult literary input for *Their Satanic Majesties Request*, as Jagger had been reading the Chinese-Taoist text *The Secret of the Golden Flower*, whose themes of light, according to David Dalton, are woven throughout *Their Satanic Majesties Request* (Dalton, *Rolling Stones*, 324).

11. From the "Hymn to Beauty" in the Baudelaire collection *Flowers of Evil*, 41, where the poem wrestles with the dualistic nature of beauty, beginning with the line: "Do you come from deep heaven or do you come from hell, O Beauty?"

12. Jimmy Page, a musician fascinated by the occult, wrote music for this that can be heard at "Jimmy Page: Lucifer Rising and Other Sound Tracks," on YouTube, https://www.youtube.com/watch?v=PSfBaLBvGCg. With its electronic timbre and repetitive structure, it seems to follow in the path of Jagger's scoring.

13. Thanks to Rob Weiner for this reference; Weiner thinks Jagger was way ahead of his time in his employment of "industrial noise," long before Lou Reed's "Metal Machine Music" (from 1975; private correspondence with Weiner, 2015).

14. Marianne Faithfull writes that Anger was "obsessed" with the Stones and that for a while Mick indulged him; in the end though "Mick took all our magic books and made a great pyre of them in the fireplace" (*Faithfull: An Autobiography*, 160).

15. Bulgakov, *The Master and Margarita*, 20.

16. Wenner, "Mick Jagger Remembers," *Rolling Stone*, http://www.rollingstone.com/music/news/mick-jagger-remembers-19951214?page=2.

17. E > D > A > E.

18. Jones's girlfriend at the time, Suki Potier, was there according to Martin Elliott, though she does not show up in other sources or in the film.

19. Richards, *Life*, 242. Richards considers Don Everly to be one of the finest rhythm guitarists of all time. Apparently Everly learned the open-G tuning from his father, who was also a guitarist.

20. For more on this topic, see Paul Trynka's interview with Dick Taylor, "Open G Tunings and Open Secrets," August 28, 2014, available on his blog at http://trynka.net/2014/08/open-g-tunings-and-open-secrets.

21. The album, basically a live jam session in the studio, was recorded during the *Let It Bleed* sessions in the spring of 1969 (appearing in 1972), featur-

ing Cooder, substituting for Richards, and Nicky Hopkins (the "Edwards" of the title).

22. In live performance, Richards puts the capo on the fourth fret; in open-G tuning the open guitar strings will sound a B chord. Thus in this performance practice he plays "Jumpin' Jack Flash" in the key of B, up from the B-flat of the original.

23. "La Bamba" is a Mexican folk song whose most popular version is by Ritchie Valens, recorded in 1958. The British group the Troggs did the first famous version of "Wild Thing" in 1966, subsequently played live by Jimi Hendrix at the Monterey Pops Festival.

24. Richards, *Life*, 238–39.

25. It must be mentioned in this context that Queen's breakthrough hit, "Killer Queen" (1974), starts with Freddy Mercury playing chords on a tack piano.

26. As with so many of the Stones' songs from this period, it is quite difficult to determine who is playing what part or instrument, especially with proper documentation lacking.

27. See, for example, "Jig Saw Puzzle, Take #12," on YouTube, https://www.youtube.com/watch?v=CMidBl9EIZ8. In this outtake, the piano part is front and center, and the slide part is still being worked out.

28. From the Greenfield *Rolling Stone* interview, 1971, as quoted in Babiuk and Provost, *Rolling Stones Gear*, 279.

29. The outtake "Pay Your Dues" is available on YouTube, "The Rolling Stones—Pay Your Dues (Early Street Fighting Man)," https://www.youtube.com/watch?v=yv2Gj6w0HWQ.

30. Wilkins also performed a version of "Prodigal Son" at the Newport Folk Festival in 1964, at the height of the country-blues revival. This was released by Vanguard on *The Blues at Newport/1964/Part 2*. The Stones could have learned the song from this record.

31. Wyman, *Blues Odyssey*, 153.

32. Ibid.

33. It is pretty difficult to tell from the song. Yet the vibrato applied does sound a lot like Cooder's—see his playing on "Memo from Turner." For a discussion of Cooder's role in *Beggars*, see "The Rolling Stones: *Beggars Banquet*," http://www.theclanmackinnon.com/ryland-cooder.com/BeggarsBanquet.html.

34. The Stones performed "Salt of the Earth" in December 1968 at the studio filming for *Rock and Roll Circus* and three times in fall 1989 with guests from Gun N' Roses, including Axl Rose, and once in 2003.

35. Wyman, *Stone Alone*, 485.

4. "THIS RECORD SHOULD BE PLAYED LOUD"

1. *Rolling Stone* wrote about the event, interviewing people who witnessed the murder; see "The Rolling Stones Disaster at Altamont: Let It Bleed," January 21, 1970, http://www.rollingstone.com/music/news/the-rolling-stones-disaster-at-altamont-let-it-bleed-19700121?page=6. According to the eyewitness, Hunter was waiving a gun in self-defense and was disarmed by the Angels when they continued to stab him. Also, note that the Grateful Dead were scheduled to play and had helped plan the event but refused to go on, as the day's mayhem only got worse.

2. Faithfull, *Autobiography*, 184.

3. Ibid.

4. Ibid.

5. Ibid., 85. Note the use of the word "supernatural" once again when dealing with the Stones!

6. "Live with Me" is very effective as a live song; see especially the one on *'Get Yer Ya-Ya's Out!'* or the recently released version from the Roundhouse in London (March 1971) on the deluxe edition of *Sticky Fingers*.

7. Quoted in Richards, *Life*, 246.

8. Babiuk and Provost, *Rolling Stones Gear*, 306.

9. Elliott, *Complete Recording Sessions*, 113.

10. C#–B–A–B.

11. On YouTube, "Gimme Shelter Merry Clayton's solo performance," http://www.youtube.com/watch?v=jqXyjbgs5rU.

12. Though DeSalvo confessed, the case of the Strangler is still open to this day; the family of Mary Sullivan, one of the victims, believes that DeSalvo was not the Strangler.

13. Caputi, *Age of the Sex Crime*, 50.

14. Adorno, *Philosophy of New Music*, 159.

15. Richards, *Life*, 268.

16. Featuring T. I. and Pharrell Williams, since this original writing "Blurred Lines" has gone on to further notoriety due to plagiarism involving Marvin Gaye's "Got to Give It Up."

17. Hellmann, "I'm a Monkey," 372. The song Hellmann refers to is Charley Jordan's "Cutting My ABC's," which can be heard on YouTube, http://www.youtube.com/watch?v=JC1JnOSRmno.

18. See Aristotle, *On Poetry and Style*, 1449b21–28. For a philosophical reading of catharsis as a psychological phenomenon, see Hans-Georg Gadamer, *Truth and Method*, where "pity and fear are events that overwhelm man and sweep him away" (130). In short, Gadamer concludes that tragic "pensiveness" is a return to ourselves; that is, it helps us to accept our fate (131).

19. Specifically I am thinking about the tragic murders in Isla Vista near the University of California, Santa Barbara, in May 2014 by a mentally deranged young student whose actions were guided by a misogynistic, delusional fantasy (note that this chapter was written before that tragedy occurred). Though the murderer does not seem to be influenced in any way by "Midnight Rambler," the subject matter of the song is quite close to the actual events. I do not think that in today's politically charged climate a song re-creating the Isla Vista murders, told from the point of view of the murderer, would be possible—in fact the co-owner of a website had to resign over comments he made praising the writing style of the murderer's manifesto. For more on this tragic event, see the *Los Angeles Times*, "Full Coverage: Isla Vista Murders Near UCSB," May 24, 2014, http://www.latimes.com/local/lanow/la-isla-vista-shooting-near-ucsb-stories-storygallery.html.

20. I > bVII > IV.

21. See "Monkey Man"; Hellmann bases this on Paul Oliver's writings on the blues.

22. In the key of C-sharp: B, A#, A, G#, or scale degrees b7, 6, b6, 5.

23. C# minor is the relative minor of E major.

24. Wilkins's version sounds in F—either he has capoed or tuned up to the key; Richards tunes his guitar to open E.

25. The extra chord is the G minor or relative minor chord (vi) of B-flat; in the live version in G major it is an E-minor chord.

26. Richards adds the F or the b7 to the G chord, thus making the tonic chord the dominant seventh (V7) of the IV chord or C, the next chord of the song. This is standard for many blues songs. The melody at "all your love's in vain" left out by the Stones is the typical blues descent, from b7–6–b6–5, or F–E–Eb–D.

27. See Edward Komara, *The Road to Robert Johnson*, 63.

28. According to Komara, Johnson often tuned his guitar down a half-step or step and played with it capoed up. For this song, he probably tuned down a half-step to open G-flat and then applied the capo to the second fret; thus the open strings would sound an A-flat chord, the tonic.

29. This can be seen on YouTube, "Rolling Stones—Love in Vain (*Stripped*, 1995)," https://www.youtube.com/watch?v=kAGnxH1dygU.

30. On disc 1 of the bootleg *Through the Vaults Darkly* (vol. 1, Godfather Records, 2007), there is a version of "You Got the Silver" with Jagger on lead vocals, recorded on February 16, 1969. It is not clear how they recovered the vocal that was allegedly wiped by the engineer.

31. This is not to mention all the songs with "Honky Tonk" in the title, from Kitty Wells to Bill Doggett among others.

32. The localized part of the progression is G > A > D, or I > V/V > V.

33. In the major-pentatonic scale of country music, the distinguishing note is the third one, which is major, which is then often combined with the flatted third of the blues. Richards does that here.

34. Richards, *Life*, 244–55, probably the most important pages on music in Richards's autobiography.

35. For the IMAX movie *Rolling Stones Live at the Max* (1991), based on concert footage from the 1990 Urban Jungle tour (i.e., the European leg of the Steel Wheels tour), there is a live cowbell version, but it does not have the same mysterious effect as the botched studio one. Watts enters with a drum-roll, and Richards seems to offer a bombastic caricature of his originally snaking entrance. This concert's version of "Honky Tonk Women" is available on YouTube, "The Rolling Stones—Honky Tonk Women," https://www.youtube.com/watch?v=CqVdRS3FCf8&index=6&list=PLKhlicDSGvk1msNKO-FCt7sEu3WoS7FOT.

5. 1970S OVERTURE

1. Other early examples of this concept phenomenon worth mentioning, and perhaps not as well known, are the Mothers of Invention's (Frank Zappa's band) first album, *Freak Out!* (1966), and an album by People!, *I Love You* (1968; see especially its B-side, "The Epic," a mini–rock opera recorded before the Who's *Tommy*).

2. In April 2015, the band appeared to be toying with the idea of playing *Sticky Fingers* in its entirety for its upcoming summer tour Zip Code. They did in fact do this at the warmup show on May 20 at the Fonda Theatre in Hollywood, though not in the order of the album. As of this writing (June), the Stones have reverted to a "greatest hits" set list for the tour.

3. Richards, *Life*, 288.

4. "We Love You" has Lennon and McCartney singing backup vocals and was meant as an answer to "All You Need Is Love," which has a prominent E-minor chord at the end of its line.

5. For example, because of shared notes, the vi chord often substitutes for the IV chord; thus in the key of C major, the A minor chord (A, C, E) substitutes for the F major one (F, A, C).

6. "Lady Jane" is in the key of D Mixolydian with a bridge section ("Just heard . . .") that focuses on A minor, while "Back Street Girl" also employs A minor but in the context of G.

7. Both songs are in the key of D minor; note that Dylan appropriated the Appalachian singer Jean Ritchie's recording of "Nottamun Town" in his "Masters of War."

8. Not well known is that King's "The Thrill Is Gone" is a cover of Roy Hawkins's song from 1951.

9. It can be heard on YouTube at "The Rolling Stones—Hillside Blues," https://www.youtube.com/watch?v=FgrdN-camN4.

10. The outtake from May 1968 is widely circulated; its prominent acoustic guitar played by Richards can be heard on YouTube, "The Rolling Stones—Blood Red Wine," https://www.youtube.com/watch?v=sXivhZmNKzM.

11. Skip James is the most prominent expert and master of the minor blues in the early blues recordings, particularly because he tuned his guitar to open D minor (the so-called Bentonian tuning/school of blues; Bentonia is a city in Yazoo County, Mississippi, eastwardly adjacent to the Delta region). His iconic and haunting "Hard Time Killing Floor Blues" and "Devil Got My Woman Blues" are both in D minor. Another powerful use of the minor in rural blues is Geeshie Wiley's "Last Kind Words Blues," on Paramount Records; the guitarist Elvie Thomas plays a prominent and devastatingly effective A-minor chord as the first verse starts (key of E, though sounding like the key of E-flat because the guitar is tuned down a half-step; hints of Em and Bm throughout the song).

12. Elliott, *Complete Recording Sessions*, 104. I am not sure what he means by "riff," and if this includes the chord progression and melody.

13. C# minor > B minor > D > A, or iii > ii > IV > I; the outro is in B minor. The version on the *Performance* soundtrack has Cooder's slide work. A song that similarly goes to C-sharp minor in the chorus is "My Obsession."

14. See, for example, Poe's "The Facts in the Case of M. Valdemar," where a dying man begs to be hypnotized with startling and shocking results. The story is available online at http://poestories.com/read/facts.

15. The note is G, which makes the chord an A-minor seventh chord.

16. That is, the interval of the minor third.

17. The chords are Am, G, F, E7, or i–(b)VII–(b)VI–V7. A good example of a popular song with this progression is the Turtles' "Happy Together," another minor-key song where it is used in the verse. Zeppelin's version of "Babe I'm Gonna Leave You" (recorded in late 1968, released in January 1969) also uses a variant of the progression. (See note 20 for more on "Babe I'm Gonna Leave You.")

18. The notes E–F are part of a modal subset of E Phrygian. After writing this chapter, I found another name for this full sequence, the "diatonic Phrygian tetrachord," in David Garland, "The World's Most-Used Musical Sequence!" WYNC, July 6, 2014, http://www.wnyc.org/story/worlds-most-used-musical-sequence. Garland also provides a handy list of fifty songs that use the sequence or tetrachord.

19. It is common to insert a passing chord in between the second and third chords, as in: Am, G, F#/D, F, E(7), or i, VII, IV6, VI, V. This is what Zeppelin's song does; a contemporaneous folk-rock pop source for this expanded progression is the Lovin' Spoonful's "Summer in the City."

20. It worth digressing on "Babe I'm Gonna Leave You," for its complicated reception history does contain another neat tie-in with the Stones. Joan Baez discovered the song sung by a young woman at a hootenanny, and when she released the song she intentionally neglected to cite her source's songwriter as Anne Bredon. Because of this, Jimmy Page maintains that he was arranging a traditional folk song when he took it from Baez; much later on the band did share credit for the song with Bredon. But Page's innocence is also somewhat difficult to believe, given the similarity of the Zeppelin version to the Association's arrangement of the song in 1965, where the latter group does credit Bredon. But perhaps Zeppelin did not want to call attention to the Association's version, which again is remarkably close to theirs, especially the A minor descending passage (on the second verse even going down to E), the melodic phrasing, and the text setting. You can listen to their version on YouTube, "The Association—Babe I'm Gonna Leave You ((Stereo)) 1965," https://www.youtube.com/watch?v=3-vOFPP0WDI&feature=kp. Finally, another tantalizing connection of this song to the Stones is Marianne Faithfull's report that she had sung Baez's version of "Babe I'm Gonna Leave You" early in her career, which uses different chords though with a minor, flamenco-styled accompaniment (probably played with a capo), complete with the modal (Phrygian) flourish. According to some web sources, she might have recorded the song (probably in Baez's style) with Jimmy Page as the session guitarist; I have been unable to locate any such recording. For this last point, see Led Zeppelin: "Babe I'm Gonna Leave You," Songfacts, http://www.songfacts.com/detail.php?id=299.

21. Both songs are in the key of G, as played by the Stones. Burke's version of "If You Need Me" is in the key of A, while Wilson Pickett's original is in C. Otis Redding's similar "I've Been Loving You Too Long" was covered by the Stones for their "live" album, *Got Live If You Want It!* but the chord progression is very different in the Redding song.

22. Of course there are glaring exceptions to this statement, especially the proliferation of metal genres in the 1980s and beyond and grunge in the early 1990s.

23. Richards, *Life,* 178. On YouTube there is a clip of Jagger playing a rudimentary version of "Brown Sugar" backstage at Madison Square Garden for Ike and Tina Turner. Comparing this to the debut of the song on December 6 at Altamont might give a sense of Richards's contribution to the riff. See

"Mick Jagger—Brown Sugar '69 MSG," https://www.youtube.com/watch?v=80H9kFUdZog.

24. Richards, *Life*, 271.

25. Again, using the familiar Mixolydian progression of I–bVII–IV, but this time twice: D > C > G for the verse, then transposed to G for the chorus, with the chords G > F > C. Note that the F chord of the chorus prefigures and helps to prepare for the shift to the parallel minor in the jam.

26. Elliott, *Complete Recording Sessions*, 130.

27. For the religious dimension of the provocative closing to the film, I am thinking particularly of the parable in John 15:4, "Jesus and the True Vine," where Jesus says, "Abide in me as I abide in you."

28. Whereas the blues shuffle style relies on the sixth and (flat) seventh scale degrees for its extension, in folk music it is the fourth degree, which is what Jagger uses here in the top voice. Note that later in the opening, he adds ninth extensions to the chords.

29. Babiuk and Provost, *Rolling Stones Gear*, 334–35, has a picture of Richards playing live in Amsterdam in 1970 on his twelve-string Martin.

30. Richards mentions that the studio in Muscle Shoals also had a guitar in Nashville tuning, so there is a possibility that Taylor recorded on the studio's guitar. See Babiuk and Provost, *Rolling Stones Gear*, 345.

31. He plays with the b7 over both the F and C chords; the notes are E-flat and B-flat respectively.

32. In his commentary to the song in *Rocks Off* (212), Bill Janovitz hears a Japanese koto in these bars, sonically the result of the plucked piano part of Jim Price.

33. Wenner, "Mick Jagger Remembers," *Rolling Stone*, 1995 interview with Jann Wenner, http://www.rollingstone.com/music/news/mick-jagger-remembers-19951214.

34. Richards, *Life*, 274. There were two studios in the area, one in Muscle Shoals called FAME studios, founded and owned by Rick Hall. Some of his session musicians split off and formed another nearby studio in Sheffield, which is where the Stones ended up. The story of these recording locales is the subject of a recent documentary, *Muscle Shoals* (Magnolia Pictures, 2013), with prominent footage of the Stones. Percy Sledge passed on April 14, 2015, as I was finishing editing of this chapter, yet another stark reminder that the era's primary musicians are dying off.

35. According to Guralnick, *Sweet Soul Music*.

36. Booth, *The True Adventures of the Rolling Stones*, 323ff.

37. Richards, *Life*, 279.

6. ELEGANTLY WASTED

1. Loewenstein (1933–2014) was the Rolling Stones' business advisor and manager from 1968 to 2007. See the *New York Times* obituary for him by Douglas Martin, May 22, 2014, http://www.nytimes.com/2014/05/23/arts/music/prince-rupert-zu-loewenstein-rolling-stones-money-manager-dies-at-80.html.

2. Rod Stewart and David Bowie also became prominent rock star tax exiles from the United Kingdom in the 1970s.

3. Faithfull, *Autobiography*, 118.

4. Janovitz, *Rocks Off*, 224.

5. For a balanced review of the film and the era that notes the conflicting evidence, see Sean O'Hagan, "The Stones and the True Story of *Exile on Main St*," *Guardian*, April 25, 2010, http://www.theguardian.com/music/2010/apr/25/stones-exile-on-main-street.

6. Refer to the revealing interview of Tarlé in the article by Charlotte Simmonds, "The Rolling Stones: The Myth and Its Makers," *New Statesman*, December 22, 2012, http://www.newstatesman.com/culture/culture/2012/12/rolling-stones-myth-and-its-makers.

7. Janovitz, *Rolling Stones' Exile on Main Street (33 1/3)*, Kindle location 262.

8. Ibid., Kindle locations 319–20.

9. Though this was surely true in the 1960s, 1970s, and the early 1980s, with the demise of the LP and rise of the CD, album packaging assumes less importance. In our age of downloading and now especially streaming, the artwork has never been less significant in the pop music world. For more on the theory of the album cover, see Ian Inglis, "'Nothing You Can See That Can Be Shown': The Album Covers of the Beatles," *Popular Music*, 84.

10. Kerouac, "Introduction," *The Americans*, http://www.camramirez.com/pdf/P1_Americans_Intro.pdf.

11. Janovitz, *Exile on Main Street*, Kindle locations 826–27.

12. Available on YouTube, https://www.youtube.com/watch?v=JsEEyeFau6Y; also see another video where Richards demonstrates "32-20 Blues," at "Keith Richards Blues Acoustic," https://www.youtube.com/watch?v=U5ANjb-yAVE.

13. "Introduction," in Marshall's *The Rolling Stones 1972*, 9.

14. The Warhol interview with Truman Capote is titled "Sunday with Mister C." *Rolling Stone*, April 12, 1973, 29.

15. Ibid.

16. Ibid., 39.

17. Ibid., 37.

18. The official download, *1973: The Brussels Affair*, is available online at the Rolling Stones Archive, http://www.stonesarchive.com/bootleg_years/1973.

19. Time Is on Our Side, "Creation: Mick Jagger, 2003," http://www.timeisonourside.com/lpExile.html.

20. Ben Ratliff, "Revisiting 'Main St.,' Rethinking the Myth," May 19, 2010, http://www.nytimes.com/2010/05/23/arts/music/23stones.html?pagewanted=all.

21. Ibid.

22. See the Harvey Kubernik interview with the sound engineer Andy Johns (the younger brother of Glyn), "Engineer Andy Johns Discusses the Making of the Rolling Stones' 'Exile on Main Street'," *Goldmine*, May 8, 2010, http://www.goldminemag.com/article/engineer-andy-johns-discusses-the-making-of-the-rolling-stones-exile-on-main-street.

23. The Stones performed this latter song with Hooker at three concerts in December 1989, in a very similar manner to "Shake Your Hips." Available on YouTube, "John Lee Hooker with Eric Clapton & The Rolling Stones—Boogie Chillen," https://www.youtube.com/watch?v=ByxJr3Z3aMI.

24. Available on YouTube, "THE ROLLING STONES/Shake Your Hips," https://www.youtube.com/watch?v=mVuKzEDnUUQ.

25. It can be heard on YouTube, from September 1970 at "The Rolling Stones—Get a Line on You," https://www.youtube.com/watch?v=6wTH1SmyIO8.

26. The song is in the key of C, and the minor chord used is the relative minor or A minor, which is a substitute chord for the C. The progression during the solo is Am > F > G.

27. Ratliff, "Revisiting."

28. Ibid.

29. See the It's Only Rock and Roll fan forum discussion of the splices at "Re: Loving Cup Alt Version," https://www.iorr.org/talk/read.php?1,1244300,1246685.

30. Richards, *Life*, 310.

31. Janovitz notes that the credited "Amyl" or Richard "Didymus" Washington was from New Orleans and brought to Los Angeles by Dr. John. *Exile on Main Street (33 1/3)*, Kindle locations 1206–7.

32. Em–Am(7)–D–G (vi–iv(7)–V–I).

33. Babiuk and Provost, *Rolling Stones Gear*, 367.

34. F, B-flat, and C (I–IV–V), with dominant-seventh alterations in the bass part of the F (E-flat) and C chords (B-flat), and a passing note (A) added for the B-flat. With the E-flat, the song is in F Mixolydian.

35. Thus: F–(F7)–Bb–G minor (instead of C)–Bb.

36. In "Us and Them," first recorded as the song "The Violent Sequence," Gilmour's intro fleshes out the chord progression as conceived by keyboardist Richard Wright.

37. Note that "Sweet Melissa" was recorded at approximately the same time and was also released in 1972. Janovitz, *Exile on Main Street (33 1/3)*, Kindle locations 1107–8.

38. The chords are A–G–D, or I–bVII–IV.

39. Richards, *Life*, 302.

40. The upper note (scale step 5) makes three vibrations for every two of the bottom note (1), expressed as the ratio of 3:2.

41. It goes down by a half step, making the interval a minor sixth.

42. The bridge has the progression F# major > C# minor, this latter chord the relative minor of E major.

43. The form of these songs is AABA, where the B section is a bridge and each section represents eight bars of music. Often bridges are called the "middle eight" from this practice; in later pop music the bridges are not always eight measures.

44. Janovitz has suggested the Leslie speaker as one possibility here for the guitar sound; *Exile on Main Street (33 1/3)*, Kindle locations 758–59.

45. Richards, *Life*, 309.

46. Available on YouTube at "Rolling Stones—Ventilator Blues—Vancouver—June 3, 1972," https://www.youtube.com/watch?v=vrsBu3RZebQ.

47. Time Is on Our Side, quoted from "Ventilator Blues: Charlie Watts, 2003," http://www.timeisonourside.com/SOVentilator.html.

48. *I Gave You Diamonds, You Gave Me Disease (Exile Outtakes)* [2008]; it can also be heard on YouTube, "The Rolling Stones—Ventilator Blues (Demo Outtake)," https://www.youtube.com/watch?v=HhaL79IQgaM.

49. With the lowering of the riff, one of the notes played is the blue note of B-flat.

7. TWILIGHT OF THE IDOLS

1. Egan, *Mammoth Book of the Rolling Stones*, 381.

2. Ben Sisario, "Sales of Streaming Music Top CDs in Flat Year for Industry," *New York Times*, March 18, 2015, http://www.nytimes.com/2015/03/19/business/media/sales-of-streaming-music-top-cds-in-flat-year-for-industry.html.

3. For more on the fascinating topic of the dance of death, see my article, Malvinni, "*Totentanz*: Notes on Adès, Lesh, and the Grateful Dead."

4. According to the interview with Jas Obrecht (see http://jasobrecht.com/?s=mick+taylor), Taylor says it is "mainly" him playing on "Angie." I take this to mean that Taylor plays the iconic introduction, which is the guitar in the right channel of the mix, versus the left channel guitar (Richards) that is less pronounced. On the official video, however, where the band sits on a stage and the guitarists adorn their instruments with roses, Richards is depicted playing the introduction—while in fact he is only playing along to a recording.

5. What makes the song appear to be in A minor is the presence of the E dominant-seventh chord as the second chord in the progressions, or i–V7. But the song ends in C, also where the verse finishes. The line beginning on the G chord also cadences to G, V/C, and so when it goes back to the A minor at the start of the verse, the A minor functions as a substitute for C major.

6. E > G (bIII) > C (bVI) > E.

7. Richards uses the E-minor pentatonic blues scale, a heavily trafficked scale in this era of blues hard rock.

8. These are played as major-seventh chords in the solos; note that the F-major seventh chord contains all of the notes of the A-minor chord.

9. Wood, *Ronnie: The Autobiography*, 112.

10. Richards also notes that Wood is from a family of water Gypsies, *Life*, 372.

11. For more on the billboard and the controversy, as well as the actual image, see Carolyn Bronstein, "Battling Pornography," Rorotoko, http://rorotoko.com/interview/20110926_carolyn_bronstein_on_battling_pornography_feminist_anti-pornograph/?page=3.

12. It's Only Rock and Roll, "Wayne Perkins on Bob Marley, 'Hand of Fate' and Auditioning for the Stones," https://www.iorr.org/talk/read.php?1,1144740,1145497.

13. Richards, *Life*, 397.

14. Ibid., 398.

15. Egan, *Mammoth Book of the Rolling Stones*, 340.

16. Richards, *Life*, 400, and Babiuk and Provost, *Rolling Stones Gear*, 466.

17. For more on the recording room and console, see Janovitz, *Rocks Off*, 294–95.

18. Elliott, *Complete Recording Sessions*, 191.

19. Ibid., 161.

20. Richards, *Life*, 399.

21. Ibid., 400.

22. It's Only Rock and Roll, "Which of the *Some Girls* Vocal Tracks Have New Vocals by Mick? [Mathijs]," https://www.iorr.org/talk/read.php?1,1518437,1518557. Note that "Petrol Gang" (as it was called on bootlegs)

features Ian Stewart on piano, and at one point Jagger castigates him for falling behind the beat; this version is cut on the Don Was remastered version.

23. It's Only Rock and Roll, "The Stones' *Some Girls* Super Deluxe Box Set Is a Disappointment—A Comment to Mr. Jagger [Turd on the Run]," November 21, 2011, https://www.iorr.org/talk/read.php?1,1515926,1516012.

24. Good examples from this time are Rod Stewart's "Do Ya Think I'm Sexy," Village People's "Y.M.C.A.," and "Dance, Dance, Dance" by Chic. In soul/ R & B, "Love Rollercoaster" (1975) by the Ohio Players had a very strong octave bass line. But funk bassist Larry Graham often used this figure, as for example his song "Hair" on *Graham Central Station* (1974).

25. McLagan (1945–2014) died while I was writing this chapter, within days of the death of an even more important sideman for the Stones, Bobby Keys (1943–2014).

26. I find the online interpretation to be quite convincing: WordReference, "Thread: A Girl with Faraway [*sic*] Eyes [Captain Kirk]," August 6, 2011, http://forum.wordreference.com/threads/a-girl-with-faraway-eyes.2205498.

27. Richards, *Life*, 402–3. Richards does sing the verses for "Coming Down Again" (*Goats Head Soup*).

28. On YouTube, "Before They Make Me Run—The Rolling Stones," https://www.youtube.com/watch?v=jFJbhtmKHHM&list=RDjFJbhtmKHHM&spfreload=10#t=4.

29. On YouTube, "The Rolling Stones—Beast of Burden (from *Some Girls, Live in Texas '78*)," https://www.youtube.com/watch?v=bj8lRssjN48.

30. The doo-wop progression is I–vi–IV–V, while this variant in "Beast of Burden" goes I–V–vi–IV.

31. The effect is similar to the entrainment of rhythm, where the pulse or the beat becomes synchronized with the listener's brainwaves.

32. Wood wrote the music and chorus, while Jagger added the lyrics. The song is credited to Jagger, Richards, and Wood, with saxophone by Mel Collins and harmonica by Sugar Blue. In keeping with the style of *Some Girls,* the song is mostly a rewrite of "Hey Negrita" with the funky exchange of two chords (C minor and F), with some interesting changes for the saxophone solo (ca. 2:04 and following). Note that "Everything Is Turning to Gold" has never been performed live by the Stones.

33. Unlike Dijon's work, the congas seem, at best, barely audible in the mix; I can hardly pick them out starting at around 1:34 during the guitar break. The hand claps in this same section are credited to "1 Moroccan, 1 Jew, 1 Wasp," (the latter two are Jane Rose and Ronnie Wood). See Elliott, *Complete Recordings,* 195.

34. This is, in my opinion, perhaps a little harsh; I know that others do not necessarily agree with this viewpoint—Rob Weiner for one, who has an amaz-

ing ear and knowledge of this material, finds *Emotional Rescue, Tattoo You, Voodoo Lounge*, and *A Bigger Bang* to be very good albums.

35. "The Rolling Stones—Never Stop (Start Me Up Demo)" can be heard on YouTube, https://www.youtube.com/watch?v=GBJ7s0QILJc&spfreload=10.

36. Janovitz, *Rocks Off*, 328.

37. The tenement building at 96–98 St. Mark's Place in the opening shots is the same one that serves as the iconic cover for Zeppelin's *Physical Graffiti* album.

38. The note D is added to the C chord, which makes it a C9 chord; held over for the next chord, F, the D turns the F into an F6 chord.

39. The doo-wop progression goes C–Am–F–G. Here, the chord preceding the verse is C, so if we count this chord, we end up with the progression. In other words, the four-bar verse of Am–F–G–C can be read as a variation on the progression.

40. For the genesis of the song in relation to the outtakes, see Elliott, *Complete Recordings*, 242.

41. Richards, *Life*, 454.

42. The Senegalese drummers are Moustapha Cisse and Brahms Coundoul.

43. The crediting of the bass part of this song is a confusing one. It is not clear to me if Wyman is on the released track; the riff does not sound like his style of playing. Also, one of the outtakes for "Undercover" has Wyman's swinging style on it without the main bass riff (the best version is on the bootleg, *Through the Vaults Darkly*, also available at the YouTube link cited below). Perhaps Wyman learned his way into the reggae/dub style the way he did with disco on "Miss You." On the Rolling Stones official YouTube channel, Wyman is credited with playing on the "B" version, and he can be seen playing in this alternative video at "The Rolling Stones—Undercover of the Night (B Version)," https://www.youtube.com/watch?v=pP1UbJ2iKLw&spfreload=10. Elliott, *Complete Recordings*, mentions that Kimsey worked with "Sly and Robbie" on effects and that Wyman's "bass sound was a vital part of the track" (242).

44. "Bill Wyman Talking to Paul Sexton," *The Rolling Stones: The Singles (1971–2006)* (box set with hardback book).

45. Sean Egan is particularly harsh in his review of the album, while Janovitz feels it is better than *Undercover*. I would go along with Egan on this one.

46. Richards, *Life*, 463.

47. *Rocks Off*, 340; Janovitz goes on say that at the time Lillywhite was making hits with Talking Heads, Simple Minds, U2 (and so on).

48. See Elliott, *Complete Recordings*, 262. For more on Clifford, who does not seem to be liked by hard-core Stones fans, see the thread at Its Only Rock

and Roll, "Matt Clifford, Why Only Two Tours with the Stones?," https://www.iorr.org/talk/read.php?1,1508621,1508666. He played second keyboards and French horn with the band on the Steel Wheels tour in 1989–1990 and apparently recently joined them on French horn again on the American tour in 2013 for "You Can't Always Get What You Want." He has also received credits on the last two Stones studio albums, *Bridges to Babylon* (1997) and *A Bigger Bang* (2005).

49. The album is called *Brian Jones Presents the Pipes of Pan at Joujouka*. Confusing matters is that there is apparently a musical schism in the town of Jajouka. The group led by Attar is called "The Master Musicians of Jajouka," while Mohammed Hamri leads another group claiming to be the "real" group, also under the name "The Master Musicians of Joujouka" (with the alternate place-name spelling). Note that Jones's album adopted the second spelling for its title, but the spelling is inconsistent in the early sources. Paul Trynka relates how Hamri was an emissary for the village and had first brought Brion Gysin to the village, perhaps the first Westerner there (*Brian Jones*, 284).

50. "The Stones in Morocco Part 1," YouTube, https://www.youtube.com/watch?v=20x1OZVofNI.

51. Trynka, *Brian Jones*, 303, mentions remarks by actress Cleo Sylvestre about Jones after he returned from Morocco: "He wanted to bring over some of the musicians he'd met. Really it was a vision of what we now call world music."

52. Olympic engineer George Chkiantz did the recording, accompanying Brian and his girlfriend Suki Potier to the village. It is not entirely clear to me what kind of effect is added to the recording, and if so who did it, whether Brian or the engineer in the studio.

53. "Rolling Stones—Love Is Strong Keith Richards on Vocals," YouTube, https://www.youtube.com/watch?v=XUpkJKhLyuI.

54. Sheffield, "Plundered My Soul," *Rolling Stone*, April 17, 2010, http://www.rollingstone.com/music/songreviews/plundered-my-soul-20100417#ixzz3LoYKvVys.

55. The only other chord in the song is a D chord, which the B minor substitutes for.

56. As a Grateful Dead scholar, I cannot resist mentioning that the Dead's so-called Beautiful Jam, part of the "Dark Star" from February 18, 1971, also contains a jam with the same melancholy quality, also on the two chords B minor and A major. I mention this as a coincidence of zeitgeist, not to infer any historical influence, though it is interesting that this progression was circulating at the time.

57. *Guardian*, "Keith Richards Wants to Make a New Rolling Stones Album," April 10, 2015, http://www.theguardian.com/music/2015/apr/10/keith-richards-wants-to-make-a-new-rolling-stones-album.

FURTHER READING

It has become impossible to separate the Rolling Stones from their mythology. Their outsider, rebellious, diabolical image was expertly crafted from the beginning. With both Richards's autobiography, *Life* (2010), and the sanctioned documentary film of band interviews, *Crossfire Hurricane* (2012), Jagger and Richards have solidified their legacy as one of the greatest songwriting teams in popular music history. Other recent efforts, such as deluxe box sets and remastered editions of *Exile on Main Street*, *Some Girls*, and now *Sticky Fingers*, have also placed the band in the spotlight once again, as have their wildly successful ongoing tours. As of this writing (June 2015), the Stones are in the midst of yet another summer tour of the United States called the Zip Code tour.

Yet the Jagger/Richards team was able to flourish because of the creative input of those surrounding them: fellow band members, sidemen and session players, and industry/sound professionals. Furthermore, the founder of the band, Brian Jones, has unfairly seen his reputation and importance for the band's hard-line R & B and blues music aesthetic become tarnished; his mistreatment goes back to the early days of Oldham's managerial manipulation of the band's image. He suffered personal indignities at the hands of Jagger and Richards, though this latter was more of a friend to him up to his seduction and subsequent relationship with Jones's then girlfriend, Anita Pallenberg.

In the run-up and after the Stones' fiftieth anniversary in 2012 there has been a flurry of writing on the band. Many of these books and articles provide a good counterpoint to the primary sources and a fleshing out of the biographical episodes that form along their timeline. Note that the one glaring lacuna in the Stones' literature is a Jagger autobiography, which at this point seems highly unlikely. Despite this, the singer has given interviews throughout the years that shed light on his own views of the band.

Babiuk, Andy, and Greg Provost. *Rolling Stones Gear: All the Stones' Instruments from Stage to Studio*. Milwaukee: Backbeat Books, 2013. The definitive book on the instruments and equipment of the Stones, at over 600 pages it features a gorgeous layout with high-quality photographs. The authors had previously done a book on the Beatles' gear. This book surpasses this first effort and grants intimate access to the band's equipment, no small achievement given the band's fifty-year legacy. But *Rolling Stones Gear* is more than a beautifully illustrated coffee-table book, offering a meticulously researched historical context for how the instruments fit into the band's biography. By seeing reproductions of the instruments and equipment, the authors provide an in-depth understanding of the behind-the-scenes circumstances for the technical aspects of how the Stones created. The book took years to compile, and the acknowledgments at the end are equally impressive and grant this volume official status.

Booth, Stanley. *The True Adventures of the Rolling Stones*. Chicago: A Cappella Books, 2000 [1984]. It is ironic that perhaps the best book on the Stones from a literary perspective also happens to be an intimate, "true" portrait of the band from an insider's point of view. As a burgeoning rock journalist working from Memphis, Booth first met the band in 1968 in England and then toured with them in 1969 with the intent of writing a book, which he could not finish for various reasons (explained in the afterword) until nearly fifteen years later. Written in a style influenced by literary giants like Norman Mailer and William S. Burroughs (the latter advised and encouraged the author early on), Booth's book captures the Stones at the most significant juncture of their career, after the passing of Brian Jones and the comeback 1969 U.S. tour that culminates in the Altamont Speedway disaster (December 6). Indeed, the book climaxes at this last concert where Booth's prose is at its best, in first-person reportage of the highest quality. He also describes the Muscle Shoals recording sessions, though humbly he does not take credit for getting the band there in the first place (Jim Dickinson, the piano player on "Wild Horses," gives him credit for this amazing Southern excursion in Richards's *Life*, 274). But the book also goes beyond relating the history of the Stones to give an exquisite portrait of music at the end of the '60s and the counterculture, an epoch-ending moment for a generation that believed that "music had the power to change people's lives," a myth that has given way to the corporate sellout of music today.

Egan, Sean, ed. *The Mammoth Book of the Rolling Stones*. London: Constable & Robinson, 2013. Bringing together writings throughout the band's career compiled by Egan, the "editor" also wrote most of the *Mammoth Book*. The book follows the chronological path of the band's musical output and is mostly organized around the band's discography. But following the historical arc of essays also gives a sense of how the band's reception history developed, from Norman Jopling's prophetic 1963 article to Barry Miles's 1968 interview with Jagger to the real centerpiece of the book, Robert Greenfield's rambling 1971 interview with Richards for *Rolling Stone*, on the cusp of their exiled days at Nellcôte and the South of France.

Elliott, Martin. *The Rolling Stones Complete Recording Sessions 1962—2012 50th Anniversary Edition*. London: Cherry Red Books, 2012. Elliott's book chronologically orders the band's studio and live recordings—numbering over 1,500, some of them only available as bootlegs or not at all—and also provides credits and liner notes for the songs and the respective era. Indeed it can be read like a history of the band. But the book's central importance is to provide a clear timeline of what was recorded when—something that can be quite daunting when dealing with such a prolific band like the Stones who did not release their material in chronological order. Finally, Elliott's book is indispensible for anyone wanting to do serious research on the band, establishing a time and place for each song.

Faithfull, Marianne, with David Dalton. *Faithfull: An Autobiography*. Boston: Little, Brown and Company, 1994. Along with Anita Pallenberg's pairings with Jones and Richards, Faithfull's relationship with Jagger played a major role in the public perception of the Stones and of Swinging London during the '60s. Her time with the band—like Pallenberg, a creative muse—has also become the stuff of legends, and her telling of the story is both articulate and revealing. Of course the most interesting parts of her book describe her time with Jagger, but she also relates what it was like to experience the Stones in concert during their formative days. For example, before she started her relationship with Jagger, she poetically observes the powerful mix of emotions unleashed at a Stones' concert: "Cases of clinical Dionysian mass hysteria were breaking out everywhere. . . . [Mick] knew exactly how to locate the North Africa of the teenage cranium . . . Mick was their Dionysus" (70). She gives a revealing account of the acid trip on that fateful day, February 11, 1967, and how the trip bonded Keith and Mick, who "saw during that trip and many subsequent ones . . . Jumping Jack Flash, the Midnight Rambler, Brown Sugar . . . the new personae that would populate their albums for the next five years" (101). Finally, she describes the lyrical impact of the literary education she gave Jagger during these years, his conversations with Allen Ginsberg and others, but is at her most revealing when writing about the film *Performance*, and especially how Mick appropriated the personas of Brian and Keith to become Turner, a "fusion of life and drama" that had "deadly after effects" (154).

Janovitz, Bill. *Rocks Off: 50 Tracks That Tell the Story of the Rolling Stones*. New York: St. Martin's Press, 2013. Janovitz tells the tale of the Stones through the songs and gives an even-handed account from the point of view of a knowledgeable, passionate fan that remains in awe of his subject matter. The narrative arc uses the standard path of Egan, Appleford, and countless others—namely, the rise and then subsequent fall of the band post-*Exile*, with one last great effort to create a great work in *Some Girls*. As a musician himself, Janovitz shows depth and insight in dealing with the musical material, something he had done a few years earlier in his monograph on *Exile*. The retrospective book is written in an appealing, accessible manner that by design will meet with fan approval.

Richards, Keith. *Life*. With James Fox. New York: Little, Brown and Company, 2010. Coming from the musical mind behind the Stones' originals, Richards does not disappoint in his discussion of the genesis of the band's songs, and especially the band's earliest blues influences. Again, he is at his finest describing how he used open tunings (especially G, with the sixth string removed) to revitalize the music of the Stones mid-career, after the band seemed moribund. He comes off bluntly on most of the points of the band's biography, seemingly without romanticizing, though he can be selective in how he chooses to recollect something. Richards can also be cavalier at times, especially in his upfront treatment of his drug addiction that in the end did much harm to the band's songwriting. Yet he is especially harsh on the death of Jones—he "was at that point in his life when there wasn't any" (272). Not surprisingly, Richards is not always kind in his assessment of Jagger and the rift that has festered between the two. But the written style oozes rock and roll sentiment and swagger by one of its seminal practitioners. Though there are points where his memory seems open to question, the book is riveting on the music and gives a precious glimpse at how it all came together.

Trynka, Paul. *Brian Jones: The Making of the Rolling Stones*. New York: Viking, 2014. A revisionary biography of Jones, Trynka interviewed numerous people who knew Brian, some famous and many of whom are essential to the Rolling Stones' story. The key events of Jones's life assume a multidimensional perspective, from the orchestrated drug busts that ruined Brian, the disastrous end of his affair with Pallenberg, and the time in Morocco, all within the shadow of the band's betrayal of him. Trynka's main aim is to show how and why Jones has been effectively airbrushed out of the Stones' story, with the corollary that his musical contributions have become less visible through the years. No mere apologist, however, Trynka recognizes that there was an unhappy, dark side to Brian, but that by seeking out the secrets of the "Devil's music," that is, the path of Robert Johnson, Jones "opened the doors to that new world" (3). Trynka argues that while Jones sought out vindication for his passionate ideas about R & B and blues music, when it came with the band's success in 1964, he had already been cruelly and unfairly shoved aside by Oldham and Jagger. The idea that Brian could not write—something substantiated by Richards, among others—is probably unfair. He was never given the space to write, while he did contribute to the band's music. The Stones' group compositional efforts, under the pseudonym Nanker Phelge (combining the group's bantering or "nankering" with the last name of their roommate and close associate from their formative Edith Grove days, James Phelge) gave way to the Jagger/Richards team, which really was the brainchild and obsession of Oldham. One interesting idea floated in the book is that Keith gives too much credit to Ry Cooder for showing him open-G tuning, when in fact Jones had played in open G and that Keith knew about it in the early 1960s. Trynka interprets this as a major ingredient in the downgrading of Jones's significance, that Keith credits an outsider and not Jones for the distinctive guitar technique that made his career moving forward (62). Furthermore, Trynka does much to show that while Jones was exhausted near the end of his life, he was also planning to embark on new projects, coming full circle to work again with Alexis Korner, who got the whole British blues scene started in the first place. Jones was also very excited about the potential for Moroccan music—indeed, Jones was one of the first down the path to appreciating the potential commercial significance of what is called "world music" today. Finally, one of the keen psychological insights of the book shows how Brian did not pity himself and never showed any public resentment toward the band for his displacement.

Wyman, Bill. *Stone Alone: The Story of a Rock 'n' Roll Band*. With Ray Coleman. Boston: Da Capo Press, 1997 [reprint of New York: Viking, 1990]. Throughout the band's career, Wyman kept a private journal and also saved newspaper and journal clippings documenting the Stones' existence. As the band's archivist, as it were, it was inevitable that he would be the first to write an insider's account of the band. In addition to *Stone Alone*, he has also authored *Rolling with the Stones*, which also contains a lot of the scrapbook items he collected over the years. His *Blues Odyssey*, another coffee-table edition, is tellingly dedicated to "Brian, the only cat who got it, and Stu, who loved them." This book traces the origins of the blues through the beat revolution in England and beyond. In *Stone Alone*, we learn of the abject poverty that scarred the childhood upbringing of Bill Wyman (William Perks). He documents the first time that the full lineup of the Stones played together on January 14, 1963, at the Flamingo in Soho (115). He also maintains that their reputation as "bad boys" came much later, and that it was not solely engineered by Oldham, but only exploited by him—in fact, their manager's first gesture was to have them wear uniforms (136). Wyman is also a great defender of Jones, and he quotes Glyn Johns in maintaining that Jagger and Richards took over the band when they started writing together in 1964 (179). He muses that it was the physical weakness of Brian—his asthma and probably undiagnosed epilepsy (Wyman diagnoses this through contact with an illegitimate child of Brian's, "Carol" or her real name, Belinda, who suffers from the disease)—that also contributed to his losing control over the band. Finally, Wyman's book chronicles in great detail, sometimes dryly (he does not have the same entertaining style of Richards), the itinerary of the band during the 1960s, and ends with the Hyde Park concert, July 5, 1969, a comeback that was made tragic by the death of Jones three days earlier.

OTHER NOTABLE BOOKS

Appleford, Steve. *The Rolling Stones: The Stories behind the Biggest Songs*. London: Carlton Books, 2010 [1997].

Loewenstein, Dora, and Philip Dodd, eds. *According to the Rolling Stones: Mick Jagger, Keith Richards, Charlie Watts, Ronnie Wood*. San Francisco: Chronicle Books, 2003.
Macphail, Jessica Holman Whitehead. *Yesterday's Papers: The Rolling Stones in Print 1963–1984*. Ann Arbor, MI: Pierian Press, 1986.
Marshall, Jim. *The Rolling Stones 1972*. Edited by Michelle Dunn Marsh. San Francisco: Chronicle Books, 2012.
McMillian, John. *Beatles vs. Stones*. New York: Simon & Schuster, 2013.
Meltzer, Richard. *The Aesthetics of Rock*. Boston: Da Capo Press, 1987 [reprint of New York: Something Else Press, 1970].
Oldham, Andrew Loog. *Stoned: A Memoir of London in the 1960s*. New York: St. Martin's Press, 2000.
Sandford, Christopher. *The Rolling Stones: Fifty Years*. London: Simon & Schuster, 2012.
Wyman, Bill. *Bill Wyman's Blues Odyssey: A Journey to Music's Heart & Soul*. With Richard Havers. London: DK Publishing, 2001.
———. *Rolling with the Stones*. London: DK Publishing, 2002.

GLOSSARY OF MUSICAL TERMS

2/4 time signature: Two beats per measure; a simple meter where the quarter note is the pulse.

4/4 time signature: Four beats per measure; also a simple meter where the quarter note gives the pulse.

6/8 time signature: Two beats per measure, where groups of three notes fill out the beat. Unlike a simple meter, in compound meter the listener perceives two layers of the rhythm, hearing both the main beat and the groups of three notes filling in the main beats.

12/8 time signature: Four beats per measure, where groups of three notes fill out each beat; similar to 6/8.

AAB lyrical scheme: Two lines of identical text (A) followed by a new line (B). The B line will complete the idea or thought of the first A line. The AAB form is especially prevalent in the twelve-bar blues.

arpeggiated: A style of playing the tones of the chord, where each note rings out consecutively and individually, yet with the cumulative effect of sounding as if the chord were struck (a chord whose tones are played consecutively is an arpeggio).

ascending scale: A scale that starts from the lowest notes and rises upward through the notes.

bar or measure: A way of grouping together a set number of beats, usually into a regular patterning that is repeated.

blues turnaround (V–IV): Common to the twelve-bar blues, it is near the endpoint of the form (measures 9–10) that signals that the pattern will start over again. The turnaround occurs over the V–IV part of the progression and the B line of the lyrics.

BPM: An abbreviation for the number of beats per minute.

descending scale: A scale that starts from the highest notes and lowers down through the notes.

dissonance: Two notes that when sounded together, usually at the same time but sometimes sequentially, will produce a resulting harmony that seems harsh to most listeners. There are two components of dissonance: 1) the psychological factor, which is culturally determined and subjective; 2) the physical properties of the sound wave, where the dissonant harmony lacks overtone (upper partial) support. Musically, a dissonant chord or interval demands some type of resolution where its held tension is released.

dominant: The note that is the fifth tone of the scale. Building a major triad on top of the fifth note results in the dominant chord, symbolized in Roman numeral analysis as "V." As indicated by the word, the dominant note and chord are the most significant after the tonic. In tonal music, the dominant also performs an oppositional role to the tonic, building tension that requires a resolution back to the tonic.

dominant-seventh chord (V7): Adds another note, the seventh, to the dominant chord. It turns out that the seventh note is actually a lowered note when it is counted from the fifth note of the scale (i.e., the dominant note). For example, in C major (C D E F G A B), starting on the fifth note, G, the dominant chord is G, B, D. If we renumber the notes starting on G, so that G A B C D E F becomes 1, 2, 3, 4, 5, 6, 7, the seventh note is an F. In the key of G major (not C!) the seventh note is actually F#; thus the F natural note as it appears in the G dominant-seventh chord is a flattened 7 (or, b7).

doo-wop progression (aka 1950s progression): Used in countless songs from the 1950s, it is a four-chord sequence that goes I > vi > IV > V. The progression contains a minor chord as its second chord (vi), and this chord imparts the nostalgia and slight sense of yearning to the chord collection. In pop music there have been numerous variations on the four-chord idea, most recently the so-called feminine progression of vi > V > I > IV.

eighth note: In common time (4/4), the eighth note is equivalent to half of a beat (where the quarter not is the beat). In simple time where the quarter note is the beat, the eighth note denotes the first subdivision of the beat, what musicians often refer to as the "and," and sometimes represented with a "+" sign.

glissando: The articulated sound produced by gliding from note to note, either descending or ascending. For example, on a fretted string instrument like the guitar or electric bass, the finger slides up on the string after the fingered note is plucked.

half step (semitone): In Western music theory, the smallest interval (pitch space) denoted between two notes. On the piano, playing two adjacent keys (e.g., from a white to a black key) produces the half step.

hammer-on: On the guitar, a technique where the lower note is plucked or picked, and the fingering hand then presses down on an upper note without replucking. The second note is considered the hammered note.

key: In tonal music practice, a key denotes a particular tonality; that is, a harmonic foundation derived from a tonic or home note. Taking the twelve chromatic notes of the keyboard, there are thus twelve possible sounding major keys (in notational practice there are fifteen, because three of these overlap).

major key and scale: The basic soundscape and scale used in Western art and popular music. Starting on the note C, the major scale goes through all the white notes on the keyboard, so C D E F G A B. A song continuing these notes with C as its tonic note would be in the key of C major.

major seventh chord: Adds another note at the interval of a third on top of the major triad. Thus taking our C-major triad, adding the seventh note of the scale, or B, will generate the C-major seventh chord. The chord is common to jazz and some soft rock. The major seventh chord is prominent in "No Expectations," heard where the slide guitar enters (measure 3).

major triad: The three-note chord that can be produced by sounding the first, third, and fifth notes of a given major scale. In the key of C, these are the notes C, E, and G. Playing the C, E, G at the same time will sound a C major chord.

minor key and scale: Closely related to the major key, the minor key and its scale have become associated with darker, more mysterious, tragic or sad moods. Every major key has a related minor one, referred to as the relative minor. The tonic note of the relative minor key is the sixth note of the major scale. So if we take the key of C major, the sixth note is A; thus A minor is the relative minor of C major. Taking this further, the resulting scale is A B C D E F G, called the natural minor because it shares the same note collection as the relative major. Contrasting this with A major (A B C# D E F# G#), the A natural minor scale has three lowered notes, specifically, on the third, sixth, and seventh scale degrees (the notes C, F, and G).

minor-pentatonic scale and the minor third: This scale forms the basis for single-note soloing in everything from R & B to blues to classic rock. The minor pentatonic also generates many of the riffs of the classic rock era. This scale is a subset of the minor scale, but only has five notes, hence the use of the Greek prefix "penta-." For A-minor pentatonic, the notes are A C D E G (1, 3, 4, 5, 7). The minor third (encompassing three semitones) is the interval that gives the scale its sonic identity, heard twice from A–C and E–G.

Mixolydian chord: A term that we are using to describe a major chord built on the flattened seventh (b7th) scale degree of a major scale. For example, in the key of E, the flattened seventh scale degree is D. Thus an example of a Mixolydian chord would be to play a D chord in the context of the key of E. As part of a progression, the Mixolydian chord or bVII is commonly found in the I > bVII > IV progression. In the key of E, this would be the chords E > D > A. The I > bVII > IV threads through numerous songs from the 1960s and beyond, from "Gloria" to "I Can't Explain" to the outro of "Hey Jude." Famous Stones' songs that use it are "The Last Time" and "Sympathy for the Devil." Since the 1960s the progression continued to develop in songs like "Sweet Home Alabama" and "Back in Black."

Mixolydian mode: The modes are ancient scales that go back to ancient Greece and beyond. The modern Mixolydian mode is based on one of the church modes from medieval times. An easy way to generate the scale is to start on the fifth note of the major scale and make that the tonic note. Thus in the key of C, starting on the note G produces the mode of G Mixolydian (G A B C D E F), which are the white notes on the piano. Another way to conceptualize the mode is to take a G major scale and lower the seventh note to make the F# the note F.

modal harmony and modal mixture: Music is deemed modal if it references a mode as the basis for its harmony instead of major or minor tonality. It is found in folk music, and in the 1950s was a major movement within jazz improvisation starting with Miles Davis and his circle. In practice, however, a modal song will usually incorporate features from the major or minor, hence the term modal mixture. In songs like "Satisfaction" or "Sympathy," the main verse progression incorporates modal harmony, while the chorus returns to major harmony.

non-chordal tones: These are notes that are not part of the chord itself. Though there are rules that govern how non-chordal tones are resolved, in rock music and in the Stones' music, non-chordal tones can come about by placing the fingers on frets above the chord, sometimes resulting in what rock musicians call a suspended or "sus" chord.

octave: An interval spanning the eight notes of a major or minor scale, where the eighth note is the same as the first—if ascending, the eighth note is double the frequency of the first. For example, if middle C is 256 hertz, then the C at the octave above it is 512 hertz.

open tuning: A way of setting the pitch on the guitar so that an unfingered strings sound a chord. These tunings go back to at least the nineteenth century and probably beyond, but became very common during the Delta blues era (late 1920s–1930s). Slide and folk guitarists continue to use them to this day. Common open tunings used by the Stones are in D, E, and G.

ostinato: A short melodic or rhythmic figure that is subject to much repetition. The repetition must be exact for it to be considered an ostinato. In modern pop music an ostinato can be referred to as a "loop," while in hard rock a "riff."

overdriven (guitar): A timbre on the guitar whereby the signal in the amplifier becomes distorted. This was originally achieved by overheating the valves on an amplifier. Manufacturers such as Gibson capitalized on the trend and made specialized effects boxes that could achieve a similar effect—thus Richards's guitar part uses one of these, a fuzz box, on "Satisfaction." Generally, there are distinctions between overdrive, fuzz, and distortion effects having to do with the overtones produced, but for our purposes these gradations of distortion are not too significant.

Phrygian: A church mode that, like Mixolydian, has its roots in the ancient music of Mediterranean cultures. The distinguishing note of this mode is the lowered second scale degree (b2), creating a half step from the tonic note to the second note. It is a common melodic sound in flamenco (usually as E F G A B C D) and some Middle Eastern music (the Kurd tetrachord, or D Eb F G).

Roman numeral analysis: A method for representing chords determined from the bass note or root of the chord. In use since the eighteenth century, it allows for the comparison of chord progressions in different keys, in that it reduces the chords to a numerical value. Thus I–IV–V, when applied to C, translates into the chords C–F–G, while starting from

G, would refer to the chords G–C–D. Structurally, Roman numerals allow for a functional comparison of harmonic events in a song or piece of music.

rubato: An Italian term that has come to denote "robbed" time, where a particular note is held for a longer time and then the next few notes are played faster.

scale: A "ladder" of adjacent individual tones, starting from low to high. The basic scale is the diatonic scale, comprised of the white notes of the piano, starting on C to the next occurrence of the same note. The most common scales are major and minor; that is, seven-note scales with a set ordering of the interval content, both of which are derived from the diatonic scale. Pentatonic (five-note) scales are common for rock soloing and as the basis for riffs.

scordatura (also see open tuning): An alternate way of tuning the strings. In this respect, open tuning is a particular type of scordatura.

solfège syllables: A system for designating the scale steps using syllables that dates back to the medieval era. In what is called "fixed do," each scale letter receives a permanent syllable—thus C D E F G A B become *do re mi fa sol la si (ti)*.

staccato (detached): A way of playing that note that shortens its duration, such that there is slight bit of silence after it.

subdominant: The note that is the fourth tone of the scale. Building a major triad on top of the fourth note results in the subdominant chord, symbolized in Roman numeral analysis as "IV." Literally meaning "below" the dominant, it is the third most important note and harmonic area after the tonic and dominant. Because the subdominant chord contains the tonic note within it (in the key of C, the subdominant triad of F has the notes F A C), it is usually perceived as a place of tonal relaxation, or an expansion of the tonic, as it were.

substitute chord: The technique of replacing a chord with one that is closely related to it. Thus in the song "Sister Morphine," the F-major chord (F A C) can be interpreted as a substitute chord for the A minor one (A C E).

syncopation: Any type of disruption to the normative patterning of the beats. It is usually accomplished by applying an accent to an offbeat or "and." It is a common rhythmic feature of much African American blues, jazz, and R & B that the Stones appropriated.

tonic: The note that is the first tone of the scale, considered "home" and the most complete place of rest in a key. The major triad built on the tonic is represented as the "I" chord in Roman numeral analysis. Most songs in a key will start and end with the tonic chord.

triplet: A rhythmic device whereby three notes are played in the space of two notes of the same kind.

tritone: Also known in medieval times as the *Diabolus in Musica* ("Devil in Music"), the tritone is a dissonant interval that historically was first frowned upon, and then later on rules were developed to handle it in composition. The interval contains three whole steps; a unique property of it is that it divides the octave in half. In the diatonic scale (i.e., the white notes on the keyboard), there is a tritone from the notes F to B. The technical name for the tritone is the augmented fourth.

vibrato: A technique on a stringed instrument whereby the pitch is slightly altered by the left hand (i.e., the hand on the fingerboard or fretboard) to produce a wavering sound. Historically it was used for expression, to increase the emotive content of a musical idea or passage. In the 1950s Fender produced amplifiers that would approximate the effect electronically; note that in the modern music products industry, the terms vibrato and tremolo (a slightly different technique, produced by rapid rearticulations of the same note) appear to be used interchangeably. Thus sometimes the vibrato arm of the guitar (the correct name), an added part to the tailpiece, is called a tremolo bar.

voicing (chord): There are many ways to vertically align the notes of a given chord on a guitar or piano. For example, taking the chord C (C E G) on the guitar, the most common ways of fingering it would be in open or first position, third position with a barring of the first finger, and eighth position, also with a bar. Notes can also appear in different orderings and octaves to generate different effects. As the Stones' music evolved with the use of open tunings and capos, the voicing of chords changed radically. This had profound implications for the larger soundscape: while the chords and underlying progressions remained virtually unchanged, the timbre and perceived sound was experienced as radically different, giving the Stones' music a unique character.

WORKS CITED

BOOKS AND ARTICLES

Adorno, Theodor W. *Philosophy of New Music*. Translated by Anne G. Mitchell and Wesley V. Blomster. New York: The Seabury Press, 1980.

Aristotle. *On Poetry and Style*. Translated by G. M. A. Grube. Indianapolis: Hackett Publishing Company, 1989.

Babiuk, Andy, and Greg Provost. *Rolling Stones Gear: All the Stones' Instruments from Stage to Studio*. Milwaukee: Backbeat Books, 2013.

Bangs, Lester. *Psychotic Reactions and Carburetor Dung*. Edited by Greil Marcus. New York: Anchor Books, 2003.

Baudelaire, Charles. *Flowers of Evil and Other Works. Les Fleurs du Mal et Oeuvres Choisies*. A Dual Language Book, edited and translated by Wallace Fowlie. New York: Dover, 1992 [1964].

Bellman, Jonathan. "Indian Resonances in the British Invasion 1965–1968." In *The Exotic in Western Music*, edited by Jonathan Bellman, 292–306. Lebanon, NH: Northeastern, 1998.

"Bill Wyman Talking to Paul Sexton." *Rolling Stones: The Singles (1971–2006)* [box set with hardback book]. N.p.: Polydor, 2011.

Blanchot, Maurice. *The Writing of the Disaster*. Translated by Ann Smock. Lincoln: University of Nebraska Press, 1995 [1980].

Booth, Stanley. *The True Adventures of the Rolling Stones*. Chicago: A Cappella Books, 2000.

Bulgakov, Mikhail. *The Master and Margarita*. Translated by Diana Burgin and Katherine Tiernan O'Connor. New York: Vintage International, 1996.

Capote, Truman interviewed by Andy Warhol. "Sunday with Mister C." *Rolling Stone* No. 132 (1973): 28–48.

Caputi, Jane. *Age of the Sex Crime*. Bowling Green, OH: University Popular Press, 1987.

Dalton, David. *Rolling Stones*. New York: Music Sales Corporation, 1972.

Dettmar, Kevin J. H. *Think Rock*. Boston: Pearson, 2011.

Egan, Sean, ed. *The Mammoth Book of the Rolling Stones*. London: Constable & Robinson, 2013.

Elliott, Martin. *The Rolling Stones Complete Recording Sessions 1962–2012 50th Anniversary Edition*. London: Cherry Red Books, 2012.

Faithfull, Marianne. *Faithfull: An Autobiography*. With David Dalton. New York: Little, Brown and Company, 1994.

Friedan, Betty. *The Feminine Mystique*. New York: Norton, 1963.

Gadamer, Hans-Georg. *Truth and Method*. Second revised edition. Translated by Joel Weinsheimer and Donald G. Marshall. New York: Crossroad, 1989.
Guralnick, Peter. *Sweet Soul Music: Rhythm and Blues and the Southern Dream of Freedom*. Boston: Little, Brown and Company, 1999.
Hale, Grace Elizabeth. *A Nation of Outsiders: How the White Middle Class Fell in Love with Rebellion in Postwar America*. Oxford: University Press, 2011.
Hellmann, John M., Jr. "I'm a Monkey: The Influence of the Black American Blues Argot on the Rolling Stones." *Journal of American Folklore* 86, 342 (1973): 367–73.
Inglis, Ian. "'Nothing You Can See That Can Be Shown': The Album Covers of the Beatles." *Popular Music* 20, 1 (2001): 3–97.
Janovitz, Bill. *Rocks Off: 50 Tracks That Tell the Story of the Rolling Stones*. New York: St. Martin's Press, 2013.
———. *Rolling Stones' Exile on Main Street (33 1/3)* New York: Continuum, 2005 [Kindle Edition].
Komara, Edward. *The Road to Robert Johnson: The Genesis and Evolution of Blues in the Delta from the Late 1800s Through 1938*. Milwaukee: Hal Leonard, 2007.
Malvinni, David. "*Totentanz*: Notes on Adès, Lesh, and the Grateful Dead." In *A Rare and Different Tune: The Seventeenth Grateful Dead Scholars Caucus*, edited by Nicholas G. Meriwether, 143–51. N.p.: Dead Letters Press, 2014.
Marshall, Jim. *The Rolling Stones 1972*. San Francisco: Chronicle Books, 2012.
Richards, Keith. *Life*. With James Fox. New York: Little, Brown and Company, 2010.
Trynka, Paul. *Brian Jones: The Making of the Rolling Stones*. New York: Viking, 2014.
Wood, Ronnie. *Ronnie: The Autobiography*. With Jack Macdonald and Jeffrey Robinson. New York: St. Martin's Press, 2007.
Wyman, Bill. *Bill Wyman's Blues Odyssey: A Journey to Music's Heart & Soul.* With Richard Havers. London: DK Publishing, 2001.
———. *Rolling with the Stones*. London: DK Publishing, 2002.
———. *Stone Alone: The Story of a Rock 'n' Roll Band*. With Ray Coleman. Boston: Da Capo Press, 1997 [reprint of New York: Viking, 1990].

INTERNET SOURCES

Bronstein, Carolyn. "Battling Pornography." Rorotoko, September 26, 2011. http://rorotoko.com/interview/20110926_carolyn_bronstein_on_battling_pornography_feminist_anti-pornograph/?page=3 (accessed June 27, 2015).
Earcandy. "A Degree of Murder—The 'Lost' Brian Jones Solo Album? [Ronnie]." N.d. http://earcandy_mag.tripod.com/rrcase-brianjones.htm (accessed June 20, 2015).
Garland, David. "The World's Most-Used Musical Sequence!" WYNC, July 6, 2014. http://www.wnyc.org/story/worlds-most-used-musical-sequence/ (accessed June 27, 2015).
Goody, Matthew Christopher. "Thames Valley Cotton Pickers: Race and Youth in London Blues Culture." Simon Fraser University: Master's Thesis, 2005. http://summit.sfu.ca/item/10216 (accessed June 27, 2015).
Guardian. "Keith Richards Wants to Make a New Rolling Stones Album." April 10, 2015. http://www.theguardian.com/music/2015/apr/10/keith-richards-wants-to-make-a-new-rolling-stones-album (accessed June 27, 2015).
Horrox, Camilla. "Historic Music Site Where the Rolling Stones Formed Could Be Torn Down by Developers." Getwestlondon, February 20, 2015. http://www.getwestlondon.co.uk/news/west-london-news/historic-music-site-rolling-stones-8681388 (accessed June 27, 2015).
It's Only Rock and Roll. "Matt Clifford, Why Only Two Tours with the Stones?" November 11, 2011. https://www.iorr.org/talk/read.php?1,1508621,1508666 (accessed June 27, 2015).

———. "Re: Loving Cup Alt Version." May 16, 2010. https://www.iorr.org/talk/read.php?1,1244300,1246685 (accessed June 27, 2015).

———. "The Stones' *Some Girls* Super Deluxe Box Set Is a Disappointment—A Comment to Mr. Jagger [Turd on the Run]." November 21, 2011. https://www.iorr.org/talk/read.php?1,1515926,1516012 (accessed June 27, 2015).

———. "Wayne Perkins on Bob Marley, 'Hand of Fate' and Auditioning for the Stones." October 31, 2009. https://www.iorr.org/talk/read.php?1,1144740,1145497 (accessed June 27, 2015).

———. "Which of the *Some Girls'* Vocal Tracks Have New Vocals by Mick? [Mathijs]." November 25, 2011. https://www.iorr.org/talk/read.php?1,1518437,1518557 (accessed June 27, 2015).

Kerouac, Jack. "Introduction." *The Americans* by Robert Frank. http://www.camramirez.com/pdf/P1_Americans_Intro.pdf (accessed June 27, 2015).

Kubernik, Harvey. "Engineer Andy Johns Discusses the Making of the Rolling Stones' *Exile on Main Street*." *Goldmine*, May 8, 2010. http://www.goldminemag.com/article/engineer-andy-johns-discusses-the-making-of-the-rolling-stones-exile-on-main-street (accessed June 27, 2015).

Los Angeles Times. "Full Coverage: Isla Vista Murders Near UCSB." May 24, 2014. http://www.latimes.com/local/lanow/la-isla-vista-shooting-near-ucsb-stories-storygallery.html (accessed June 27, 2015).

Martin, Douglas. "Prince Rupert zu Loewenstein, Rolling Stones Money Manager, Dies at 80." *New York Times*, May 22, 2014. http://www.nytimes.com/2014/05/23/arts/music/prince-rupert-zu-loewenstein-rolling-stones-money-manager-dies-at-80.html (accessed June 27, 2015).

The Master Musicians of Jajouka Led by Bachir Attar. "The Full Story." N.d. http://www.jajouka.com/the_full_story.html (accessed June 27, 2015).

Mullen, Jethro. "Is Rap the Most Important Music Since 1960? Scientists Say They Have Proof." CNN.com, May 6, 2015. http://www.cnn.com/2015/05/06/tech/pop-music-study-hip-hop-the-beatles/ (accessed June 27, 2015).

Myers, Marc. "Still Picking Up Good Vibrations [interview with Brian Wilson]." *Wall Street Journal*, October 7, 2011. http://www.wsj.com/news/articles/SB10001424052970204524604576609000066845070 (accessed June 28, 2015).

Obrecht, Jas. "Mick Taylor on the Rolling Stones, John Mayall, and Playing Guitar." Obrecht Music Archive, June 22, 1979. http://jasobrecht.com/?s=mick+taylor (accessed June 28, 2015).

O'Hagan, Sean. "The Stones and the True Story of *Exile on Main St*." *Guardian*, April 25, 2010. http://www.theguardian.com/music/2010/apr/25/stones-exile-on-main-street (accessed June 28, 2015).

Poe, Edgar Allan. "The Facts in the Case of M. Valdemar." Poe Stories, n.d. http://poestories.com/read/facts (accessed June 28, 2015).

Ratliff, Ben. "Revisiting 'Main St.,' Rethinking the Myth." *New York Times*, May 19, 2010. http://www.nytimes.com/2010/05/23/arts/music/23stones.html?pagewanted=all (accessed June 28, 2015).

Rolling Stone. "100 Greatest Rolling Stones Songs: [no.] 7 'Jumpin' Jack Flash' (1968)." October 15, 2013. http://www.rollingstone.com/music/lists/100-greatest-rolling-stones-songs-20131015/jumpin-jack-flash-aa968-19691231 (accessed June 28, 2015).

———. "500 Greatest Songs of All Time: [no.] 1 Bob Dylan, 'Like a Rolling Stone.'" April 7, 2011. http://www.rollingstone.com/music/lists/the-500-greatest-songs-of-all-time-20110407/bob-dylan-like-a-rolling-stone-20110516 (accessed June 28, 2015).

———. "500 Greatest Songs of All Time: [no.] 2 Rolling Stones, '(I Can't Get No) Satisfaction.'" April 7, 2011. http://www.rollingstone.com/music/lists/the-500-greatest-songs-of-all-time-20110407/the-rolling-stones-i-cant-get-no-satisfaction-20110516 (accessed June 28, 2015).

———. "The Rolling Stones Disaster at Altamont: Let It Bleed." January 21, 1970. http://www.rollingstone.com/music/news/the-rolling-stones-disaster-at-altamont-let-it-bleed-19700121?page=6 (accessed June 28, 2015).

The Rolling Stones. "12th July 1962." http://www.rollingstones.com/release/12th-july-1962 (accessed June 29, 2015).

"The Rolling Stones: *Beggars Banquet*." N.d. http://www.theclanmackinnon.com/ryland-cooder.com/BeggarsBanquet.html (accessed 20 June 2015).

Sheffield, Rob. "Plundered My Soul." *Rolling Stone*, April 17, 2010. http://www.rollingstone.com/music/songreviews/plundered-my-soul-20100417#ixzz3LoYKvVys (accessed June 28, 2015).

Simmonds, Charlotte. "The Rolling Stones: The Myth and Its Makers." *New Statesman*, December 22, 2012. http://www.newstatesman.com/culture/culture/2012/12/rolling-stones-myth-and-its-makers (accessed June 28, 2015).

Sisario, Ben. "Sales of Streaming Music Top CDs in Flat Year for Industry." *New York Times*, March 18, 2015. http://www.nytimes.com/2015/03/19/business/media/sales-of-streaming-music-top-cds-in-flat-year-for-industry.html (accessed June 28, 2015).

Songfacts. Led Zeppelin: "Babe I'm Gonna Leave You." N.d. http://www.songfacts.com/detail.php?id=299 (accessed June 20, 2015).

Time Is on Our Side. *Exile on Main Street*: "Creation: Mick Jagger, 2003." N.d. http://www.timeisonourside.com/lpExile.html (accessed June 20, 2015).

———. "Paint It Black." N.d. http://www.timeisonourside.com/SOPaintIt.html (accessed June 20, 2015).

———. "Ventilator Blues: Charlie Watts, 2003." N.d. http://www.timeisonourside.com/SOVentilator.html (accessed June 20, 2015).

Trynka, Paul, and Dick Taylor. "Open G Tunings and Open Secrets." August 28, 2014. http://trynka.net/2014/08/open-g-tunings-and-open-secrets/ (accessed June 28, 2015).

Wenner, Jann S. "Mick Jagger Remembers." *Rolling Stone*, December 14, 1995. http://www.rollingstone.com/music/news/mick-jagger-remembers-19951214?page=2 (accessed June 28, 2015).

WordReference. "Thread: A Girl with Faraway Eyes [Captain Kirk]." August 6, 2011, http://forum.wordreference.com/threads/a-girl-with-faraway-eyes.2205498/ (accessed June 27, 2015).

YouTube. "The Association—Babe I'm Gonna Leave You ((Stereo)) 1965." https://www.youtube.com/watch?v=3-vOFPP0WDI&feature=kp (accessed June 28, 2015).

———. "Before They Make Me Run—The Rolling Stones." https://www.youtube.com/watch?v=jFJbhtmKHHM&list=RDjFJbhtmKHHM&spfreload=10#t=4 (accessed June 28, 2015).

———. "Cutting My ABC's CHARLEY JORDAN, Blues Guitar Legend." http://www.youtube.com/watch?v=JC1JnOSRmno (accessed June 28, 2015).

———. "Gimme Shelter Merry Clayton's Solo Performance." http://www.youtube.com/watch?v=jqXyjbgs5rU (accessed June 28, 2015).

———. "Jig Saw Puzzle, Take #12." https://www.youtube.com/watch?v=CMidBl9EIZ8.

———. "Jimmy Page: Lucifer Rising and Other Sound Tracks." https://www.youtube.com/watch?v=PSfBaLBvGCg (accessed June 28, 2015).

———. "John Lee Hooker with Eric Clapton & The Rolling Stones—Boogie Chillen." https://www.youtube.com/watch?v=ByxJr3Z3aMI (accessed June 28, 2015).

———. "Keith Richards' Blues Acoustic." https://www.youtube.com/watch?v=U5ANjb-yAVE (accessed June 28, 2015).

———. "Mick Jagger—Brown Sugar '69 MSG." https://www.youtube.com/watch?v=80H9KFUdZog (accessed June 28, 2015).

———. "The Rolling Stones—32-20 Blues (Robert Johnson Cover)." https://www.youtube.com/watch?v=yZ8nPYyvsuk (accessed June 28, 2015).

———. "The Rolling Stones—Beast of Burden (from *Some Girls, Live in Texas '78*)." https://www.youtube.com/watch?v=bj8lRssjN48 (accessed June 28, 2015).

———. "The Rolling Stones—Blood Red Wine." https://www.youtube.com/watch?v=sXivhZmNKzM (accessed June 28, 2015).

———. "The Rolling Stones—Get a Line on You." https://www.youtube.com/watch?v=6wTH1SmyIO8 (accessed June 28, 2015).

———. “The Rolling Stones—Honky Tonk Women.” https://www.youtube.com/watch?v=CqVdRS3FCf8&index=6&list=PLKhlicDSGvk1msNKO-FCt7sEu3WoS7FOT (accessed June 28, 2015).

———. “The Rolling Stones—Love in Vain (*Stripped*, 1995).” https://www.youtube.com/watch?v=kAGnxH1dygU (accessed June 28, 2015).

———. “Rolling Stones—Love Is Strong Keith Richards on Vocals.” https://www.youtube.com/watch?v=XUpkJKhLyuI (accessed June 28, 2015).

———. “The Rolling Stones—Never Stop (Start Me Up Demo).” https://www.youtube.com/watch?v=GBJ7s0QILJc&spfreload=10 (accessed June 28, 2015).

———. “The Rolling Stones—Paint It Black—Live 1990.” https://www.youtube.com/watch?v=QCgwCJt5NQI (accessed June 28, 2015).

———. “The Rolling Stones—Pay Your Dues (Early Street Fighting Man).” https://www.youtube.com/watch?v=yv2Gj6w0HWQ (accessed June 28, 2015).

———. “THE ROLLING STONES/Shake Your Hips.” https://www.youtube.com/watch?v=mVuKzEDnUUQ (accessed June 28, 2015).

———. “The Rolling Stones—Undercover of the Night (B Version).” https://www.youtube.com/watch?v=pP1UbJ2iKLw&spfreload=10 (accessed June 28, 2015).

———. “The Rolling Stones—Ventilator Blues (Demo Outtake).” https://www.youtube.com/watch?v=HhaL79IQgaM (accessed June 28, 2015).

———. “Rolling Stones—Ventilator Blues—Vancouver—June 3, 1972.” https://www.youtube.com/watch?v=vrsBu3RZebQ (accessed June 28, 2015).

———. “The Stones in Morocco Part 1.” https://www.youtube.com/watch?v=20x1OZVofNI (accessed June 28, 2015).

INDEX

ABOUT THE AUTHOR

Musicologist **David Malvinni** teaches courses in music history and African American studies at Santa Barbara City College. As a classical guitarist and violinist, he teaches at the Santa Barbara Suzuki Violin School. He also directs a music appreciation outreach program reaching about one thousand students per year, "Music Matters," for the Community Arts Music Association, for which he has written the curriculum, *A Classical Music Journey for Young People*.

David received his bachelor's degree in philosophy from Rice University, master's in musicology from the University of Massachusetts, Amherst, and a PhD in musicology from the University of California, Santa Barbara. As an undergraduate he was awarded a scholarship to study music and literature at the University of Heidelberg in Germany (1990–1991). While a graduate, he was a member of philosopher Jacques Derrida's seminar at the University of California, Irvine (1998–2001).

His work focuses on topics connecting classical, world, and popular musics, and continental philosophy remains a vital interest. As a scholar of the Grateful Dead's music, David gave talks at the *Unbroken Chain* (2007) and *So Many Roads* (2014) conferences and maintains a related blog at *Grateful Dead World*. His many publications include two books, *The Gypsy Caravan: From Real Roma to Imaginary Gypsies in Western Music and Film* (2004), and *Grateful Dead and the Art of Rock Improvisation* (2013).

David lives in Santa Barbara with his wife and two children, who are also musicians. They enjoy playing music together and also give concerts. His favorite activities outside of music include hiking and fitness.